The Dialogues of Sancho and Quixote

MYTHICAL Debates On Global Warming: 1997-2010

Daniel H. GOTTLIEB

Canopy Publishing
Post Office Box 1645
Lake Oswego, Oregon
www.canopypublishing.com

Books by Daniel H. GOTTLIEB

The GALILEO Syndrome
The FIRES of Home
The Dialogues of Sancho and Quixote
    MYTHICAL Debates On Global Warming: 1997-2010

The Dialogues of Sancho and Quixote
    MYTHICAL Debates On Global Warming: 1997-2010
© 1997-2010 by Daniel H. Gottlieb

Library of Congress Control Number 2010911029
ISBN: 978097536550-2-6

Printed in the United States of America

The Dialogues of Sancho and Quixote

MYTHICAL Debates On Global Warming: 1997-2010

Daniel H. Gottlieb

CANOPY PUBLISHING

Oregon   2010

Sancho and Quixote began debating the topic of global warming on the Internet in 1997

The layman's confusion with anthropogenic forcing of our planet's radiative balance has been fostered by the synthesis of a fallacious argument that frames human-induced climate change as suspect, not science. In conjunction, by framing humanity as belligerent to the environment--not integral to it-- the economic realities have also been obscured. The result is the global warming debate has become an exercise in propaganda technique--for all sides. And that is a tragedy.

Unfortunately, one gives credence to a debate--regardless of how absurd the premise--when one enters the debate. So rather than deny the absurd, I present the changes to the discussion from 1997 to 2010--as a way of decoding the carnival of intercourse. To further clarify the madness, since the only item certain about the synthesized debate is its absurdity, I have engaged two maniacs, Sancho and Quixote to represent the warring camps: Sancho, for sanctimonious environmentalism, and Quixote, for maniacal capitalism.

Their subjects are born of madness and displayed as such. Some humor has also been injected for the sake of our collective sanity.

The reasons for the synthesized debate on human induced climate change remains obscured behind a greasy ceiling, and I do not attempt to unravel the motivation for the debates in this book; however, some amount of elucidation on motive did creep into the work. I apologize beforehand for any clarity inadvertently delivered to the public on the topics of science, balance, a healthy market-based economy, or non-linear systems.

Daniel H. Gottlieb
July, 2010

For La

Chapter 1
1997

December 11, 1997
Sancho, Quixote, and Coal

Sancho:	"So Quixote, how was Kyoto?"
Quixote:	"I love coal."
Sancho:	"What?"
Quixote:	"Sancho, I love coal. I love everything about it. It's shiny and it's black..."
Sancho:	"Try that again? I thought you hated fossil fuels because they emit greenhouse gases."
Quixote:	"I love oil as well. I love the smell of..."
Sancho:	"Are you feeling all right?"
Quixote:	"I do have a case of the Asian flu. Are my eyes puffy?"
Sancho:	"No they're fine. What happened, Quixote? Why the sudden love of fossil fuels?"

QUIXOTE: "Money."

SANCHO: "Money?"

QUIXOTE: "I've decided to take a job lobbying for the fossil fuels industry. 'Slide Along With Us, Or Else!' That's going to be my first campaign. Like it?"

SANCHO: "Charming."

QUIXOTE: "From now on it's light lunches, golf, and strategy meetings to corrupt the truth. I'm an executive fighting the commie eco-freak madness that's taken over our land. No more of this chicken little stuff for me. Did you know climate change is just a plot to take the world away from oil companies?"

SANCHO: "I didn't know they owned it."

QUIXOTE: "See, you're so naive. Don't you know the cost of producing oil is less now than in 1947?"

SANCHO: "But we're paying ten times more than what we were paying in 1947."

QUIXOTE: "Pretty smart, huh? Believe me, they own the world. Guess what my second task is?"

SANCHO: "What?"

QUIXOTE: "I'm organizing the 'Bangladesh Don't Matter' marketing campaign. Want to help me? Where are you going? You can't leave. I've signed you up to lead our new campaign targeting teenagers. Remember Joe Camel? Well he originally came from the desert and we executives figured since we're probably going to a hotter place..."

December 24, 1997
Sancho and Quixote on Rhetoric and Litigation

QUIXOTE: "Guess what Sancho? I've been promoted to the Rhetoric Department. Very important in an oil company. In fact I'm in charge of a bunch of pros from the tobacco industry. Seems they were given early retirement from their old companies."

SANCHO: "Good of you to help the unemployed."

QUIXOTE: "The rhetoric fight has moved to climate change. So battered and scarred, we continue the fight to help the American people."

SANCHO: "Try that again? What are you referring to?"

QUIXOTE: "Sancho, you don't understand the workings of corporate America like I do."

SANCHO: "Enlighten me, Quixote."

QUIXOTE: "Did you realize the oil companies know their products cause climate change?"

SANCHO: "I suppose so."

QUIXOTE: "And you think they're a bunch of greedy bastards don't you, Sancho?"

SANCHO: "The thought had crossed my mind."

QUIXOTE: "Wrong. Look they can't admit their products cause global warming because if they did they'd be up to their pumps in litigation. Heck, they recalled toys for lead, cars for faulty systems, heaters because they burn homes down, they even sued the tobacco folks into a corner because of a little cancer. Can you imagine what they'd do to the oil and coal companies for screwing up the entire planet?"

SANCHO: "Oh, that would be dreadful."

QUIXOTE: "Exactly, lawyers would sue the pants off the oil companies."

SANCHO: "We can't let that happen."

QUIXOTE: "Exactly, Sancho, the oil companies can't admit it and so therefore they cannot help you solve the problem of climate change. Why are you laughing?"

SANCHO: "Have you considered therapy?"

QUIXOTE: "No, listen. We in big oil have to keep muddying the water and bringing out shills to confuse things on climate change until we can get our necks out of the litigation wringer."

SANCHO: "Oh, of course--you wouldn't want to pay for your mistakes."

QUIXOTE: "Sancho, we're here to help. We sacrifice a few shills of course. Make a few deals and viola we're set. We strike a deal then we can continue our mission of helping the people of the world get cheap energy. We're learning a lot from the tobacco boys."

SANCHO: "I can tell."

QUIXOTE: "It's just a matter of time before we can come to the rescue-- with a lot of rhetoric."

SANCHO: "But people may die."

QUIXOTE: "Prove it."

SANCHO: "What?"

QUIXOTE: "Prove it. No, don't bother. Sancho, all it takes is a few phone calls and I can have guys doing an op-ed in the Wall Street Journal, the LA Times and the Washington papers saying exactly the opposite of anything you can prove--"

SANCHO: "In less time than it takes to say casket."

QUIXOTE: "Exactly--and who is going to believe you over those bastions of the public trust."

SANCHO: "I see your point."

QUIXOTE: "So you see I'm right. I'm helping the oil companies so they can help us. Want to join our crew? We're planning an anti-UN rally next week. The theme is: Help the Oil Companies Protect the Poor."

SANCHO: "Quixote, you need a vacation."

CHAPTER 2
1998

January 4, 1998
Sancho, Quixote, and Oil

QUIXOTE: "I swear, Sancho, sometimes you positively paranoid."

SANCHO: "Listen, Quixote, right after you joined the oil companies, it all went to hell in a hand basket."

QUIXOTE: "I swear, you are so uninformed about technology it's laughable."

SANCHO: "My windmills are still messed up, Quixote."

QUIXOTE: "You're too tense. Have some of my Prozac."

SANCHO: "No thanks."

QUIXOTE: "Umm, that was cherry flavored. I get these prescriptions for a dollar, you know."

SANCHO: "Ah, perqs."

QUIXOTE: "Look Sancho, you need to understand large transnational companies care about you."

SANCHO: "Like a spider cares for a fly. But okay, Quixote, whatever you say. You're the guy in the suit."

QUIXOTE: "The armor of the 20th century knight."

SANCHO: "Chivalry in the service of lucre, Quixote. Hardly a noble steed."

QUIXOTE: "You're just jealous because of my income. It sets me free, you know."

SANCHO: "Met a lot nice people at corporate, Quixote?"

QUIXOTE: "It's a dog eat dog world."

SANCHO: "Didn't used to be before you became an executive."

QUIXOTE: "I was blind."

SANCHO: "Now you're deaf as well as blind. If money frees you how come you're so careful about what you do and say now?"

QUIXOTE: "It's prudent. We in large enterprises are conservative in thought and action because we treasure the public trust."

SANCHO: "You mean because of the stockholders."

QUIXOTE: "Where? Is my tie tight enough? Straighten up. And think nice thoughts about the future."

January 13, 1998
Sancho and Quixote on Climate Disinformation

QUIXOTE: "I love disinformation, Sancho."

SANCHO: "I'm worried about you, Quixote. First it was the Armani suits, then the 'Fossil Fuel Is Your Friend Program,' now it's that group of clowns that lead you around by the nose, or should I say the purse."

QUIXOTE: "Fred and his friends are scientists, not clowns--though they are a gas at a party with those matching sets of lamp shades. You ought to hear Bob do his urban heat island speech after a few belts. Absolutely the funniest thing you've ever heard."

SANCHO: "Sounds like a real hoot."

QUIXOTE: "It is. Besides, Sancho, Spreading disinformation is imperative in dealing with the internet. Great new job opportunities for those who can be flexible with the truth. Man, we've got you eco-freaks spinning like tops. You know they call me the Kafka of climate change."

SANCHO: "Quixote, you and your buddies belong in a Kafka novel."

QUIXOTE: "Prove it! References? Got any, huh? See, I'm gettin' pretty good at it. Want to hear my new one: NOAA and NASA, the big Universities, the UN, NCAR, all of them are shills for Al Gore. Personally I liked calling them socialists but with elections coming--you know."

SANCHO: "So it's all just a game."

QUIXOTE: "No. We are just a bunch of working stiffs out to make a living. That way when the climate gets fierce we have the bucks to ride it out."

SANCHO: "What about those without the money?"

QUIXOTE: "I assure you we'll make certain the people who suffer from climate change will be displayed as lazy and deceitful. Ever notice how all the pictures of storm damage shows trailer parks getting hammered? It's the 'ghetto thing' all over again."

SANCHO: "Loathsome."

QUIXOTE: "Those of us in R&D don't care about such things. Besides you don't get it: The whole point of what we're doing is to slow things down, not stop progress."

SANCHO: "R&D? Try that one again?"

QUIXOTE: "If things move too fast, certain interests might get left with the dinosaurs and you know what happened to them?"

SANCHO: "You mean the comet that got them?"

QUIXOTE: "No, unleaded gas got them! I heard that joke at Stanford recently. Just loved it. You know what else I'm proposing? Putting up our own sources of data that we've--how shall I say it? delicately tweaked."

SANCHO: "You mean like the data about 1997 being a cold year?"

QUIXOTE: "Don't you love that one? The same day NOAA came out with their reports saying things were getting warmer, my contractors were all over the place spreading different data. The people out there don't know who to believe. I'd really like to do the 'Black is White thing' but it has already been done."

SANCHO: "By Orwell."

QUIXOTE: "Right, too bad he went to the dark side--but, that's the key for us. That and keeping you eco-freaks tied up in the same pointless arguments about whether the planet is warming or not."

SANCHO: "You mean you know it is?"

QUIXOTE: "Of course. But don't you see? If you guys get by the basic arguments you might be able to prove things that my benefactors might find embarrassing."

SANCHO: "Like what?"

QUIXOTE: "Don't be a dolt."

SANCHO: "You won't tell me?"

QUIXOTE: "If you don't know, there's no way I'm going to tell you."

SANCHO: "I thought we were friends."

QUIXOTE: "There are no friends in the boardroom."

SANCHO: "Oh, that's right up there with your newfound freedom. Look, Quixote, we're messing up the planet and you don't care. Why not?"

QUIXOTE: "There's money to be made and with money you can insulate yourself against the problems brought on by climate change. So why should I care? The rest of it: the science, the public good, storms, and the public--that's just a bunch of chickens running around with their brains shot full of nonsense--it just don't matter. They're noise anyway. And I assure you, we in Rhetoric & Disinformation mean to keep it that way."

January 21, 1998
Sancho, Quixote,
Climate Change, and Cows

QUIXOTE: "Sancho, we have the climate change problem solved. And you can thank the fossil fuel industry."

SANCHO: "That's great news, Quixote, What has your band of seppalytes at Rhetoric and Disinformation come up with now?"

QUIXOTE: "Well, we've...What's a seppalyte?"

SANCHO: "Oh, Quixote--as someone high up in the obfuscation racket you should have a better vocabulary than that."

QUIXOTE: "What is a seppalyte, Sancho? Tell me, or I'll get them to raise gas prices again."

SANCHO: "A seppalyte is someone who, because of selfish need, ignores facts. Or it can also be someone who purposely ignores facts because of a job requirement."

QUIXOTE: "I like it. Now let's see how can I turn all that on you environmentalists..."

SANCHO: "You are without peer, Quixote."

QUIXOTE: "I know. Did I tell you I won last month's 'Corporate Knight Award'? It is a very handsome stereo system that drowns out anything I don't want to hear."

SANCHO: "The perfect gift for you. So what great breakthrough have you achieved?"

QUIXOTE: "Cow farts."

SANCHO: "Excuse me?"

QUIXOTE: "Cow farts. They are going to be identified as a major contributor to climate change."

SANCHO: "You admit there is climate change?"

QUIXOTE: "Only to an old friend like you."

SANCHO: "So what have you fossil fuel folks facilitated for methane?"

QUIXOTE: "Plenty. We've got a genetic engineering team that can eliminate methane from cows."

SANCHO: "Won't they blow up or something?"

QUIXOTE: "We did have a problem with exploding cows for a while. The lightning problem in Australia was a particular problem. Fortunately we sold the patent to the military. In any case we've solved that in the most ingenious way."

SANCHO: "Oh, oh."

QUIXOTE: "We've put in a protein in their genes that changes the methane into Texas Light Sweet Crude. And, we've also found a way to funnel it into the milk and out the cow's teat."

SANCHO: "What? Are you mad?"

QUIXOTE: "I know, we're geniuses. Think of it. A field full of Bessie-cows going into the barn. Their teats laden with Texas Light Sweet Crude. It's a dream come true."

SANCHO: "What happens to the milk?"

QUIXOTE: "We throw it out."

SANCHO: "No, what about the milk? You know, like for kids?"

QUIXOTE: "Remember what I said? The cow farts are going to identified as a main cause of climate change. In a few months my branch will start a campaign showing cows are partially responsible for global warming, the storms, El Nino, unemployment, you name it. The list is endless. And with a little deft work, we might even place all the blame for climate change on cows and their farts. Then we're off the hook for litigation. We've learned a lot from the tobacco wars."

SANCHO: "Brilliant, Quixote, so where do we get milk from?"

QUIXOTE: "We've got a guy in Kuwait working on that. He's the same guy who invented the Camak."

SANCHO: "What's a Camak?"

QUIXOTE: "A cross between a camel and a yak. It's fertile too."

SANCHO: "What was he trying to produce, a sweater that spits twenty feet?"

QUIXOTE: "Sancho, you don't get it. We're seizing the future."

SANCHO: "You're seized--that's for sure--Quixote, what about other animals and their methane?"

QUIXOTE: "That's the beauty of our plan. Once we get acceptance that cow farts are a huge problem, we can begin to genetically engineer cats, bats, dogs rodents, people, you name it. It will be fossil fuel companies again coming to the rescue of mother Earth by eliminating the evil gas that threatens us all. Once again fossil fuels will be king, and firmly fixed in the hearts and minds of our citizenry--to say nothing of people's bodies. Ah, a knight at last!"

SANCHO: "Won't all these other creatures all have a problem like the cows?"

QUIXOTE: "Like what, Sancho?"

SANCHO: "They need to pass gas."

QUIXOTE: "Who told you?"

SANCHO: "Told me what?"

QUIXOTE: "Gas, how'd you know we are working on getting unleaded?"

SANCHO: "Gasoline? From people and animals?"

QUIXOTE: "It's great isn't it? I can see the campaign now: Technology marching side by side with the market embracing the planet and its ecology. And no more flatulence. Think of all the anal retentives that will embrace us. And it's made possible by the fossil fuel industry. It all brings a tear to my eye."

SANCHO: "As it should, Quixote."

February 22, 1998
Sancho, Quixote, and the Dead

SANCHO: "Nice office, Quixote."

QUIXOTE: "Bigger space and a better view than the last office. I also have more stock options--and word is--I'm in line for a golf date with the big boys."

SANCHO: "Doesn't get better than that. What are you reading?"

QUIXOTE: "E-mail--those damn reports on the storms in California. Sancho, I'm sick and tired of all this El Nino stuff. So what if this is the strongest El Nino ever? So what if more people are starving than before? So what if the California produce harvest is getting battered? So what if it rains a bit more in California and it's a tad cooler in Florida? Who cares?"

SANCHO: "The people in California and Florida, Quixote."

QUIXOTE: "Bah, they've had good times. They made big money. Let them eat tofu."

SANCHO: "You know they say the El Ninos come more often now. And that I heard that NOAA was saying there is a correlation between increased hurricanes and climate change."

QUIXOTE: "Who cares? We have the situation in hand, Sancho. I've got the people at Western Fuels pumping money out like waste water. I've got more declarations than you can swing a cat at. I've got articles in the Journal and the Times. I practically have the Post purring like a kitten and the networks are so well controlled that it's become an embarrassment. Cato, Heritage, and Hoover are spitting out opinions like oil wells in the Gulf--"

SANCHO: "Cato, Heritage, and Hoover? Who are they, the three stooges?"

QUIXOTE: "Those are respected institutions, Sancho."

SANCHO: "Really?"

QUIXOTE: "I keep telling you not to make jokes like that here--even if they are true. In any case, I've got the situation in hand. Best of all I've got time."

SANCHO: "Not really, Quixote."

QUIXOTE: "Prove it. Ha, got you again. And if you say one word and I'll get a dozen articles written to the contrary. I'll get a declaration signed by a hundred notable initials. Fight me and I'll get a special prosecutor to grill you about your children. Debate me and I'll wear you down with paid hecklers. Let's talk solar cycles? How about satellite data? What about the reliability of models? Chaotic systems? Hell, I've got a million of 'em. Besides, I've got so many politicians lined up you couldn't pass gas without my boss' okay. And we've got the campaign dollars to back it all up. You have got nothing."

SANCHO: "Just the truth."

QUIXOTE: "It means nothing, Sancho."

SANCHO: "It's still the truth."

QUIXOTE: "It's useless, as long as we can keep labeling it speculation and throwing up a wall of silence around anything that makes sense. Remember, this is a battle of perception, not truth. Power at its best. Face it. We've won. Let me just finish this e-mail and we can go to lunch. I swear, you eco-freaks...Oh, my cell phone."

SANCHO: "Quixote? Quixote? What's wrong? Quixote, you're all white."

QUIXOTE: "My niece just died in a tornado, in Sunnyvale. The winds were a hundred and fifty miles an hour and the rain came in buckets. In Sunnyvale--a tornado! It touched down for just a moment, caught an automobile and dumped it on top of her. It took an hour to get the car off her because all the emergency crews were busy. She kept calling for her mommy. She died on the way to the hospital. I'll be damned."

SANCHO: "I think so, Quixote. I really think so."

April 12, 1998
Sancho, Quixote, and Control

QUIXOTE: "Who cares about people dying, Sancho. There's money to be made."

SANCHO: "Your own niece died in a tornado in Sunnyvale, Quixote. How can you be so heartless?"

QUIXOTE: "It's easy. I have money. I have power. I have ego. I have control issues. The rest doesn't matter."

SANCHO: "Quixote, you lie. You cheat. You falsify facts for your own purpose. Thirty-nine people were killed in a series of tornadoes down south. Then you put out a news report that said there is no connection to climate change. Are you mad?"

QUIXOTE: "Don't you see, Sancho? I have nothing anymore. Why should I care if my policies and my misinformation kill others or that I bastardize the truth? The end means relief to me. So damn the icebergs and the storms. Our technology is unsinkable. To my dying day I shall say global warming is a myth."

SANCHO: "You mean you want it to all fall apart, Quixote?"

QUIXOTE: "Of course. That's why my boys work so hard to label you environmentalists as wanting to go backwards. We don't want anyone to know our sadness. Remember what William F. Buckly said when asked how he would like to be reincarnated?"

SANCHO: "How did he want to be reborn, Quixote?"

QUIXOTE: "Stillborn, Sancho, stillborn."

June 28, 1998
Sancho, Quixote, and the Herd

QUIXOTE: "Sancho, for a while I thought your friends in the news groups might get somewhere. And I have to say it had me and my patrons worried. Thank God, they've just turned out to be a bunch of clowns who only want to pontificate."

SANCHO: "That's not fair, Quixote. There are many more people who recognize that climate change is killing people. The internet has had a lot to do with that. Awareness is coming--it just happens slowly."

QUIXOTE: "Slow enough for us, thank you. But it is too bad so many will die over the years from climate change."

SANCHO: "Quixote, you mean that bothers you?"

QUIXOTE: "Sancho, you jaded eco-freak, of course it bothers me. Less consumers means less profits."

SANCHO: "Lovely, but you were talking about the news group. New people come to the internet and they are educated by facts so it looks like the same old argument goes on and on. In fact people are learning a great deal here."

QUIXOTE: "You know, I see that. But I have to laugh at how little pressure exists for change even with all this education. I swear this is the most dickless generation--"

SANCHO: "Quixote, that's not true."

QUIXOTE: "Sancho, haven't I convinced you the public has abdicated its right to say anything about what goes on in this country?"

SANCHO: "No."

QUIXOTE: "Oh look around you--the proof is obvious: The wealthy murder their children and nobody cares that the police are powerless. We bribe politicians and we talk openly about it and nobody does anything. Every other nation agrees there is climate change, but here in the U.S., it's still considered junk science. We have the right to buy guns but not affordable health insurance. Racism is becoming the law of the land and wrestling garners more interest than truth."

SANCHO: "Something is being done."

QUIXOTE: "Like what--line item veto? Anything we don't like we tie up in idiotic debates; then we have our buddies in the tabloids, oops, I mean news organizations, give our side weight while they toss disapproving glances at any view we oppose. We follow up with some corruption, make a few movies, and if it really gets tough we start a war. Buy a judge here, sell a favor there--I swear my job is just getting easier."

SANCHO: "Change is occurring, Quixote, it's just happening slowly."

QUIXOTE: "Sancho, you just keep telling your friends that and I'll put you on the payroll. I love the grease that makes the free market system work."

SANCHO: "I thought you said it wasn't really a free market."

QUIXOTE: "Hey if you'll buy it--I'll sell it."

SANCHO: "You're a cold-hearted bastard, Quixote."

QUIXOTE: "Of course. And that's another thing that I love. You fools see bastards get ahead, run things, then commit the most heinous of crimes but you sit on you duffs. Sancho, you get what you deserve."

SANCHO: "That viewpoint makes it easier for you, doesn't it, Quixote?"

QUIXOTE: "While your viewpoint makes it easier to be a coward, doesn't it Sancho? You see I don't need rationalization, Sancho. We define the facts of life. Oh, by the way, if you can't reach me for a few weeks try me at the tobacco companies' picnic."

SANCHO: "What are you doing there?"

QUIXOTE: "We're having a problem with that new report that says 560,000 people died from cancer this year in the U.S., and 450,000 deaths are cigarette related."

SANCHO: "That's terrible."

QUIXOTE: "I'll say--we're almost sure it will cut into profitability."

SANCHO: "You don't care about your fellow humans, do you?"

QUIXOTE: "Actually that leads to my next big campaign: Basically, we have too many humans and they are the real cause of all our problems."

SANCHO: "Meaning what?"

QUIXOTE: "Someone's gotta' go. Any suggestions which part of the herd should be culled?"

SANCHO: "I think that would be obvious, Quixote."

CHAPTER 3
1999

May 5, 1999
Sancho, Quixote, and Wacky Weather

QUIXOTE: "Where have you been, Sancho?"

SANCHO: "Busy, Quixote--very busy. I've decided that argument is pointless. Mourning is appropriate."

QUIXOTE: "Good. I'm glad you agree with us. We've just got too much money for you eco-nuts to win any argument about climate change. Wait, mourn what?"

SANCHO: "I used to think the facts mattered."

QUIXOTE: "Now you know they mean nothing. I'm proud of you. Hey--but if it makes you feel any better we're making substantial investments in solar power and fuel cells. Did you know they emit water vapor? Not that we agree that greenhouse gases matter--ah, it's just good business. You know what I mean. Say what's that ribbon on your chest. Green and black--looks like something from a 60's black power meeting."

SANCHO: "I'm in mourning, Quixote, for the people in Oklahoma and Kansas. They died as a direct result of global warming: A big energetic storm moving real slow--that's its signature. And you know that's true."

QUIXOTE: "I don't know that's true and if you start pushing it, Sancho, I'll have my friends flood the airwaves with misinformation--"

SANCHO: "No problem, Quixote. You asked about why I wear green and black some days. I wear green and black whenever a person dies from one of those storms--the ones you claim aren't caused by man-made climate change--"

QUIXOTE: "Now, Sancho, let's not get into that. Every storm is not caused by greenhouse gases. Those tornadoes are just part of a weather cycle."

SANCHO: "True, every storm does not bear the signature of climate change. But more and more storms do..."

QUIXOTE: "Not true. Didn't you watch the channels last night? They said the tornadoes were part of a natural cycle. Of course they couldn't have said anything different, regardless of the facts, but that's an economic issue not a truth issue."

SANCHO: "What else did they say? I can use a laugh."

QUIXOTE: "They said that 'wacky weather' is at it again and we are cycling into a period of difficult weather. They went onto say: Sure there will be more weather disasters but it's natural. Man, some people look so professional when they feed their masters and pander to the trusting."

SANCHO: "So slow moving highly energetic storms are becoming the norm and it is a cyclic event? Oh, spare me, Quixote. You can spout that nonsense out on the airwaves but don't feed it to me. We both know the facts."

QUIXOTE: "Sancho, speak quietly, you know facts can be a problem. Look, the big boys are not ready to face this issue yet. Don't you get it? Good. Now that you've come to terms with the reality of our situation let me clue you in a little further: The systems aren't in place to deal with this scale of man made disaster. Cripes, think of the liability. When, or if, they have those kinds of issues solved, then we'll deal with the truth. But don't hold your breath. The truth has become vestigial."

SANCHO: "I'm sure that's correct as well."

QUIXOTE: "Sancho, people are going to die as a result of corporate policy. So what? Keeping the economy, and my friends, healthy are all that matters. The rest of you--well that's life these days. We have won. So you all wait on us until we're ready to do anymore than give band-aids to the dying. Sancho, we need to take care of our own kind in times like this."

SANCHO: "That's why I mourn those killed by 'that wacky weather'."

QUIXOTE: "Mourn all you want, Sancho. Just keep quiet. You know that green and black looks good together. I bet I could make a small fortune registering the design of those green and black stripes then selling them to eco-nuts like you and your friends. I wonder if I could get a Star Wars tie-in. Say, you're a smart man, Sancho. Why didn't you register the ribbon design and make a killing?"

SANCHO: "You mean you think I should make money off the dead and maimed by taking advantage of the grief? No thank you, Quixote. You can do that if you want."

QUIXOTE: "I do have all the necessary experience..."

November 15, 1999
Sancho, Quixote, and True Believers

QUIXOTE: "...And, make sure to try the pina coladas. They're fabulous."

SANCHO: "Quixote, I didn't allow you to drag me out here to this resort to ply me with tropical drinks and smoothies to be bribed. I came here to talk issues. What do you really want? And please take off that stupid sombrero."

QUIXOTE: "Easy Sancho, you never could appreciate the good life. Listen up here. We want your people to go easy on Lenny."

SANCHO: "Lenny who?"

QUIXOTE: "Lenny--the hurricane that just formed. My friends don't want you taking any cheap shots saying it's a global warming event."

SANCHO: "But that's exactly what it is."

QUIXOTE: "So you understand then. Look, we took it in the shorts with that damn Mitch and then that beating North Carolina took. How about this? You guys shut up about Lenny and we'll see what we can do about Kyoto."

SANCHO: "No deal."

QUIXOTE: "Too bad. You like my shirt?"

SANCHO: "What? No, it's a little gaudy--all those multicolored winged dollar bills flying around make me nauseous."

QUIXOTE: "I got the shirt here in Boise: At Tropical Tom's Northwest Hula Shop. It's a franchise we're thinking about opening all over North America. We can get you in on the ground floor if you'll shut up about the climate. What do you think?"

SANCHO: "You are shameless."

QUIXOTE: "Thank you. Listen let me clue you in. There is no way anything is going to be done on climate change before my friends are ready. The population is confused and the lobbies are strong. Anyone-but-Gore is going to be elected president. Why keep beating your head against the wall?"

SANCHO: "Because people are dying due to climate change and your organizations are lying to them so you can feather your own nests. As a result, you're condemning generations to worsening storms, disease, flooding, and a host of other horrible events. Quixote, why don't you try and stop it?"

QUIXOTE: "The economy will suffer."

SANCHO: "That's a lie. Only the industries entrenched in the current carbon based economy will initially suffer."

QUIXOTE: "Those are my benefactors. Therefore they are the economy."

SANCHO: "Then, your economy is a myth."

QUIXOTE: "Blasphemer! Know yea' that more will suffer if the economy falters! Trust me. My friends guarantee it."

SANCHO: "How can you face your God spouting that heehaw?"

QUIXOTE: "My God is the free market--may it be blessed and kept. And you blaspheme with talk of making it suffer for some humanistic goal. Oh forgive me, Great One, for even uttering such blasphemy! You know, by me making such a statement my portfolio could suffer."

SANCHO: "You are truly sick."

QUIXOTE: "Here is the bottom line: We don't a give a crap about people. Our God--the market--preaches the economy will provide. The economists say it. I believe it. That's all there is to it. You know that might make a good bumper sticker. Wait, let me write that down."

SANCHO: "I'm going to leave."

QUIXOTE: "No wait. Look, Sancho, so long as we can keep the population quiescent--their wants, or don't wants, will not matter. After that, we don't care what they do. They think it's freedom and we are happy."

SANCHO: "And the suffering and dying, Quixote?"

QUIXOTE: "Most of all the suffering and dying, Sancho. Too much press on their dying and suffering could hurt our economy--may it bless us and keep us. Besides, there are too many people anyway."

Sancho: "Time for me to go."

Quixote: "Are you sure you don't want another rum drink, Sancho?"

Sancho: "No thanks. Rum on a cabana here in Boise with the temperature at 75 in mid-November, just doesn't seem right."

Quixote: "Just a blip, Sancho. There is no pattern here."

Sancho: "Sure, whatever you say."

Quixote: "Sancho, try thinking of climate change as another opportunity for the free market to weave its mysterious and glorious ways."

Sancho: "Bye now, Quixote..."

Quixote: "Believing in the free market works, you know. Without it I doubt I could sleep at night."

CHAPTER 4
2000

January 26, 2000
Sancho, Quixote, and the
White Rabbit

QUIXOTE: "Sancho, if I've told you once, I've told you a thousand times, do not waste energy. Turn off that moped. Don't you know excess expenditures of energy are going to cause serious problems now that we have global warming."

SANCHO: "Excuse me, Quixote? Have I driven my little electric motorbike into the white rabbit's forest? Is Alice going to appear around the corner arguing with the Queen of Hearts? Since when can you agree there is global warming?"

QUIXOTE: "I always knew it was a possibility. I just wanted time to examine the science of it all."

SANCHO: "Maybe those mushrooms we had at the restaurant were bad. Would you try that again, Quixote?"

QUIXOTE: "Look, I've always been on your side, Sancho. I'm your master. I wanted to be sure about global warming and now I am certain it is real. We all are."

SANCHO: "Incredible."

QUIXOTE: "Think about it, Sancho, if I and my friends admitted to this earlier there might have been panic in the streets. You know how much I care for the common man. That reminds me: Come on let's go inside and listen to my new Aaron Copeland CD."

SANCHO: "Wait. Quixote, do I look like I took a stupid pill this morning? Are you telling me that you--and your patrons-- now agree that the climate is changing?"

QUIXOTE: "Absolutely, Sancho. And I want to say we are very concerned. Now about that new CD, there is a great 'Fanfare for the Common Man'. We're thinking about using it during the acceptance speech at the convention."

SANCHO: "Slow down. Quixote, let's try and deal with one catastrophe at a time: So you agreeing that there is a discernible human influence on the climate?"

QUIXOTE: "Of course. Sancho--we're very convinced."

SANCHO: "Quixote. When you were in that snow storm in North Carolina, did a tree branch fall on you or something?"

QUIXOTE: "No. It was nothing of the sort. Although I am a bit concerned about our forecasting ability."

SANCHO: "I bet so. Models fail in rapidly changing chaotic system, Quixote."

QUIXOTE: "I can't comment on the rapidity of the changes."

SANCHO: "I can just see the absurd output as the software tries to cope with the atmospheric patterns. Ever find out why the models failed so gracelessly?"

QUIXOTE: "Sancho, it wasn't the models; it was a glitch. I talked to the geeks and their managers."

SANCHO: "So you looked into their deep blue eyes, Quixote, and asked them if their software can really handle rapidly changing open-ended chaotic domains and they kept a straight face?"

QUIXOTE: " 'A model is a model.' They said."

SANCHO: "Flux-fostered weather might be a bitch to deal with if your software doesn't take it into account..."

QUIXOTE: "Looks that way to me, Sancho. To get back to your earlier point: It wasn't the storm that convinced me global warming is real. Besides, a given weather event cannot be traced to global warming..."

SANCHO: "Bull, Quixote..."

QUIXOTE: "Well, I have been taught to believe that a single weather event can't be linked to global warming. I'll not question that until I'm told to. But really I do believe in global warming-- which by the way, I do believe in and always have."

SANCHO: "I see."

QUIXOTE: "You do admit, Sancho, we have to be cautious on how we approach it."

SANCHO: "Of course, Quixote. I congratulate you and your friends on your new respect for science. But I have a question: Now that we all agree we have a global warming problem what are you going to do about it?"

QUIXOTE: "Take some serious investment positions in alternative energy companies. What did you think we'd do? I swear Sancho, sometimes you are a romantic."

April 9, 2000
Quixote, Sancho and the Antarctic Icebergs

QUIXOTE: "B13, that's B13. Mark your cards, ladies and gentlemen. Straight up and down. Straight from side to side--or on a diagonal. They are all winners. And remember the winner gets a big salami and a trip to Winnipeg."

SANCHO: "Quixote? Are you kidding me, Bingo? And where did you get all those ice cubes?"

QUIXOTE: "Quiet, Sancho, My great aunt Albedo is at table four and I'm trying to help things work out. Okay, did we all get that last number? Auntie? Okay, let's spin the cage and see what comes up next. Here we go: B-14. That's B-14. How odd. Look Sancho, this Bingo game is getting complicated and I could use some help here. Auntie Albedo hasn't won yet."

SANCHO: "You're trying to fix a Bingo game, Quixote? Are you joking?"

QUIXOTE: "Look do you want to help me or not, Sancho?"

SANCHO: "I'd be glad to help, Quixote."

QUIXOTE: "Well then sit down at the table and help me help my Auntie Albedo to lose. But please don't make any commotion about the damn planet. I'm here to relax and so is the rest of the gang, so keep your moralizing to a minimum."

SANCHO: "I promise to behave, Quixote."

QUIXOTE: "Good. Or maybe I should just I hand you the white ball and you can put the ping-pong ball in the slot. You think you can do that?"

SANCHO: "I believe so. Quixote, how come all the tables are filled with business people playing Bingo? I thought Bingo was for old ladies with nothing do."

QUIXOTE: "Everyone likes to gamble now and then, Sancho. So quit being so uptight. Any Bingos out there? Okay, the next number is B-16. That's B-16. You got that Auntie? Damn, she missed it again. Sancho, you're sweating."

SANCHO: "Maybe it's the warmth in here."

QUIXOTE: "We'll take care of that later. Go Auntie! I've got to think positive. You know I can't see her mark her card. I'm getting worried."

SANCHO: "You've only called three numbers in this game, Quixote. There's still hope to fix the game."

QUIXOTE: "You think so? Okay, the next number is B-17. Darn, she missed that one too."

SANCHO: "Quixote. Have you noticed all your ice cubes are melting?"

QUIXOTE: "The heater is screwed up. Okay the next number is B-18."

"Bingo!"

QUIXOTE: "Damn. Okay, Sancho you can try to cool things down now."

SANCHO: "I'll do my best. So who won? I don't think it was your Aunt Albedo."

QUIXOTE: "Nope. Aunt Albedo never had a chance. She didn't even get a single mark on her darn card that last round."

SANCHO: "So who won, Quixote?"

QUIXOTE: "The fat guy in the corner with the green suit who looks like a small dinosaur. But I think he cheated, Sancho."

SANCHO: "Heaven forbid, Quixote. But what makes you think he cheated?"

QUIXOTE: "He's been smiling at me all during the game like he knew something I didn't know about the game."

SANCHO: "Never. You're in control of your fate. That's for sure."

QUIXOTE: "Wait, now you've got that same smile, Sancho. Is there something you haven't told me?"

SANCHO: "Not a thing, Quixote. Perhaps you could ask your Aunt Albedo? Say, is she shrinking?"

October 4, 2000
Sancho, Quixote, and the Hurricane Joke

QUIXOTE: "Sancho. I have a joke for you. What do you get when you fire a high powered microwave into a hurricane?"

SANCHO: "I don't know, Quixote, what do you get when you fire a high powered microwave into a hurricane?"

QUIXOTE: "A secret that never happened."

SANCHO: "A secret that didn't work? I see. Try cold water. Is this supposed to mean something to me, Quixote?"

QUIXOTE: "Is what supposed to mean something?"

SANCHO: "This thing about the microwave and the hurricane?"

QUIXOTE: "I don't know what you're talking about, Sancho."

SANCHO: "Are you feeling all right, Quixote?"

QUIXOTE: "Never better. Did you like the debate between Gore and Bush? I think we found a lot of common ground."

SANCHO: "A bad case of cynicism, maybe?"

QUIXOTE: "I liked the part where the Republican said he trusted the man in the street."

SANCHO: "I think you're drinking too much coffee."

QUIXOTE: "Oh come on; it was hilarious, Sancho. I'll bet there weren't a thousand people watching who understood the irony of a Republican candidate saying he trusts the man in the street to take care of himself."

SANCHO: "You right, Quixote, genuine belly laughs all the way around. It was a real hoot."

QUIXOTE: "Oh lighten up; no one pays attention to civics."

SANCHO: "It's not just civics, Quixote. What do you think would happen if people understood a candidate for President called the population a bunch of fools? And it might easily happen if people took the time to understand what a Republican form of government means."

QUIXOTE: "You mean as opposed to a Democratic form of government? Or that we live in a Republic and not a democracy."

SANCHO: "Exactly, Quixote."

QUIXOTE: "Well it wouldn't be pretty, Sancho. That is for sure. But who cares? And it will never happen. Heck I'll bet if you posed that question to 50,000 science PhDs, less than 1% would understand the difference between a Republic and a Democracy. But that's good. You can't trust the masses to make their own decisions. We live in a Republic. That's the fact. The media tells people it's a Democracy and they buy it. Tell me that's not a terrific joke."

SANCHO: "It is not funny."

QUIXOTE: "What can I say? Sancho, a Republic works."

SANCHO: "I partly agree with you, Quixote. A Republic does seem to be the best form of government. But there also seems to be mounting abuse in our Republic."

QUIXOTE: "Oh, Sancho, relax. The big problem is not the total disrespect for the American people. It's not the duplicity. It's not the corruption. It's not the abuse of public trust. It's the jokes. People miss too many jokes so it's lonely at the top."

SANCHO: "You're a sensitive guy, Quixote."

QUIXOTE: "No, seriously, I feel sorry for them. You too. You're all so serious. Look, do you know the best joke of the night?"

SANCHO: "Lay it on me, Quixote. I can't wait to break out into gales of uncontrollable laughter."

QUIXOTE: "NBC. They showed a baseball game instead of the debates. Man, now that was funny."

SANCHO: "I'm rolling in the aisles."

QUIXOTE: "And almost no one will question it, Sancho."

SANCHO:	"You're probably right, Quixote. I'm laughing so hard tears are coming to my eyes."
QUIXOTE:	"I'm telling you, Sancho. Drop this idealistic quest you're on about the environment, about the government, and about the truth. Deal with the facts."
SANCHO:	"The facts according to you, Quixote."
QUIXOTE:	"No. Not just me, Sancho. Me and my friends. Because without us--there are no facts. That's why this climate change thing is still being debated. The truth no longer exists."
SANCHO:	"Quixote, aren't you a wee-bit worried about that abuse-of-power thing?"
QUIXOTE:	"Should I be? Does a major corporation worry it stuck it's corporate tongue at the people of the United States and ignored the future President of the United States for a baseball game? Of course not. Was it an abuse of power to shirk responsibility? Of course it was. But there's no problem with that. We have the reins. We have the cash. Hell, we have a microwave oven on steroids for God's sake! Damn the planet and full speed ahead! Cash, megalomania, and technology uber alles. Lighten up Sancho. We're good for a thousand year run here."
SANCHO:	"Now that was a good joke, Quixote."

October 30, 2000
Sancho, Quixote, and the Keystone COPS

SANCHO: "Nice camera, Quixote, planning on getting pictures of some oil wells for the den?"

QUIXOTE: "You're way too cynical, Sancho. I've gotten this camera because I've got a new assignment. I'm going to be a director for a movie."

SANCHO: "And I'm Clark Gable. I thought you were doing that marketing on those coral reefs..."

QUIXOTE: "I was selling dead pieces of coral reef as hood ornaments on SUVs. We've made a ton of money on that one. More dead reefs every year and a growing demand. I love it. But, that project is well underway and I'm not needed anymore. You know we've killed 40% of the world's coral reefs? All that raw material for free."

SANCHO: "A triumph of the will, Quixote."

QUIXOTE: "The free market at work. No, this Keystone COP project needs my special help: I am the director in charge of building consensus among the COPs--or at least that's what Ol' man Sennett says."

SANCHO: "Are you sure you are spelling that right? No matter. What don't the COPs agree about?"

QUIXOTE: "Oh the usual stuff: ego, self importance, profits. On the other hand, the COPs do agree they're getting nowhere artistically. That's where I came in. They're finger-pointing at each other about their tempo being off."

SANCHO: "Is their tempo off, Quixote?"

QUIXOTE: "Their tempo means nothing, Sancho."

SANCHO: "I don't understand, Quixote."

QUIXOTE: "It's their timing, not their tempo that matters. You know that thing about Nero fiddling while Rome burned?"

SANCHO: "I do."

QUIXOTE: "Our COPs have it all over Nero."

SANCHO: "So are you going to fix the timing?"

QUIXOTE: "Sancho, you should know me better than that. I'm going to tell them their timing is perfect. I need acting, not results."

SANCHO: "You'll lie to them. Now that's the Quixote I know."

QUIXOTE: "Sancho, it will not matter if I lie to them. That's why they've picked me. This a plum job for me. I know comedy: I know humor, giggles, pratfalls, gouges in the eyes, laughter, pie throwing, and deceit. Or don't you enviro-freaks understand the concept of humor?"

SANCHO: "I know humor, Quixote, and I know you. You'll lie to the participants telling them they are doing cutting-edge work and how it is all going great--while you run them straight into a brick wall."

QUIXOTE: "They are the Keystone COPs, remember? Running into walls is what is supposed to happen to them. But as you know, I know art. It will be done with grace."

SANCHO: "Well you have a sense of humor. You're lying to the actors to produce a watered down version of progress because you have a zillion police run in circles and get nothing done."

QUIXOTE: "Well we haven't got a zillion COPs yet, but we are hiring our 6th COP in a few weeks--a Dutch guy, very popular. Problem is he doesn't want to be neutered like the other COPs. I'll need to work on that one."

SANCHO: "You must be kidding. Neutered as in...?"

QUIXOTE: "Neutered. Non-viable. Inactive. Unable to, ah, reach one's full potential. Castrati."

SANCHO: "So then the other COPs were neutered? Didn't they mind that little requirement?"

QUIXOTE: "They didn't seem to. Besides, it makes them funnier when they say their lines. We've got a milestone in creativity here, Sancho. The Keystone COPs with their output modified by 21st century creativity and first century practice!"

SANCHO: "Quixote, you cannot be serious."

QUIXOTE: "Oh it'll be great. I hear the rewrite on the script is dynamite too."

SANCHO: "You hear it's great? Aren't you the director? Haven't you read it?"

QUIXOTE: "Of course not. I have only heard about the script in top level discussions--at lunch. But I don't have access to the actual script for the COPs. That's high level stuff, Sancho."

SANCHO: "But you're involved in the production?"

QUIXOTE: "I'm directing it."

SANCHO: "How can you direct it without seeing the script?"

QUIXOTE: "It's on a need-to-know basis, Sancho. And you know me. I'm a good corporate knight."

SANCHO: "Until you're extinct of course."

QUIXOTE: "There you go again, Sancho. You don't get it. I saw the film rushes. It doesn't take an idiot to recognize the COPs need a new script. But I'm not a script writer so I leave that alone and trust in TPTB. Besides, my real job in this is to keep the production company, Bread and Circus Productions, in business for a while longer."

SANCHO: "Why?"

QUIXOTE: "Education is an unending task for we of the elite. See, you can laugh at it too."

SANCHO: "Film can be a funny business, Quixote. Can you tell me, is this a remake of an old movie or is it a new script?"

QUIXOTE: "We never vary the script, Sancho. We just change the car chases and move the venue to whatever city needs tourist dollars. Sometimes we change the romantic leads, update the jokes, and show the latest weaponry, but then of course we get money from the products we showcase."

SANCHO: "And where's the art?"

QUIXOTE: "Commerce breeds art. We support commerce. Commerce breeds a better life for all."

SANCHO: "Hallelujah!"

QUIXOTE: "Sancho, you are not in step with art as it is being envisioned for our century."

SANCHO: "That's obvious. So who's writing the script--do you know that much?"

QUIXOTE: "I can only guess-- I think it's a joint venture between the CFCs--Carbon Fuels Consortium, Ol' man Sennett, and some guys from the UdotNdot. You know I have seen some of the comedy routines. We have COPs running around in circles. COPs falling in the street. COPs getting run over by vehicles. COPs in a big limousines racing through towns. COPs trying to get paid. But humor is based on the actors you know. My favorite actor is from Japan. He is so funny I just giggle whenever I see him. He's this big fat guy like a Sumo wrestler. Anyway, we have this one scene where all the other COPs pretend the fat guy is skinny and they run around trying to get the fat guy into a seat that doesn't fit. He also has this problem with flatulence; that makes the scene a real rib-tickler."

SANCHO: "All class, Quixote."

QUIXOTE: "Okay, we still have a lot of editing to do. But I need to be careful about who does the cutting and by how much."

SANCHO: "Does it really matter?"

QUIXOTE: "With the guidelines we use--not a bit. But it adds drama."

SANCHO: "So has there been much cutting?"

Quixote: "No, that's funniest part of all. There hasn't been any cutting, even as temperatures are sky-rocketing in our discussions. Sancho, you should hear those people howling about the depths of the cutting that are planned. It's a hoot."

SANCHO: "And why is that funny?"

QUIXOTE: "None of it is going to happen. I can't help but giggle."

SANCHO: "And so that's funny because?"

QUIXOTE: "That's what the COPs say to me. Here's what I tell them: I tell them even with no cutting, we are taking a step forward for art and cinema."

SANCHO: "It doesn't sound like a step forward to me."

QUIXOTE: "Of course not. This is the Keystone COPs remember? They achieve nothing other than provide amusement and distraction to the audience. So I am merely trying to keep the actors in the right spirit."

SANCHO: "So how does the film end?"

QUIXOTE: "I'm not sure but you ought to see all the stuff that's being put aside for the big conclusion. Believe me there will be all kinds of mayhem."

SANCHO: "So is that what COPs do? Lead us quietly into the mayhem of the end?"

QUIXOTE: "For some. For others the COPs and their antics represent a kind of hope."

SANCHO: "So then it is hope that will come from the COPs--not just humor."

QUIXOTE: "Don't be silly, Sancho. At the rate we are going there is almost no hope at all. But we can all guffaw at their antics. Carpe Diem, Sancho!"

October 30, 2000
Sancho, Quixote, and the Corporates

QUIXOTE: "Hey Sancho, great news! You know all my lobbying against global warming?"

SANCHO: "How could I forget, Quixote?"

QUIXOTE: "Well I am finally getting my reward."

SANCHO: "Quixote, that thing of beauty can be all too rare. Do tell me of your just reward."

QUIXOTE: "They're making more of me."

SANCHO: "Beg pardon? Is this a joke? Have I died and gone to liberal hell? Or perhaps this is just a nightmare?"

QUIXOTE: "I'm being cloned, Sancho. They're taking bits of my mucus and making more of me. If my snot is truly viable then they'll make millions of me."

SANCHO: "Be fruitful and multiply--I think some ancient said that--but I doubt the ancients will approve of the method, Quixote."

QUIXOTE: "Huh?"

SANCHO: "With mucosa? I thought is was full of white blood cells and germs."

QUIXOTE: "Best way to clone a human. No wait, that's not what they said. They said it was the best way to clone me, something to do with strong genes in my mucosa. But I still don't know why they were laughing when I entered the room. Hey what are you laughing about?"

SANCHO: "I guess even the macabre has a sense of humor. How did you arrive at this vaulted level, Quixote? Did you find some oil under a homeless shelter and have it condemned?"

QUIXOTE: "Not yet, but we're still looking. Oh, that was a joke."

SANCHO: "You found me out, Quixote. So why you?"

QUIXOTE: "TPTB considers me the perfect donor."

SANCHO: "What's TPTB: Toilet Paper To Be?"

QUIXOTE: "Very funny. TPTB stands for: The Powers That Be. It's an acronym. Anyway, to answer your question of why I was chosen: I'm a team player--a consensus builder. I'm only after what I can get. I listen to and accept TPTB. I have shown myself more than willing to screw over generations of children by my opposition to climate change, and a certain family down south knows that I know just when smack booty."

SANCHO: "Your glories light the night sky. So are you the first human, and I use that term with tongue in cheek, to be a test subject?"

QUIXOTE: "Don't be stupid. I'm flying coach on this one. The real money is in first class already and they have had their clones underway for years."

SANCHO: "Amazing what your friends can do with money, snot, and an ego the size of Greenland."

QUIXOTE: "No you don't understand. Actually, they didn't use snot, eh mucus--though they won't tell me what excretia they did use. I think there is some sensitivity about that."

SANCHO: "I can well imagine. So what else are the first class passengers on the clone express getting that you are not receiving?"

QUIXOTE: "Well everyone wants to live longer. So they will get arms, legs, organs that kind of thing before anyone else. I guess if you take an organ from your cloned self it's not considered a problem in polite society."

SANCHO: "Excretia not withstanding. Taking an organ from a version of yourself and putting it into the original model to live longer sounds like the ultimate in screwing oneself--but I am not in polite society."

QUIXOTE: "I can buy you a PSR--a Polite Society Rating."

SANCHO: "No thanks, Quixote."

QUIXOTE: "Sancho, I know how to work the system. I know all the acronyms. All you need to do is support my team on a few key issues."

SANCHO: "I don't think working for the truly twisted is my path."

QUIXOTE: "Hey these are pioneers, not monsters. Giants working to make life better for you, me, and our children. Ah, choo!"

SANCHO: "Gesundhite. Anything else the front-seaters get on the clone express?"

QUIXOTE: "Nothing, the field is still too new for the real weirdness to have taken hold--but don't worry--we'll get there. Oh, there is an interesting idea floating around. Some of our finest minds think perhaps that the best solution is to clone a body and then transfer consciousness to the new body. That way you never get old and you remain always young. But you know, I don't think they plan to just use their own clones."

SANCHO: "Aren't there laws about this stuff?"

QUIXOTE: "Just enough to make sure only the richest and most powerful can do as they desire."

SANCHO: "Silly of me to think otherwise."

QUIXOTE: "Now, you're making fun of me."

SANCHO: "Oh never, Quixote."

QUIXOTE: "Hey it's not all yachts and Beluga at the top. There are lots of problems with the procedure, but I'm not privy to them."

SANCHO: "I can well imagine, Quixote. Getting the right buggers can be a daunting task."

QUIXOTE: "It's rough at the top sometimes."

SANCHO: "And all that bickering..."

QUIXOTE: "Exactly, Sancho."

SANCHO: "So all we get is a multitude of you, Quixote? Do you get an organ or two if you have the right snot?"

QUIXOTE: "Very funny. Nope, no longevity, but I might be the prototype of a whole class of corporate servants."

SANCHO: "An honor from above the clouds."

QUIXOTE: "Hey. We work all week long. Then we would shop all weekend long. We do as we are told--leaving the powers that be to guide us along to a new and more prosperous future."

SANCHO: "No wonder the clone thing is so easy for your type. Well regardless, your mantra sounds like the makings of a new national anthem."

QUIXOTE: "Global anthem, Sancho."

SANCHO: "Of course, Valhalla comes to Mother Earth. Gaia in her proper place."

QUIXOTE: "Bliss-ninnies, beware!"

SANCHO: "It's frightening to see you happy, Quixote."

QUIXOTE: "Tell me about it, Sancho."

SANCHO: "You know, Quixote, suddenly your stand against global warming has some real appeal to me, now that you have elucidated this alternate version of our future--as envisioned by your friends."

QUIXOTE: "Trust me, Sancho, I know truth. I work in the world's largest corporations. I know what's going on. I know what I am doing. I know how to get what I want."

SANCHO: "Of course, Quixote. Sure you do."

November 9, 2000
Sancho Quixote, and the Elections

QUIXOTE: "Sancho, give me a hand will you. I'm going to Florida on the next plane."

SANCHO: "What's the problem, Quixote?"

QUIXOTE: "What do you think is up, the sun?"

SANCHO: "Oh, the election. Going down there to straighten things up, are you?"

QUIXOTE: "You know Sancho, this is the messiest one of all. I swear those, kids. Now I know why TPTB had me put together that marketing program for TV saying a little vote fraud is better than upsetting the nation with an investigation into facts."

SANCHO: "I like that one commercial where Ed and Edna were sitting in the kitchen loading their machine pistols..."

QUIXOTE: "And then they go out to the pistol range and shoot holes in the truth. I like that one too. Why are you grinning, Sancho? It's not meant to be funny."

SANCHO: "Don't strain yourself, Quixote. Oh, I almost forgot. A guy called earlier to say the plumbers are all set. Do you have any problem with leaks?"

QUIXOTE: "We're working on it already."

SANCHO: "I'm sure."

QUIXOTE: "Any other calls?"

SANCHO: "Just that one call from Publisher's Clearinghouse. They wanted to make sure you got your book: 'Misleading Old People'."

QUIXOTE: "Yup. Let's see my bags are packed. Is that my 'Book of Shills: On Think Tanks and Their Rates' sitting on the table?"

SANCHO: "Yup, just underneath of the Stanford catalogue."

QUIXOTE: "Put it here next to my notes on things-to-say-the-other-guy-did-that-we-really-did. Better yet stuff it into the liner of that other book."

SANCHO: "'The Fine Art of Puppetry: Media and Elections.' Some light reading, Quixote?"

QUIXOTE: "No for that I have this."

SANCHO: "'The Joys of Living in a Banana Republic'."

QUIXOTE: "Bound to be a classic. Got a lot of work to do so I thought some light reading was called for. Oh that reminds me, do you still have the receipts for those boxes I shipped down to Tallahassee?"

SANCHO: "Here, Quixote. Why are you flushing them down the toilet?"

QUIXOTE: "There, I feel better already. Now where's my book of yiddish sayings?"

SANCHO: "Let's see. Ah, over there by that postal meter--the one you got from the army surplus store."

QUIXOTE: "Spanish sayings?"

SANCHO: "Same place."

QUIXOTE: "I swear, I don't know what they would do without me. And where is my gallon jug of White-out?"

SANCHO: "In the living room under the Al Gore posters."

QUIXOTE: "Oh, that remind me, the posters that say 'Vote for Buchanan'? Burn those for me while I'm gone, will you?"

SANCHO: "Count on me. I wouldn't want to stand in the way of you--or any other megalomaniac--flushing our American way of life down the toilet."

November 25, 2000
Sancho and Quixote on Climate Modeling and New Orleans

QUIXOTE: "Sancho, what is that music?"

SANCHO: "La Marseillaise. So welcome back from Florida, Quixote. How come no sun tan?"

QUIXOTE: "Oh I was sidetracked away from Florida at the last minute, and sent over to the Hague. We almost lost it, Sancho. Thank goodness we tied the place up in knots."

SANCHO: "Florida?"

QUIXOTE: "The Hague. It's been a tiring but productive two weeks for me and my teams."

SANCHO: "So then you did get to work on the election, Quixote?"

QUIXOTE: "I left a lieutenant in charge--but I sent out a few ballots in my spare time. Though I lost track of the dates and sent some too late. I'll have to answer for that at some point, I tell you. But, what the heck--I'll just tell them I was too busy throwing monkey wrenches into the gears at the Hague."

SANCHO: "How so?"

QUIXOTE: "Too much science--not enough rhetoric. I hate that. Most days I was busy keeping the troops in line. Sancho, some of my people even had the audacity to suggest that we might be wrong putting our economic well-being ahead of the environment. Damn scientists."

SANCHO: "Did you have them shot, Quixote?"

QUIXOTE: "Worse. I had to show them who is boss so I sent them off to Dade County to scream at the canvassing board."

SANCHO: "Talk about rotten duty."

QUIXOTE: "Oh, the worst. Look do me a favor will you? I need you to feed the piranhas while I'm gone."

SANCHO: "Which friends in specific?"

QUIXOTE: "No--my fish."

SANCHO: "Oh, sorry I get confused some times. Still feeding the little devil's those mutated frogs they send you?"

QUIXOTE: "Got to get rid of them somehow. I get a shipment every week."

SANCHO: "It's amazing how well you can cover your tracks--regardless of the number of feet--with a few carnivorous creatures. So where are you off to, Quixote?"

QUIXOTE: "Sancho, I can't say--but I'm trying to corner the market on beads. Did you know they float and can get caught in the propellers of oil tankers?"

SANCHO: "What are you talking about?"

QUIXOTE: "Forget I said that. Actually, we're closing down our offices in the great state of Louisiana. I'm selling some real estate and liquidating some assets--that kind of thing."

SANCHO: "Why are your friends selling their real estate holdings in New Orleans?"

QUIXOTE: "I didn't say that."

SANCHO: "What happened, your address get given out to Greenpeace?"

QUIXOTE: "Nope. All I can say, Sancho, is one of the boys from Bermuda Biologicals got a little too loud in a Karaoke bar the other night and so I'm off to liquidate assets."

SANCHO: "Something going to happen there I should know about?"

QUIXOTE: "Where? What do you mean?"

SANCHO: "What's going to happen in New Orleans, Quixote?"

QUIXOTE: "I know no-thing, Sancho. Because, as you know, there is no way to predict the impact of a chaotic system, like weather, on an area as small as a city more than a few days hence..."

SANCHO: "So who said climate models are the only way to see?"

QUIXOTE: "If anything was going to happen it would be years out. So of course I wouldn't know anything is going to happen. Also computer models can't resolve a small area or the effects of time."

SANCHO: "Something is not right here. I notice you frame everything in climate modeling terms."

QUIXOTE: "Those are the rules, Sancho. Get it?"

SANCHO: "How do you sleep at night, Quixote?"

QUIXOTE: "Are you saying I am some kind of vampire, Sancho? Look-just feed the fish will you. And keep the doors closed or the piranhas might catch a cold..."

SANCHO: "We wouldn't want that would we? Quixote, I have relatives in New Orleans."

QUIXOTE: "Fish food...."

SANCHO: "What?"

QUIXOTE: "...In the greenhouse."

SANCHO: "What are you saying?"

QUIXOTE: "The greenhouse, Sancho. Put the frogs in the greenhouse a few days ahead of the feeding. The piranhas will leave some and you can use the wet rot for fertilizer for the lilies. I want the lilies healthy and strong. I'll need lots of them by the time it's all over."

SANCHO: "You've started growing lilies, Quixote?"

QUIXOTE: "I'm thinking about starting a new business. So I am learning how to cultivate the lily."

SANCHO: "You are growing flowers? Why does that strike me as odd? What kind of business are you starting?"

QUIXOTE: "Among other things, I'll be selling lilies to graveyards."

SANCHO: "I should have known. You exude charm, Quixote."

QUIXOTE: "Thank you. Do you know if any lilies float?"

SANCHO: "I think they're called water lilies."

QUIXOTE: "Water lilies would be perfect. I'll make a note of that. I'll sell them as floating remembrances. I could hire a boat and throw them over the side. They'll grow well in muddy water, I bet. I could get some videos of the service, maybe some deeply religious jazz riffs. I could put it on DVD with some news pictures. Man, there's money to be made in that! Hell you know, I could just show the same damn lily being tossed in the water and sell it over and over. The profits will sink right to my bottom line."

SANCHO: "Quixote, walk with me to the fish tank."

CHAPTER 5
2001

March 18, 2001
Sancho, Quixote, and Foliage

QUIXOTE: "Sancho, What are you doing spitting at that bush?"

SANCHO: "Oh, it's you. I was wondering when you'd get here."

QUIXOTE: "I would have been here earlier but I was attending a series of seminars at the Coal and Oil Intermediate Training for Unprincipled Supervisors, Unleashed and Allied, or COITUS U ALL--as one of the wily-boys call it."

SANCHO: "Seems to me another name fits as well."

QUIXOTE: "You have no idea how well. Did you know it's a think tank with the specific purpose of finding ways to reduce the population."

SANCHO: "Interesting goal. How's that going, reducing the population?"

QUIXOTE: "Getting better every day."

SANCHO: "So you're recommending birth control, education, access to information, that kind of thing?"

QUIXOTE: "Sancho, you are a funny man."

SANCHO:	"I had a feeling you might see it that way. So what's COITUS U ALL's plan for culling out unwanted humanity?"
QUIXOTE:	"Did you hear that if the coal plants operators burn coal as they wish, that the IPCC suggests maybe a 10 degrees C rise in global temperature?"
SANCHO:	"I'm confused. You are quoting the IPCC, is this a joke? Last thing I knew your people branded them kooks and hysterics."
QUIXOTE:	"Wait till you hear the jokes on Letterman and Leno. Anyway, look. I said our purpose is to reduce the planetary population. Climate change will do that job admirably."
SANCHO:	"So you do agree it is happening."
QUIXOTE:	"We've discussed that in private."
SANCHO:	"Oh, I get it--so that's why your people fight it? To kill off a portion of the next generation? I thought it was just to get so obscenely rich you and your buddies can play Caligula for years to come."
QUIXOTE:	"Stop being so melodramatic, Sancho. Think about it. Who really gets hurt by the storms, the diseases, the famine and the disasters of climate change?"
SANCHO:	"The insurance companies?"
QUIXOTE:	"Don't be a fool. It's the poor, the weak, the less educated--those that do not have access to good information, so in other words, human chaff. Your mouth is hanging open. Now sure there will be a few 'normal' people getting hurt but we're talking acceptable losses with a continued strong global economy. And it's a dream come true for my folks at COITUS U ALL and the Alumni."
SANCHO:	"But people are going to die."
QUIXOTE:	"So? And what's with the spit on the bush. God, that is a disgusting plant. Did you deposit all that phlegm on those branches, yourself?"
SANCHO:	"I've spit at every branch for 3 weeks, but it has done no good. I am beginning to see why."
QUIXOTE:	"Why in the name of OPEC does that surprise you? And why are you spitting at a stupid bush anyway?"

SANCHO:	"This was once a cherry tree. Then some people came along and grafted this bush on it. I've been trying to convince the bush to turn back into a cherry tree and I thought spitting at it might motivate a change. But it doesn't seem to work."
QUIXOTE:	"You have got to be kidding me. And who cares anyway?"
SANCHO:	"The problem is the root structure. You see how the branches are all rotting?"
QUIXOTE:	"I did, but I thought that was a function of the graft or your fusillade of spit."
SANCHO:	"You are right it's the graft. Every living thing around here is going to be affected. I wanted to stop it and finally saw I needed to get my frustration out so I began to spit at the bush. Then I realized the bush didn't give a tinker's damn about me, or my spit. The rotting roots are everywhere, and spreading."
QUIXOTE:	"Awe relax, Sancho. It's just the way of things now. Plants, people, and institutions all change."
SANCHO:	"Rot and change are not really the same thing."
QUIXOTE:	"You and I just happen to be here to watch the latest change. And that spit-covered bush and its bad roots spreading everywhere are not the problem. They are merely a symptom of change. Ignore it."
SANCHO:	"So the problem is the graft, not what comes after it."
QUIXOTE:	"It's a fait accompli, my friend. I keep telling you to go with the flow. Caring is out; the Me-generation is back."
SANCHO:	"For some perhaps, not I."
QUIXOTE:	"Listen. I can get you into the inner circle, no problem. Soon your life will be a cascade of money that you don't really control, an illusion of power you don't really have. Women sleeping with you who hate you and themselves-- and a patina of meaninglessness that will transmute to every decent human feeling into spite, jealousy, mean-spiritedness, as well as a competitive frenzy that would make a gladiator blush. But there's paid dental and paid medical insurance."
SANCHO:	"I'll pass on the wonderful opportunity. But I do think I'll go back, catch a taxi home, and leave the dumb bush alone."

QUIXOTE: "And I do have to get back to classes. You know COITUS U ALL calls louder than you could ever imagine. What are doing now? Why are you leaning over the bush like that? What are you doing, talking to a plant?"

SANCHO: "I just had to explain that I was going. After three weeks of spitting day after day I've developed a responsibility for closure, I guess."

QUIXOTE: "Closure huh? So did you tell the bush you were going?"

SANCHO: "In a way. I said to the bush COITUS U ALL. I'm sure it understood."

QUIXOTE: "Tree-huggers. I'll never understand them. Come on, let's get going I'll be late for my seminar on how to market genocide to preschoolers."

July 15, 2001
Sancho, Quixote, the Great Bear, and Sinks

SANCHO:	"Quixote, what in the name of Paul Bunyon are you doing with a chain saw?"
QUIXOTE:	"Sinks, Sancho."
SANCHO:	"You're going to cut up a sink with a chain saw?"
QUIXOTE:	"Yup."
SANCHO:	"Kitchen, bath, or utility sink?"
QUIXOTE:	"Very funny. But yes, that's right we will be cutting up sinks--don't ask me why. But first, I need to practice. Open that big box then stand back, Sancho."
SANCHO:	"The one with the BC on it? That must be one huge sink you're cutting into--holy cow, Quixote, what's in that box? It's moving."
QUIXOTE:	"It's a bear, Sancho. And don't give me a bad time about what I have to do. I feel bad enough about this that I don't need to hear your bleeding-heart-liberal-bleat."
SANCHO:	"Ahh, what are you going to do to the bear, Quixote?"
QUIXOTE:	"I'm just following orders. Now open up the box and stand back. You may want put on a mask and keep your mouth shut. It might get messy. Oh darn it. My chain saw just seized. I need a better balance of oil."
SANCHO:	"Quixote, why do you care about a chain saw or some bear, if you're planning to cut up sinks? And why in the name of Thomas Crapper are you going to cut up sinks anyway? Last time I checked cutting into a sink severely diminishes it's function."
QUIXOTE:	"Well we'll make more sinks, Sancho. I hear there's a bug that will spit them out like paper clips."
SANCHO:	"Like Australia needs more rabbits. So you're going on the theory that if it works then why not break it?"

QUIXOTE: "Exactly--though this doesn't make as much sense as you might think--if you look at the long term costs of trading those sink parts for operative sinks we might be better keeping the sinks whole. I checked."

SANCHO: "So, you think there's more value to whole sinks than cut up sinks. That's good, Quixote. Your holistic approach to plumbing makes you practically a tree-hugger."

QUIXOTE: "Insulting me will get you nowhere. And I'm still going to cut sinks up--that's what I am doing with the bear."

SANCHO: "Doing with the bear? What are you going to do to the bear, Quixote?"

QUIXOTE: "You know nothing about economics and the creation of wealth, Sancho. Neither do I--so I do as I'm told."

SANCHO: "You can't mean you are going to use that chain saw on that bear, Quixote?"

QUIXOTE: "You're worried the chain saw isn't big enough to do the job on such a large bear? Don't worry. I'll be okay. It's the quality of the bar, not the size."

SANCHO: "Right. This whole thing makes almost no sense--even by your standards--Quixote. What about the bear?"

QUIXOTE: "Look, Sancho. I received a note the other day that said my associates will need my help in cutting up sinks so they can make more money. Then the chain saw came in the mail. A note inside said: 'We're going to cut up the Great Bear as practice for dealing with sinks and tree-huggers.' Then I saw this bear out in the forest by my property that same day and I put it all together. So I trapped the bear and made preparations to chain saw the bear so I can help figure out how to deal with sinks and tree-huggers. I'm always ahead the curve, you know."

SANCHO: "Quixote, you're lost in a sea of corporate zealousness. Tell me this isn't so."

QUIXOTE: "Can't do that, Sancho. Step aside, or look away if you can't take the heat."

SANCHO: "Quixote, you can't use a chain saw to cut up a bear! It's not right."

QUIXOTE:	"Don't worry. I'll be okay."
SANCHO:	"Not you. If you take a chain saw to a bear-- you'll kill it."
QUIXOTE:	"Prove it."
SANCHO:	"Quixote, you are need of serious medical attention. What makes you think you can cut up a bear and not kill it?"
QUIXOTE:	"I'm a corporate knight, Sancho. I'm not paid to think."
SANCHO:	"Obviously."
QUIXOTE:	"There, I've gotten the oil myself. Hear those teeth running along the bar, Sancho? It's a beautiful sound isn't it? Okay, open up the box and let me at that great bear."
SANCHO:	"Think, Quixote. Soon those steel teeth will be ripping into that bear at a hundred miles an hour. Ripping its limbs apart, cutting through it's bones, destroying tendons, kidneys, bones, heart, stomach, intestines. It'll be bear guts everywhere. You might mess up your yard."
QUIXOTE:	"Well, messes can't be helped when there's money to be made and sinks to be cut, Sancho."
SANCHO:	"Do you think it might be a mistake cutting up a huge bear like that here, on the ocean, windward, side of your property?"
QUIXOTE:	"Should I?"
SANCHO:	"Think about it, Quixote."
QUIXOTE:	"Okay yes, of course. Any idiot can see the problem: flying bear guts. Look, Sancho, they told me to do this. And as a good knight I have to do as I am told--no matter how idiotic it seems. Step aside."
SANCHO:	"Quixote--I think you're missing something here. Tell me again why the bear has to die so you can cut up sinks."
QUIXOTE:	"Sancho, what do you think of me? Do you really think I'm going to kill that bear? All I'm going to do is rip it apart with my chain saw and cut it up into little pieces. It will still be a bear. Now open that box--I've got some cuttin' to do."

SANCHO: "Do you really presume to tell me you're going to cut that bear into pieces with a chain saw and then claim you didn't know you would kill it?"

QUIXOTE: "I don't have time to model it on the computer. Besides, no one can predict the future, Sancho, though I will admit there is some possibility I might curtail its functions."

SANCHO: "Curtail its functions? You plan to kill a living breathing organism for something you don't understand."

QUIXOTE: "'We will not kill it We may however curtail its function a bit.' They told me to say that. Another is: 'The Great Bear will be all right.' Sounds positively mystical doesn't it? We are getting so soulful ever since geebee was elected."

SANCHO: "Who writes your stuff, Kafka?"

QUIXOTE: "Sancho, it's just a bear. Like a sink is just a sink. Who needs to worry about the details--especially when there's money to be made? You tree-huggers, how about I use a no-regrets policy? There, now I've set the safety on the chain saw. The bear will be all right. Safety first, Sancho. Get out of the way."

SANCHO: "No."

QUIXOTE: "Heck, I'll cut the lock off the box, myself. I don't need your help."

SANCHO: "With that chain saw and your myopia you're invincible, Quixote, I can see that now. Of course that moldy cheese in your skull helps also."

QUIXOTE: "No reason to get hot under the collar, Sancho."

SANCHO: "You're right, it does seem to be getting warm quick."

QUIXOTE: "Ah, you're a tricky one Sancho. You're trying to save that bear with that old global warming story. They mentioned that too in the letter. It was under the heading of: Dealing with eco-freaks. But forget it. The increased heat you feel doesn't mean anything. Heck, maybe it's just a tiny heat island effect--caused by my chain saw. Hmm, I better send that off so we can use it on CNN. Now let me at that flesh. And don't worry it will be all right."

CHAPTER 6
2002

February 22, 2002
Sancho, Quixote, and the Giggles

QUIXOTE: "Sancho, what's wrong? You look like you are about to burst."

SANCHO: "It's laughter, Quixote. I have been sitting here watching and listening to you and your friends these last few months and for the most part I just had a few smiles-but the humor of what I'm seeing recently is just too much to deal with."

QUIXOTE: "We don't appreciate humor. You need to remember that."

SANCHO: "Humor can be counter productive."

Quixote: "Unless they say it is okay. Then it's splendid of course. Unless they change their mind--in which case they never said what they said unless they say they said it differently--in which case that's also okay. You're laughing again."

SANCHO: "I can't help it. Your friends are just too much."

QUIXOTE: "Sancho, they're serious business people and government officials. Now quit that--I said quit laughing. Sancho, I'm serious. We have ways to make you stop laughing."

SANCHO: "Quixote, I just can't stop. Let me ask you a question: Is it really true that Junior proposed a global warming control plan that exempted carbon dioxide but included mercury?"

QUIXOTE: "Well, Junior and the Boss did that, yes, and we are sorry for that. The mercury lobby is really pissed at us. Guess who had to calm them down?"

SANCHO: "You?"

QUIXOTE: "Of course, but I'd rather be floating on the top of the spittoon than down in the mire with the rest of you. What are you laughing about now?"

SANCHO: "Why did you-all include mercury but not CO_2 Quixote?"

QUIXOTE: "The mercury lobby is lots smaller. Their junkets are boring too. Their lunches are bad and their campaign contribution suggestions were not met."

SANCHO: "I see how that might bring about negative legislation for a lobby."

Quixote: "It's a tough job. I pity the guys from mercury. I mean think about it: they're competing with fossil fuels, aluminum, autos, transport, and the rest of the gang."

SANCHO: "Sounds like ritualized extortion."

QUIXOTE: "And that's not the worst of it. Did you know Junior and the Boss like petroleum."

SANCHO: "As in Vaseline?"

QUIXOTE: "Hey without petroleum, Junior and the Boss might do some real harm. The petroleum smooths things out."

SANCHO: "You don't need to tell me."

QUIXOTE: "I can't anyway. But let me say it is thanks to petroleum that what Junior and the Boss are doing to the country isn't quite as bad as it might be. Quit laughing, Sancho."

SANCHO: "Quixote. It is just too absurd."

QUIXOTE: "But of course--that's American politics at the dawn of the 21st century. Trust me. I know."

SANCHO: "We're a banana republic. It's all extortion and blackmail."

QUIXOTE: "Sancho, we are not racist. We are honest business people concerned with environment and the welfare of our ghettos."

SANCHO: "You should do stand up comedy, Quixote."

QUIXOTE: "We do. Did you see our last set of interviews? They were a hoot. Did you know I, and the guys from an unnamed energy company with minor financial problems, had popcorn during the last public speeches--I swear Ken almost spit up a couple of times. He thinks Junior is one of the funniest men he has ever met."

SANCHO: "No doubt, Quixote. Is it true you guys put out a report the other day saying Junior was concerned that a group of dissident scientists who opposed the theory of anthropogenic forcing of the climate were not being heard from because they were being gagged by the liberal news media?"

QUIXOTE: "That was a good one wasn't it?"

SANCHO: "I can always recognize your work. So how come those dissident scientists got the op-ed page of the NY Times and the Wall Street Journal?"

QUIXOTE: "Damn liberal media never cuts us any slack."

SANCHO: "Absurd, Quixote, absolutely absurd."

QUIXOTE: "And those guys at Fox--sooo liberal. Sancho, if you laugh any harder, you'll need oxygen."

SANCHO: "So what about that Enron thing, Quixote?"

QUIXOTE: "Who?"

SANCHO: "Enron."

QUIXOTE: "Never heard of them, Sancho."

SANCHO: "Is it true a group of think tank buffoons released a report that said Enron conspired with the Clinton Administration to push legislation on climate change?"

QUIXOTE: "Oh them. Enron. Horrible people. They are the anti-corporation you know. We're getting tons of mileage out that trading screw-up of theirs."

SANCHO: "What do you mean trading screw-up, Quixote?"

QUIXOTE: "They screwed up a few trades in the energy market then they
            tried to cover it. Things went from bad to worse and that's all
            she wrote."

SANCHO: "Energy trading is tough?"

QUIXOTE: "Brutal, Sancho. I doubt anyone really knows how to do it
            well besides the people in arbitrage."

SANCHO: "New markets are tough."

QUIXOTE: "Especially when the prices are impacted by climate change.
            Oops, I didn't say that."

SANCHO: "Of course not, Quixote."

QUIXOTE: "You know I think we might pin Osama Bin Laden to Enron
            with just a little more spin."

SANCHO: "You're kidding?"

QUIXOTE: "As a stockholder. And I never kid about good propaganda.
            Remember stocks have no sense of humor."

SANCHO: "You underestimate yourself."

QUIXOTE: "But not just propaganda--it's our lifeblood."

SANCHO: "When the emperor has no clothes it's the only recourse."

QUIXOTE: "No there is lots more we can do, Sancho. Have I told you
            about our Ghettoization of America plan?"

SANCHO: "Oh no."

QUIXOTE: "What happened, you stopped laughing?"

March 20, 2002
Sancho, Quixote, and the Greenhouse

QUIXOTE:	"Sancho, I'm telling you for the last time there is nothing to worry about."
SANCHO:	"Quixote, the water is dirty, the air is dirty, the electrical system is failing, and we keep losing shelves. Don't you think they are hints that maybe this place isn't as safe as you and say."
QUIXOTE:	"The design is sound. The system will continue to function. We are safe."
SANCHO:	"Quixote, I'll say it again--those shelves keep breaking so we have a problem. A big one."
QUIXOTE:	"There's nothing wrong with the shelves. They function exactly as they are supposed to, Sancho. It was just time for those shelves to collapse."
SANCHO:	"But what about the shelf that's over the dynamite in the basement. If it breaks the water main will break and we will be flooded."
QUIXOTE:	"Nonsense. This is a three-story mansion. There is no way the water in the basement will reach the critical rooms of my bedroom, my play room or the kitchen. I designed the house so all that will be safe from rising water."
SANCHO:	"Ah, Quixote, don't you think that if the shelf falls into the dynamite we might have bigger problems than a flood?"
QUIXOTE:	"All my friends say not to worry about it. I do as I am told. I don't want to lose privileges so I don't think about that."
SANCHO:	"Our home is falling apart."
QUIXOTE:	"Nonsense. Everything is fine."
SANCHO:	"My bedroom is downstairs. Does that matter?"
QUIXOTE:	"We should move you upstairs so you will be safe."
SANCHO:	"What about the people down the hill?"

QUIXOTE: "They matter? Look, I'm willing to save you, my servant. That makes me a good guy doesn't it? In fact all my friends are going to save their servants. We are good and decent people, but we can't worry about everyone--especially when there's money to be made."

SANCHO: "Quixote, you ninny! There are dishes on the floor in the kitchen, the entertainment systems has been punctured by the computer in the study, all the sinks seem to be shrinking, the bug problem is out of control. All the frogs near our house each have three legs. You almost died from West Nile Fever last year and the plants are all over the floor in the greenhouse because of those shelves you refuse to worry about keep breaking."

QUIXOTE: "The shelves are going to be fine. This place we live in is going to be just fine."

SANCHO: "Our home is coming apart, you dumb bunny. Don't you get it?"

QUIXOTE: "It's a cyclical thing. You just don't understand."

SANCHO: "The shelves keep breaking, Quixote--and they are breaking faster than you can spin lies that say they are not collapsing. If you can't deal with that, then at least think about your upcoming party. It's going to be a disaster when all this is too horrific to ignore."

QUIXOTE: "Oh the party, thanks for reminding me. Still, people will forget. There's wrestling, baseball, internet porn, cigarettes, and booze. Everything is fine."

SANCHO: "If the shelves collapse too quickly they might just collapse in the middle of your party. If that happens there is no way anyone is going to forget your party because of kitty litter and drugs."

QUIXOTE: "Well, we want it to be a memorable party."

SANCHO: "Kind of like the Nazi party, Quixote?"

QUIXOTE: "Don't worry about that one. With the plans my friends and I have the Nazi party will seem like a bunch of also-rans."

SANCHO: "People may die, you mean?"

QUIXOTE: "Now there you go, heh, heh. Everything is fine."

SANCHO: "Everything is not fine. Get it?"

QUIXOTE: "I'm talking with my experts. They assure me the shelves are fine. In fact they say the greenhouse is not really there. Crimeny. What was that?"

SANCHO: "That big shelf in the greenhouse just fell. I think it was the one with the Larsen bees on it."

QUIXOTE: "We don't own a greenhouse, Sancho."

SANCHO: "Really, so what's that room on the south side of the mansion that's covered with glass and heats from the sun and stays warmer than the rest of this place?"

QUIXOTE: "That room doesn't exist Sancho, therefore the problem with the shelves does not exist either. And frankly, the Larsen bees don't matter. By the way, is the Ross shelf still okay?"

SANCHO: "I'll go look."

QUIXOTE: "Hmmm, don't bother. We don't own a greenhouse, Sancho."

SANCHO: "You said in 1998 if the shelf with the Larsen bees collapsed quickly you would do something."

QUIXOTE: "I lied."

SANCHO: "What?"

QUIXOTE: "Better luck next time. Oh, don't be so glum. The shelf was a floater anyway."

SANCHO: "What does that have to do with anything? It collapsed in a month you, dunderhead."

QUIXOTE: "But it took a month. That's the way I will spin it next week. Imagine, an entire month for a collapse! Heck I can hear the anchor on NBC now. 'Imagine a whole month!' You know as I think about it...In time that will seem like a long time for one of those shelves to collapse. Hell, it will become commonplace if I have my way. Besides there is no greenhouse so the bees don't exist, and the shelves don't matter so neither does their collapse. Especially since that last shelf was a floater. By the way, what's a floater?"

SANCHO: "Quixote, you and your friends are floaters, you know that?"

QUIXOTE: "Was that an insult?"

SANCHO: "Quixote, you have to do something about this place falling apart."

QUIXOTE: "Not really."

SANCHO: "When are you going to pay attention to the problem?"

QUIXOTE: "That's just it, Sancho. I don't have to pay attention to the problem. Neither do my friends--so stop bothering us with problems you don't have the money to enforce."

SANCHO: "Money? Do you really think the misery you are in the process of creating will not catch up with you in spite of your money?"

QUIXOTE: "Perhaps, but we're too far into it now to go back. And we all know now that if anybody tries to blow the whistle on us I can assure you they will sink faster than call options on Enron stock. No one will do anything. Get it?"

SANCHO: "That's it?"

QUIXOTE: "That's it. I will just stall for time now and hope for a viable exit strategy."

SANCHO: "That's heinous."

QUIXOTE: "By the way I heard an interesting notion on that comparison to the Nazi party. It's come up before."

SANCHO: "I bet it has. What's the spin, Quixote?"

QUIXOTE: "You know the problem wasn't what the Nazis did. The problem was they got caught and how they were remembered."

SANCHO: "You are certifiable, Quixote."

QUIXOTE: "No, listen, I've got it solved. If we really mess this house up right--there won't be any history to recall what we have done. Pretty slick, huh?"

SANCHO: "Said one dinosaur to the other..."

CHAPTER 7
2003

June 19, 2003
Sancho, Quixote, and Casa Blanca

SANCHO: "Quixote, welcome back to Casa Blanca…"

QUIXOTE: "Nice to be back, Sancho."

SANCHO: "Was the snooker competition fun; how did you do?"

QUIXOTE: "Not so good, we only just won the pool competition. The rest of the competition was tough, especially on geebee. Some of the other participants insisted he not cheat--so we compromised on pool after I told geebee needs to play by our rules or he gets confused. They balked at first."

SANCHO: "Which pool rule didn't they like, Quixote?"

QUIXOTE: "You know, I rack or else."

SANCHO: "So what happened?"

QUIXOTE: "They claimed it was Fascism. And I think I made a mistake, when I agreed we are Fascists."

SANCHO: "You are--but sometimes it takes hard love like that to show how decent you really are, Quixote."

QUIXOTE: "Then I told them what is real. And just to prove my point I reminded them that it was me, who, just a few years ago, looked at them over-the-counter and took all their money."

SANCHO: "That must have gotten their attention."

QUIXOTE: "The TV was on--most of them missed it."

SANCHO: "Lucky you. Quixote, what's wrong?"

QUIXOTE: "Sancho, they insisted we not cheat."

SANCHO: "Horrors. No egomania? No bullying? No graft? Bet you must have had a good laugh over that one, Quixote."

QUIXOTE: "I did, but can you imagine it: Us, not cheating?"

SANCHO: "It dimples my chads just to think about it. Were they trying to ruin your way of life?"

QUIXOTE: "I don't know. I made contact with GITS, Goebels Institute for the Terminally Stupid, just in case. I wanted to make sure geebee and his friends were okay to stay in the competition."

SANCHO: "That would be a tragedy if they missed it. They play 'Lord of the Flies' so well."

QUIXOTE: "In truth, they'd never keep geebee from playing; he won the butt-kissing award the other day from API for editing that climate thing Christine wrote."

SANCHO: "I thought she was a member of the club, Quixote."

QUIXOTE: "Some times bad people go good--it's one of the horrors we have to face in this life."

SANCHO: "You amaze me, Quixote. How is the butt-kissing award awarded anyway?"

QUIXOTE: "One has to show exemplary cowardice in the face of decency and present the proof of your cowardice to the public. The API, the Accumulating Pissants Institute reviews the entrants and makes its decisions accordingly."

SANCHO: "That's a pretty high level award. And I read that editing job-
-it was quite thorough. He really shined."

QUIXOTE: "I was proud of the way he ignored the essence of truth and
gutted the facts. Frankly, I think there is no way the Nobel
Prize people can ignore that and keep him out."

SANCHO: "Where's your young ward anyway? He hasn't peed on himself
again has he?"

QUIXOTE: "No, geebee's still in the car trying to figure out how to use
the door handle. He sat on the other side of the car again by
mistake."

SANCHO: "Oh you made him get in the car by walking around the
front and not the back. That wasn't very nice, Quixote. But
very funny. Sooner or later he'll get it."

QUIXOTE: "I don't know he insists that everyone sit on the right side
and he begins to tantrum when anyone says there is another
place to sit."

SANCHO: "How are you going to get him out."

QUIXOTE: "We're working on that. Got any ideas, Sancho?"

SANCHO: "I think I do, Quixote. Have you considered shining a bright
light on him?"

QUIXOTE: "We may need to try that. Truth is, I can't stand it when an
idiot stands in the way of getting things done."

SANCHO: "I know that feeling, Quixote."

CHAPTER 8
2004

August 2, 2004
Sancho, Quixote, and the Bases

SANCHO: "Quixote, what are you doing?"

QUIXOTE: "Who, what me? Oh, Sancho. Long time no see."

SANCHO: "What in the name of Lou Gehrig are you doing on that truck? That looks like home plate in your hand."

QUIXOTE: "I took it from Yankee Stadium--after a baseball game. Don't worry nobody saw me. It was during one of those horrific rainstorms."

SANCHO: "Why did you take it?"

QUIXOTE: "Truthfully, Sancho, they said I need to add bases to the ocean. They said nothing about home plate. You think I'm in Dutch with them?"

SANCHO: "Why are you adding baseball base bags to the ocean?"

QUIXOTE: "Look Sancho, I do as I am told. They said the ocean was getting too acidic and I should add some bases to it."

SANCHO: "You are one funny lackey, Quixote. Are you sure they said bases? As in the plural?"

QUIXOTE: "You mean I should just add first base? What difference does it make? You're so picky."

SANCHO: "Quixote, how do you and your friends stay in power being so, how shall I put it: inelegant"

QUIXOTE: "Terror."

SANCHO: "You've become more honest, Quixote."

QUIXOTE: "You know Sancho, you were right about the climate--where have you been?"

SANCHO: "I went to work for the GBC."

QUIXOTE: "What's that?"

SANCHO: "The Global Bifurcation Council."

QUIXOTE: "Who are they? A bunch of nuts who just go off at a moment's notice about climate change."

SANCHO: "Not quite at a moment's notice."

QUIXOTE: "Are you going to help me put these bases in the ocean or not? I really need a hand. I have truckload of bases here."

SANCHO: "Quixote, the climate--we have a serious problem developing."

QUIXOTE: "Oh, not again. Sancho, we have plans to stabilize CO_2 at 550 ppm and take the US output down to 1.3 gigatons a year by 2050. Of course Kyoto is a load of lime."

SANCHO: "550 PPM by the year 2050?"

QUIXOTE: "So, it's something. We're at least addressing the problem."

SANCHO: "Said one dinosaur to the other.....Quixote, do you remember when I used to talk about the "Phase Shift' and how we need to consider what might happen?"

QUIXOTE: "Oh, you mean the 'Tipping Point'? That was in the global warming movie the boys at Fox put out. We're on this one, Sancho--trust me. Climate change will never happen that fast and it was only fiction."

SANCHO: "I can think of one piece of fiction that has it right."

QUIXOTE: "Huh? I think you're beginning to bifurcate."

SANCHO: "Something is. The so-called 'Tipping Point' isn't like a ledge. It is a set of nonlinear events, Quixote. Rogue wave frequency or a two-foot deep hailstorms in July in Edmonton for example. It's the frequency of hyper-energetic events that matter. It's not like the movies. Get it? Count on it."

QUIXOTE: "You worry too much."

SANCHO: "You said that same thing when I told you climate change was due to human forcing."

QUIXOTE: "Bah, so what! Who cares? I don't think anyone will notice if I throw the wrong base in the ocean, do you?"

SANCHO: "Quixote, do you know what happens when you put...Ah... Second base in an acidic solution."

QUIXOTE: "Sliding is out of the question?"

SANCHO: "Cute. It creates water and something else. Think about it."

QUIXOTE: "Sometimes, Sancho, your discussions aren't worth any more than salt. Besides, I never concern myself with thought. I follow my orders...But you have me curious. The ocean is an acid?"

SANCHO: "You really are a comedy, Quixote. Of course the oceans are not acids but the CO_2 is causing an increase in acidity. Things are dying and things are changing as a result."

QUIXOTE: "So what? Are you saying my bases are going to pollute it? Believe me, my bases are not going to hurt a thing."

SANCHO: "There might be lots of, uh, bases in the ocean."

QUIXOTE: "I know. We have lots of other lackeys beside me tossing things in the oceans. I have one friend who tosses dead mad cows in the ocean, but he is very careful, believe me. He never lets anyone know when he's doing it."

SANCHO: "Tossing diseased carcasses in the ocean--that's careful?"

QUIXOTE: "The sin is to be caught. Still he keeps lists of everything he does. I keep telling him: Be careful of those cattle-lists."

SANCHO: "You are a funny one, Quixote."

QUIXOTE: "Look, Sancho. You are my best servant, but I need to tell you: You are crying wolf again, Sancho."

SANCHO: "Wolf, Quixote. Wolf."

September 24, 2004
Sancho, Quixote, and the Big Mower

QUIXOTE: "Sancho, do you have time to listen to some slogans?"

SANCHO: "Sure, Quixote, let me just finish making out my check to Amnesty International."

QUIXOTE: "Not with my money, you're not."

SANCHO: "Quixote, it's my money I got it as an inheritance from Grandpa George and Grandpa Tom. Besides, what's the problem with Amnesty International?"

QUIXOTE: "My friends are angry with them. We're starting a campaign that centers on the notion that Amnesty International does not exist and never will exist. The plan is to show some evil environmentalist created Amnesty International as a way to spread fear and mistrust."

SANCHO: "Seems I have heard this somewhere, Quixote. How could Amnesty International not exist?"

QUIXOTE: "I don't know. I admit it's kind of a stretch. My friends figured they got away with it for global warming so now they are trying to broaden the scope of the campaign to include human rights. Some of the guys from Heritage and Marshall are sure this will wotk."

SANCHO: "Oh, no wonder. Well good luck--but I don't think it'll fly."

QUIXOTE: "Why not?"

SANCHO: "It didn't really work before. Human induced global warming is accepted by every reputable institution out there."

QUIXOTE: "The U.S., government says it is not proven."

SANCHO: "My point, exactly."

QUIXOTE: "Hmmm. I see. Even so, we have convinced much of TV-America there is nothing to worry about with global warming. How difficult can it be to claim there is no such thing as Amnesty International?"

Sancho: "Well for one they exist."

Quixote: "So does global warming--but that hasn't stopped us from convincing the public we have it under control."

Sancho: "Touche. So what kind of slogans do you have for me to critique?"

Quixote: "Well a few of them will relate to the so-called organization allegedly named Amnesty International, but for now I have some others for you to hear."

Sancho: "I see you're on task, Quixote."

Quixote: "Always. Okay the first one relates to nuclear power as an answer to global warming. Ready?"

Sancho: "I'm all a-glow."

Quixote: "Okay, Ready? 'Nuclear Power: It takes 20 years to get going--by that time the need will be obvious. Why wait?'"

Sancho: "Ah prudent risk assessment, I love it, Quixote. What's next?"

Quixote: "How about: Global Warming will kill you in the future--why shouldn't we?"

Sancho: "Perfect. I think you're on a roll."

Quixote: "Okay this is my favorite: 'We screwed around for so long with global warming you have no other choice: Go Nuclear or die!'"

Sancho: "Your use of the imperative is profound. I'd say you're hitting on all cylinders."

Quixote: "Okay here's one we're not sure of--it relates to the amount of concrete used in a nuclear power plant, ready?"

Sancho: "Hit it."

Quixote: "Concrete adds far more CO_2 to the atmosphere than you think. So don't think about it...Or else."

Sancho: "Hmm, it has a certain ring to it, Quixote. I like the way your friends use threats to get your message across."

QUIXOTE: "Also we have a plan to form a new think tank to push the overall of lies, deceit, greed and stupidity. We're calling it the Guantanamo Electricity Nearly-Nuclear Intelligent Think Tank Affirming Lies."

SANCHO: "Too long--but the acronym is interesting. Anymore slogans?"

QUIXOTE: "Kind of--how do you like: 'We screwed you on your pension so why not go to war and die for us?'"

SANCHO: "Not very elegant, but it is to the point.'"

QUIXOTE: "I have trouble with that one."

SANCHO: "Why?"

QUIXOTE: "It leaves out our plans to rape Social Security."

SANCHO: "So it's the full disclosure thing that bothers you."

QUIXOTE: "Exactly. I'm thinking we need a certain level of openness to make this campaign work."

SANCHO: "You could be right, Quixote. Why not say something like: 'Corporations are godless soulless beings that exist solely to make money'?"

QUIXOTE: "Can't, Sancho, then we would have to admit humans have become subservient to corporations. That makes corporations look a bit demonic."

SANCHO: "Ya' think?"

QUIXOTE: "Definitely."

SANCHO: "So you worry people will see the transnational corporate legal structure as evil because it has no culpability, no social responsibility, no soul, and no guiding principles beside making money? And then there is the problem that it has the right to influence public policy inside national boundaries?"

QUIXOTE: "Exactly. That's it in a nutshell. They can't have you all working together. We need you all to keep fighting each other."

SANCHO: "As in wars?"

QUIXOTE: "Wars, religious intolerance, ethnic intolerance, right vs. left, you name it, Sancho."

SANCHO: "Otherwise, we might see that the inhuman structures called transnational corporations are ruining our planet, killing people, corrupting the U.S., and turning humans into their puppets. Hell, with clarity on the lack of responsibility for corporations all kinds of things might make sense, Quixote."

QUIXOTE: "Exactly--and we can't have that, can we, Sancho?"

SANCHO: "We, Quixote? Who is we? Your friends?"

QUIXOTE: "My friends are people, Sancho, not corporations."

SANCHO: "Amen to that, Quixote."

October 12, 2004
Sancho, Quixote, and the Fog

SANCHO: "Nice glasses Quixote--they look a bit like running shoes for the nose. Of course everything plastic does. What are the little windshield wipers for?"

QUIXOTE: "Sight. We have seen the future, Sancho, and we want to make sure a little dampness doesn't fog the market."

SANCHO: "I see. And which part of the future have you and your friends become so enamored with that you seek clarity over spin?"

QUIXOTE: "Sancho, I know we have been at odds sometimes on this global warming issue but at this point you need to see we are all on the same page. What are you grinning at now?"

SANCHO: "There is a big difference between what you say and what you do, Quixote. Your acceptance of climate change means, what exactly?"

QUIXOTE: "We are working to gain the upper hand. We are seeking solutions. We are--to be honest--working the problem."

SANCHO: "I hope that's a joke."

QUIXOTE: "No."

SANCHO: "And the problem is?"

QUIXOTE: "That global warming is our friend and you all need to recognize it that way."

SANCHO: "I think I am about to lose my lunch."

QUIXOTE: "And that all the stink over it--especially those hurricanes-- was way out of line. Those little puffs of wind had nothing to do with climate change."

SANCHO: "Beg pardon? The four hurricanes that hit Florida were, puffs of wind?"

QUIXOTE: "And some rain. They were a fluke--a once in a life time event."

SANCHO: "Why not just say they never happened?"

QUIXOTE: "That was my point exactly! You think it will work, Sancho?"

SANCHO: "Quixote, I've seen you and your friends proceed on notions so ludicrous George Orwell would blush."

QUIXOTE: "Thank you, Sancho. I had no idea you were so impressed by my work."

SANCHO: "Quixote, the Nazi's were efficient in their practices. It doesn't mean I find them laudable--by any means."

QUIXOTE: "So then you think we can blame the hurricanes on the Nazis?"

SANCHO: "I don't think so, Quixote."

QUIXOTE: "You're right. Europe is too far away. Africa then. Hmm I like that. An assault on us by Africa perhaps. I could get some shill to say the hurricanes are someone else's problem instead of linking the hurricanes to global warming. I bet I could make a stink that way. Maybe another op-ed or a news release might do it. I could say: the hurricanes are the fault of... Hmm...An evil empire?"

SANCHO: "No that's been done. I'd be surprised if you could achieve even a bit of odor with that old tactic. Wait, I thought you were going for clarity here?"

QUIXOTE: "Sancho--when it comes to clearing the waters I have no trouble in raising a little pew to confuse the issue of storms and global warming."

SANCHO: "Wait, Quixote, I'm confused. You said you were on-board about global warming."

QUIXOTE: "Right, Sancho--we are green as green can be--in a corporate kind of way."

SANCHO: "Do you agree the size, speed, frequency, and intensity were boosted significantly by the increased energy in the system caused by the increased heat retention of the atmosphere and the decrease in the differential between the temperature in the poles and the equator?"

QUIXOTE: "I will not agree, but of course I do agree--you understand why, Sancho."

SANCHO: "So why not say global warming has had a significant impact on the hurricane season?"

QUIXOTE: "Don't you get it? My job is to make sure we admit to nothing--except between you and I--master and servant. Of course you know we're more than that."

SANCHO: "Oh, sure, Quixote--but what do you have to lose?"

QUIXOTE: "If we start tying weather events into global warming than it will become more than just a vague scientific notion that is years off."

SANCHO: "Exactly--then the sacrifices we need will make sense to people and we can all work together on solving the problem."

QUIXOTE: "My friends don't understand the word sacrifice. Besides, global warming isn't a problem."

SANCHO: "And the so-called Tipping Point, Quixote?"

QUIXOTE: "The Tipping Point, that's Phase Shift--oh yes, your arcane notion of things getting out of control."

SANCHO: "Exactly."

QUIXOTE: "Sancho, we will never let that happen."

SANCHO: "Oh. So it's ego that really stops us from addressing global warming? The admissions are a scam?"

QUIXOTE: "Of course it's real. We admit there is global warming. We will not admit that current weather events are tied into it. That would be too much."

SANCHO: "Why?"

QUIXOTE: "Sancho, think about it. Let's say my friends admit global warming is causing billions of dollars in damage every year and that the damage is increasing."

SANCHO: "To say nothing about the increase in human misery and death."

QUIXOTE: "Not ever--not a single word."

SANCHO: "Got it. Why not?"

QUIXOTE: "We might be forced into doing something about it."

SANCHO: "And what's wrong with that?"

QUIXOTE: "Some of the changes might be unpopular. No one wants to take the heat for that. My friends are good and decent people--but we're pragmatic."

SANCHO: "So you'll let people die and human suffering increase because it's convenient for your sense of self."

QUIXOTE: "Correct. But we are not without feeling, Sancho."

SANCHO: "How could I have ever thought different?"

QUIXOTE: "Here look closer at my glasses--the ones with the little windshield wipers."

SANCHO: "The ones that allow you to see so clearly."

QUIXOTE: "Exactly. There, turn them over--do you see?"

SANCHO: "Odd. The windshield wipers are on the inside. What for?"

QUIXOTE: "Tears, Sancho, tears."

SANCHO: "For your friends? I guess in a way that's touching."

QUIXOTE: "Not for us, Sancho. I swear if you don't get over that sappy notion of caring you will always be a servant."

SANCHO: "Heaven forbid."

QUIXOTE: "These glasses are for the rest of you. They'll keep the tears out of your eyes so you can continue to do your job. See that little misting device by the nose bridge."

SANCHO: "Yes."

QUIXOTE: "Nitrous-oxide. Our tag line will be: 'Just get out there and do work!' Do you like it? The glasses are also recyclable."

SANCHO: "Incredible."

QUIXOTE: "And you thought our think tanks were filled with buffoons and stooges."

December 23, 2004
Sancho, Quixote, and the Book

SANCHO:	"Quixote, were you laughing, or crying? Quixote?"
QUIXOTE:	"Quiet, Sancho, I'm being uplifted."
SANCHO:	"You told me to tell you when I finished putting the biodiesel stock portfolio in the safe. Is that really a book you're reading?"
QUIXOTE:	"Of course."
SANCHO:	"You, and a book? What is the name of Adam Smith pulls you from your focus group reports?"
QUIXOTE:	"The book is called 'Killing the Poor."
SANCHO:	"What's so funny about that?"
QUIXOTE:	"Humor can be serious literary work, Sancho."
SANCHO:	"So why the giggles?"
QUIXOTE:	"'Killing the Poor' is a straightforward look at the environmental movement."
SANCHO:	"Straightjacket view sounds more to the point."
QUIXOTE:	"The book uncovers the facts: The global warming problems are all the fault of you environmentalists. You evil guys."
SANCHO:	"Quixote, do you need an aspirin?"
QUIXOTE:	"No, you greedy tree-hugger."
SANCHO:	"Something's odd here. So, this book you're reading is a critique of the environmental movement, Quixote?"
QUIXOTE:	"Hard hitting literature and to the point."
SANCHO:	"So why are you laughing?"
QUIXOTE:	"The avarice, the lust that permeates the environmental movement, the mad need for power, the total control of the media and the poor government's kowtowing to the fascist enviro-dogs. It's all here. Finally, the truth, ah ha!"

Sancho:	"Quixote, you're laughing at a book that says killing the disadvantaged is okay? You're laughing at my reaction?"
Quixote:	"Don't be so rash, Sancho. Did you know Mephistopheles House put this book out?"
Sancho:	"Now there are the seeds of credibility."
Quixote:	"Sancho, Mephistopheles House is a well respected name."
Sancho:	"Right after Moe, Larry, and Curly."
Quixote:	"My point, exactly."
Sancho:	"And that's what you are laughing at?"
Quixote:	"Sancho, you environmentalists live in a state of fear. I swear!"
Sancho:	"Awareness of the environment does not equal fear."
Quixote:	"For some it does. But that's not the point. You environmentalists control the media. It says it right here in the book! Therefore we need to kill the disadvantaged. Sancho, have you ever heard anything so idiotic in your life?"
Sancho:	"You're putting me on, Quixote."
Quixote:	"This is the funniest book I have ever read. Still I knew it would get your goat. I love the way things like this crank you environmentalists up--just like little wind-up dolls. A few assaults on your cherished dogma and off you spin certain of your moral imperatives and our Machiavellian ways."
Sancho:	"Is the author in on the joke?"
Quixote:	"Of course not."
Sancho:	"See. It's not a very funny title either, Quixote."
Quixote:	"Get over it. Nobody takes junk like this seriously. Fact is the pendulum has started swinging your way. My guess is it's just someone's idea of a joke. They wanted to spread some Christmas cheer. We corporatists do love watching the righteous enviro-wrath rising through your pedantic gorges and spilling out in high-minded hearsay coated in pure indignation."
Sancho:	"Fair enough, Quixote. But a joke?"

QUIXOTE: "Look, I'll prove to you it's a joke. Did you see the review where the guy said: It reads like Ayn Rand's 'Atlas Shrugged' only this book has more than just one idea--it has information in it?"

SANCHO: "All right I see the humor in that one--Ayn Rand is your world's Gandhi. I wish I'd seen that posting before your little joke."

QUIXOTE: "I hid it, Sancho. You were so down after COP-10 I wanted to cheer you up. You've got to quit taking the shift of power so seriously."

SANCHO: "I have trouble finding humor in a book that purports killing the disadvantaged as little more than a lark."

QUIXOTE: "Look at it this way, Sancho. It's not a lark--it's the swan song of the bankrupt viewpoint that says global warming is a myth. Grant us this graceless exit--and enjoy the humor."

SANCHO: "Fair enough. Sometimes the cloak of darkness does bind. Merry Christmas, Quixote."

CHAPTER 9
2005

January 5, 2005
Science, Truth, and Other Circuses as Seen By Sancho and Quixote

SANCHO: "Quixote, what is that? Another book? 'Burning Witches for Fun and Profit'?"

QUIXOTE: "Great little book."

SANCHO: "And what's this? 'McCarthyism--Can Paranoia Again Become a National Imperative?' What kind of circus are you and your silly friends up to now?"

QUIXOTE: "It's all in the game plan for you eco-freaks. Just in case we can't convince everyone that environmentalists are the cause of everyone's problems we go to plan B--Paranoia."

SANCHO: "Nice, Quixote. Why?"

QUIXOTE: "Why what, Sancho?"

SANCHO: "Why the headlong attack on environmentalists?"

QUIXOTE: "Relax. It's not really you guys. No one will get burned at the stake."

SANCHO: "How nice of you all. Who is the target then?"

QUIXOTE: "The insurance companies, maybe scientists."

SANCHO: "You lost me."

QUIXOTE: "Look. Here is the geopolitical landscape as of the new year. Global warming causes big storms and big insurance damage claims. Costs are mounting."

SANCHO: "And people suffer and die."

QUIXOTE: "Don't cloud the issue with minutia. Where was I? Oh. The insurance companies are taking a big hit on the bottom line. So they are looking for someone to blame and take to court."

SANCHO: "I don't get it. Why does the insurance industry feel like supporting the trial attorneys in addition to spending 60 billion dollars in storm claims per year?"

QUIXOTE: "That was the old number Sancho. It's much larger now."

SANCHO: "And then there's that pesky dead people problem."

QUIXOTE: "Not for us."

SANCHO: "Regardless, Quixote, why is industry targeting the scientists environmentalists while supporting the trial lawyers?"

QUIXOTE: "You miss the point. The insurance industry is looking for deep pockets to help pay the costs of the disasters. It's not the environmentalists; they are targeting CO_2 emitters."

SANCHO: "Now I am lost. We all emit CO_2 when we breathe."

QUIXOTE: "The insurance industry is beginning to target oil, gas, aluminum, coal, power companies and the rest of the carbon-economy leaders for litigation."

SANCHO: "Oh, I see. Because they are putting out the CO_2 and the insurance companies are paying the damages for that."

QUIXOTE: "That's correct. If the insurance companies can prove a culpable link to the large scale CO_2 emitters then they can recover storm costs through the courts."

SANCHO: "Got it. But I still don't get it. The environmentalists support the insurance industry and their position on global warming."

QUIXOTE: "Yes. They have been. The problem is the environmentalists are beginning to make headway and people now mostly believe climate change is happening."

SANCHO: "So then shouldn't the insurance companies like them?"

QUIXOTE: "Of course. But the CO_2 companies are getting stung."

SANCHO: "For good reason. Oh I see: awareness makes it easier for the insurance companies to win against the CO_2 emitting companies in court."

QUIXOTE: "Exactly."

SANCHO: "So your friends target the environmentalists, and therefore undercut public support for the insurance companies so the insurance companies are less likely to win in court."

QUIXOTE: "Precisely."

SANCHO: "So, the potentially culpable corporations are targeting the environmentalists. But, in the end, they don't really think the environmentalists are a problem?"

QUIXOTE: "Not a bit. But economics says we need to protect our assets. Therefore: attack the environmentalists and science."

SANCHO: "Quixote, won't that strategy slow down our response to global warming, and...Kill more people?"

QUIXOTE: "Of course."

SANCHO: "Don't any of your friends care?"

QUIXOTE: "Not a one. Remember the only reason the walls have tumbled on climate change is its inescapable conclusion. My friends now need to slow things down now so we don't get eviscerated in court."

SANCHO: "So then remediation isn't a priority for either of the warring parties, Quixote?"

QUIXOTE: "Not for anyone important, Sancho."

SANCHO: "Except the environmentalists."

QUIXOTE: "Radical dogs."

SANCHO: "Very funny. So we are back where we were a decade ago only this time it isn't a debate on global warming. It is a negotiation about when and if we should expect anything to get paid for."

QUIXOTE: "Exactly. And as soon as one of you rabid tree-huggers claim we need to move quickly, my friends are going to label them as an extremist--and I understand it the plan is to exile them into the same cell as Martha Stewart. I hear the curtains are death."

SANCHO: "Now that is scary. So what if the response to global warming didn't focus on blame?"

QUIXOTE: "You mean just work the problem? Sancho--you are naïve. Think about it. The insurance industry can save a pile of cash by finding villains. The CO_2 emitting companies are a big fat target--even though they might not be culpable."

SANCHO: "Quixote, how do you figure that?"

QUIXOTE: "Some of them were just trying to supply us with affordable energy. Others just didn't know. Some truly didn't care and still do not care. But, regardless, they are all in the same boat now. We're trying to kill or control the process for our own good. As a result my friends and I stone wall efforts to raise awareness of climate change."

SANCHO: "So neither group cares that people are going to die in increasing numbers because the CO_2 emitting companies and the insurance companies are only protecting their assets."

QUIXOTE: "Happy New Year, Sancho."

SANCHO: "Don't they care they are fostering hardship and death for the sake of an extra dollar?"

QUIXOTE: "You are a servant, and you have always been a good servant. But you need to see truth, science, decency--they're jokes to us."

SANCHO: "Quixote, death is pounding on humanity's door and it's getting louder every day."

QUIXOTE: "All the more reason for my friends to protect their assets. We have a storm to ride out."

SANCHO: "They are mad…"

QUIXOTE: "Quite so."

SANCHO: "Quixote, you know I never interfere with your vanity-fair of geopolitical power. But that said, in this case, the truth is more than a joke."

QUIXOTE: "You need to shut your radical environmental mouth, Sancho."

SANCHO: "Quixote, you need tell your friends and their playground partners to start playing nice. It's time for them to get off their assets and really work the problem. Quixote we're running out of time."

QUIXOTE: "Ain't that the truth, Sancho?"

January 28, 2005
Sancho, Quixote, and the Emperor

SANCHO: "Quixote, I have a question for you."

QUIXOTE: "Shoot, Sancho."

SANCHO: "Why not work together to fix global warming?"

QUIXOTE: "Why should we? My friends are beginning to find ways of making money off global warming."

SANCHO: "That's the same global warming you say isn't really happening, Quixote?"

QUIXOTE: "Of course. We've discovered denial is a great way to keep the opportunities of global warming to ourselves."

SANCHO: "Brilliant--if a bit greedy and sad."

QUIXOTE: "You dummies fall for our nonsense so why not?"

SANCHO: "I'm not buying it, Quixote."

QUIXOTE: "Listen: Every time we finalize an economic coup handed to us by the changing climate we go public saying global warming, if it were real, is bad for the economy."

SANCHO: "I guess it doesn't matter to a vampire if it sleeps at night?"

QUIXOTE: "Not a bit. Heck, we're scrambling to get our piece of the arctic shipping lanes, without agreeing that global warming is the reason the Arctic will be ice free in the summers. That's tough work."

SANCHO: "Look at that plan, Quixote. Easier availability to oil will just increase the severity of global warming. Why do it?"

QUIXOTE: "We will resplendently say global warming is not necessarily a bad event showing how some companies are making a killing on it. But tell me, why do you think more oil availability will increase the severity of global warming?"

SANCHO: "More supply, less cost. Less cost, more usage. More usage, more CO_2, more CO_2, more warming."

QUIXOTE: "I really do admire the dogmas you embrace. What would be the worth to us of us lowering prices?"

SANCHO: "Doesn't increased supply mean prices have to go lower?"

QUIXOTE: "Only in a college Econ class, Sancho."

SANCHO: "What about the free market?"

QUIXOTE: "What about the tooth fairy?"

SANCHO: "I see--it's all myth."

QUIXOTE: "Sancho, we all have myths. Besides, every capitalist strives to control their market--it's a reward built into the system now."

SANCHO: "Now that's what I am talking about. You and your megalomaniac friends need to control--yet you are letting the climate spin out of control. That doesn't make sense to me."

QUIXOTE: "You've a mistaken assumption there, Sancho."

SANCHO: "Quixote, isn't there a point where the economics are outweighed by increased mortality, destruction of lives, the economic impact of a decaying infrastructure?"

QUIXOTE: "Merely opportunities for revenue growth in developing markets, Sancho."

SANCHO: "That's demonic. Or, it's a load of bull."

QUIXOTE: "Those are the facts, Sancho. Accept it or not. And to be clear it's not really evil. It is just the way our society functions. Everyone makes the choice to be cattle or not."

SANCHO: "And you slaughter cattle."

QUIXOTE: "Not us. Cattle get slaughtered because they don't have the wit to recognize that the big hammer coming straight towards their skull isn't a crown."

SANCHO: "And you see the hammer?"

QUIXOTE: "Of global warming? More than you'll ever know."

SANCHO: "Doesn't it seem to you that your consent to global warming mayhem is a killing of the innocent?"

QUIXOTE: "By the boatload. And of course consent is evil. But that's not our problem."

SANCHO: "Something isn't right here. Since when do you admit to being evil? Usually you blame the imperatives of the omnipotent marketplace."

QUIXOTE: "Praise be to the marketplace."

SANCHO: "Quixote that's a dumb joke. Get off your knees. Wait, you meant that? Are you crazy?"

QUIXOTE: "Look, Sancho, at least the market place works."

SANCHO: "So that's it, Quixote. You didn't just admit to being evil. You admitted to not knowing what to do. That's it isn't it? Your friends know they have screwed it up with global warming and they don't know what to do next."

QUIXOTE: "Sancho, don't go there."

SANCHO: "Quixote, you really do see the marketplace as holy. But not just because you are slime. The marketplace is the only functioning system you have left. It's the only thing you understand. You hold onto a quarterly report like a child holding a security blanket."

QUIXOTE: "Know the market and the market will set you free."

SANCHO: "With apologies to Tolstoy. You use your own actions to justify a lack of meaning as the facts of life. You claim freedom is a lack of meaning because you don't know what else to say. Then, armed with those absurdities you put fresh paint on the corroding foundations of our society and its proof: global warming. Then you fill the media with the mantra: 'Go buy something.' And you call it good."

QUIXOTE: "And that makes us evil?"

SANCHO: "You just don't know what else to do, Quixote."

QUIXOTE: "Sancho, everything is fine--except for a few insurgents of course. Things are getting better. I swear."

SANCHO: "Quixote, you're justifying a downward spiral as progress. Finding scapegoats at every turn, and in truth, what you are really saying is you don't have the slightest idea of what to do next. Except pray to your deity: the marketplace."

QUIXOTE: "The marketplace isn't my deity. Besides, the marketplace can't solve global warming. Technology will solve global warming, Sancho."

SANCHO: "You no longer believe that, Quixote. You and your friends once thought Deus Ex Machina could fix the climate. Then you figured out the changing climate just had too much inertia to be nudged back into line and now you're scared. Quixote, you aren't really a nihilist or vampire. You and your friends are just terrified and your vanity will not let you admit it. You haven't the slightest idea of how to fix of global warming. Do you, Quixote?"

QUIXOTE: "Why else would we burn resources at every turn. Why you are laughing at me, Sancho?"

SANCHO: "It's irony, Quixote. You're not even a good servant."

QUIXOTE: "Too sad a truth, Sancho."

February 16, 2005
Sancho, Quixote, and the Rug

QUIXOTE: "Sancho, help me burn this rug will you?"

SANCHO: "Burn that beautiful Persian rug? It was the one in the library, Quixote."

QUIXOTE: "I'll pay the huff fees. I know you don't like to lug around big weights like that."

SANCHO: "Quixote, the weight doesn't bother me. That rug is ancient, and it's so well made. The fabric is in good shape, the knots are a bit tightly wound, but what can you expect from a rug as old as that?"

QUIXOTE: "It's not just this one, Sancho. We're going to burn all of them. Think of it as a cogeneration project."

SANCHO: "What?"

QUIXOTE: "Sancho, I'm not here to debate policy. My friends have made a decision to burn the rugs."

SANCHO: "Given up on books?"

QUIXOTE: "Not funny."

SANCHO: "Quixote, just tell me why?"

QUIXOTE: "My friends say it's a matter of national security."

SANCHO: "Persian rugs, national security? You are kidding, right?"

QUIXOTE: "It's all because of our enemies. They tell us they are going to use the rugs to keep warm. In fact there is really an insidious plot--too terrible to tell most people. Sancho, they are going to put the rugs in a plane, or a suit case, and bomb our cities with megatons of rugs."

SANCHO: "Who gives your friends these notions? Bozo the Clown?"

QUIXOTE: "Close, our intelligence support. Sancho, it's all the fault of environmentalists anyway."

SANCHO: "Heavens have we sinned again? Do tell, Quixote."

QUIXOTE: "This global warming mess they have created."

SANCHO: "Us? Oh, of course, a joke."

QUIXOTE: "It's no wonder you are still a servant. Sancho. You fear truth."

SANCHO: "You mean I am inept in understanding the ways of brutal dictatorships, Quixote. Enlighten me."

QUIXOTE: "By burning rugs we cut down on our dependency for foreign oil--we also take another small step in controlling another planetary game token."

SANCHO: "How?"

QUIXOTE: "My friends don't share that kind of information with me."

SANCHO: "They're probably worried you'll laugh yourself to death."

QUIXOTE: "They also have a plan to generate fake rugs using some new genes that didn't quite work out for corn. The next year the rugs disintegrate into compost--how's that for being green?"

SANCHO: "Blackmailing others to force them into buying the products of your friends to is not recycling. It's wasteful."

QUIXOTE: "No. I mean using some bad genes over again in a different product. It saves energy and carbon dioxide We expect to receive carbon trading credits for that one."

SANCHO: "Geopolitics at its finest."

QUIXOTE: "Okay, you win. Truth is, we've wanted to control the rug market for years now."

SANCHO: "I remember that."

QUIXOTE: "Shaa, Sancho. We don't talk about our failures."

SANCHO: "Your friends are manic, Quixote. How did a bunch of ignorant bullies lacking a conscience, morals, or shame turn us all into such ignorant Oakies."

QUIXOTE: "The list is endless, Sancho. You know, if this bothers you we could go watch TV?"

SANCHO: "Funny. Aren't you ashamed of being associated with those thugs?"

QUIXOTE: "If they aren't doing rotten tricks to someone, then someone will do horrible things to them."

SANCHO: "So your friends, justify brutality by their own brutality, Quixote?"

QUIXOTE: "We're fighting tooth and nail to save the planet from the scourge of global warming. And truth is the first casualty of war, Sancho."

SANCHO: "Quixote, why not try to spin your friends into expanding their viewpoint away from aggression as a primary policy tool? Perhaps you could tell them they need to remember cultures and citizens have a right to self-determination. Then, instead of wasting energy feeding their megalomania they can channel resources into important problems--addressing them with old fashioned values like hard work and ethics--instead of turning us all into global vampires."

QUIXOTE: "Sancho--that's un-American."

SANCHO: "Only these days, Quixote."

March 3, 2005
Sancho, Quixote, and Rigor

SANCHO: "Hmmm WAIS Ice Company. Okay, Quixote, here is the last bag of ice. Man, this ice is heavy. Where do you want it?"

QUIXOTE: "On the scale over there, Sancho. Put it next to the other bags of ice. I need to track the weight of the ice as it melts. One of your radical eco-freaks friends says that as ice melts the weight of ice will change as the water flows off the scale and into the bucket that is sitting on the plate."

SANCHO: "And your people say not?"

QUIXOTE: "We seek only the truth. So we plan to take a 'wait and see' position on these important questions of science because science is all truth. Praise be to science. Ommmm."

SANCHO: "I think you've been working too hard, Quixote. Should I get other plate? There's a curve to the floor. The change in weight might crack that plate even more."

QUIXOTE: "No. I've done this same experiment with rocks on the scale and the weight doesn't impact the plate."

SANCHO: "Did the rocks melt?"

QUIXOTE: "Of course not. Put that last bag of ice on the west side."

SANCHO: "Quixote--might the plate's crack change and the plate break even more from the movement of ice mass to water mass?"

QUIXOTE: "No religion, Sancho."

SANCHO: "Not that kind of mass--oh forget it. What about the water temperature, does that have an impact on the plate?"

QUIXOTE: "The plates are too big--therefore irrelevant--science marches on, Sancho. We'll be doing this all spring and summer."

SANCHO: "Soon the floor will be covered with water and mud."

QUIXOTE: "We men of science take risks like that all the time."

SANCHO: "Quixote, since when are you a man of science?"

QUIXOTE: "I experiment therefore I science."

SANCHO: "Ah, not quite. How do you know you have the experiment well bounded and it's safe? Safety is a part of science also."

QUIXOTE: "Look if you are worried just get da' cart. The instructions are in there."

SANCHO: "Very funny. You're going to make a mess."

QUIXOTE: "You have no proof and we need proof before making any decisions. The rocks didn't cause a mess, so why should the water? Just let the ice sit on the plate--and if I'm wrong what the heck, you can still use a mop to clean up the mess. I mean that's what servants are for right, Sancho?"

SANCHO: "There you go, Quixote, 25kg of ice. Oops, more cracks in the plate. And I think were getting some leaks of water."

QUIXOTE: "Get the insulation from the shed and put it around the ice."

SANCHO: "Quixote, I still don't get it. Why mess with ice on some old cracked plates in a greenhouse?"

QUIXOTE: "Research and development--I'm helping the team out."

SANCHO: "Soon the greenhouse heat will render the insulation useless; the ice is still going to melt."

QUIXOTE: "Well that's what we are here for: the pursuit of knowledge."

SANCHO: "Huh?"

QUIXOTE: "Truth is…A few of the guys want to see if I can spin a byte or two saying ice will not melt in a warm greenhouse."

SANCHO: "You cannot be serious."

QUIXOTE: "Look, I do as I am told. Okay now put the insulation around the ice bags and keep one bag uninsulated. There that's good. It's only good science to make sure you have a control group."

SANCHO: "Quixote, how is one bag of ice a control group?"

QUIXOTE: "If it doesn't melt then we know that the insulations does not matter because heat does not melt ice and we are in business."

SANCHO: "Quixote, of course the ice will melt."

QUIXOTE: "Some of my people think not. In fact I need you to turn on the sprinkler. If we raise the humidity, some of the guys are suggesting the ice will grow in size."

SANCHO: "In a warming environment like this greenhouse? The laws of thermodynamics might take an exception to that notion."

QUIXOTE: "I've friends who change laws."

SANCHO: "It will not work, Quixote. The laws of thermodynamics are sacrosanct."

QUIXOTE: "So was social security. Wake up to the new reality, Sancho."

SANCHO: "Quixote, there are some laws your friends cannot rewrite."

QUIXOTE: "Don't you believe that for a second, Sancho. Oh oh, look. The ice that's uninsulated is melting faster. Damn, there goes another Nobel Prize. I really wanted one of those too."

SANCHO: "They're all melting; the uninsulated ice is melting faster."

QUIXOTE: "Yes, but look the insulated ice bags are melting slower. Whoa--what in the name of the Australia was that?"

SANCHO: "A bag of ice--the change in the orientation from the melting ice shifted the bags. Oops, there they all go. After the first one moved, the other bags of ice moved also. There's mud everywhere--and it's not even summer."

QUIXOTE: "Not my fault. Ha! I made a joke. Well, regardless we can call the experiment a complete success."

SANCHO: "How's that?"

QUIXOTE: "We have proved that when ice melts the remaining ice has less mass. I need to get this off to the think tank people."

SANCHO: "Absurd. I'll go get the mop and start cleaning this up."

QUIXOTE: "You know, Sancho. I wonder if it was only a matter of time before we messed up."

SANCHO: "Definitely, Quixote, definitely,"

April 6, 2005
Sancho, Quixote, and the Sponges

SANCHO: "Quixote, I suppose your people put out the report that says poor people who make fires to cook and heat their home are responsible for global warming?"

QUIXOTE: "Sancho, you know we never admit to propaganda. But that said, how do you think it played?"

SANCHO: "First you were blaming farm animals for global warming, now poor people. Does the term shameless mean anything to you?"

QUIXOTE: "Does the term power mean anything to you, Sancho?"

SANCHO: "They have a right to live, Quixote--and their carbon footprint is tiny compared to a multinational corporation."

QUIXOTE: "But they don't have a lobby. They don't have a media budget. None of my friends sit on the board of directors for Poor Folks Inc., and that makes them fair game. Think of it as just another adaptation to climate change. Which reminds me, have you seen the sponges? They were in the greenhouse the last time I saw them."

SANCHO: "Gone. All used up."

QUIXOTE: "Well please go out and buy some more, will you? We have appearances to keep and dirt will ever do."

SANCHO: "I tried. The sponges were gone. It's global warming, I guess."

QUIXOTE: "Now I see what you mean by environmental tragedy. I hate loofahs."

SANCHO: "You misunderstand. I think people living in low lying coastal countries are refusing to sell us sponges anymore."

QUIXOTE: "What? That's outrageous! That violates the free market rules. I want a government investigation. They just don't get to do this."

SANCHO: "Maybe they know what they are doing, Quixote."

QUIXOTE: "How dare they do that to us? Where is our government when we need it?"

SANCHO: "Quixote, perhaps they're angry that their countries are disappearing under water and they'd like to let us know. Look, I'll just go to the market and buy some synthetic sponges."

QUIXOTE: "Sancho, do I look like a synthetic sponge kinda' guy? I'm rich. I'm powerful. If I don't get what I want someone is going to get hurt."

SANCHO: "You must have been fun on the playground."

QUIXOTE: "It was my basketball. Bah! We need to fix this. We need to make the world safe for sponge usage. No--that's been used-- how about we attack because we think they have SMD? "

SANCHO: "Sponges of mass destruction? Quixote, you can't use that--it fits your friends too well."

QUIXOTE: "Egad you're right. I know we'll claim their sponges emit too many greenhouse gases and we need to sequester them in the homes of the rich--a sacrifice on the part of the wealthy to keep greenhouse emissions down. I bet if I do it right we can claim it as a Clean Development Mechanism."

SANCHO: "Corruption as a way of life?"

QUIXOTE: "The floor is dirty in the greenhouse. You see, this is just what we were talking about earlier. Poor people emit too many greenhouse gases when they cook and now they can't even manage a simple thing like selling sponges the way we say they should. Boy are they going to pay. I can hardly wait. Is Grenada one their countries? I loved those beaches."

SANCHO: "If the beaches are not under water, Quixote. What is it about you and your friends that makes you think its okay to take something just because you want it?"

QUIXOTE: "I'll need to get together with the Goebbels Institute for Moral Misalignment and Enterprise Extension, on that one."

SANCHO: "Funny. Quixote, but you do need a morality transplant."

QUIXOTE: "You can't stop us, Sancho. We have the guns. We have the money. We laugh at ethics and morality then use them like smart bombs in our media spin campaigns."

Sancho: "Every time you and your friends do something like that you conscript us into your mayhem all because we don't stop you."

Quixote: "Sancho, my old friend, it's not your fault. It's my friends and I who have made the population of the United States impotent; they're so scared of us. No one can blame you all. We own you--so don't worry."

Sancho: "Quixote, that's like getting dispensation from the devil after you've sold him your soul."

Quixote: "Now there was someone who had a bad media campaign."

Sancho: "Quixote, do you really believe that if people can't defend themselves you can use them up and throw them away?"

Quixote: "We call it recycling opposition. Boy I love these knee-jerk conversations."

Sancho: "It's still not right. And sooner or later people will learn to defend themselves."

Quixote: "Bah, if they don't like it let them do as Marie Antionette said."

Sancho: "Which was, Quixote?"

Quixote: "'Let them eat cake'--or was it: 'Let them burn ice'? Hmm, same thing I guess."

Sancho: "Better a knee jerk than a neck jerk, Quixote."

April 18, 2005
Sancho, Quixote, and Rogue Waves

QUIXOTE: "Sancho, give me a hand, will you?"

SANCHO: "Sure, Quixote, what can I do for you?"

QUIXOTE: "Sit in this nice barber chair and let me buzz-cut your hair."

SANCHO: "Nice chair. And it doesn't have a joy buzzer in the seat. Hmm, what's up?"

QUIXOTE: "I can't believe it. The guys want me to take up the beauty business. I told them I don't do that--but they kept insisting it was right up my alley.

SANCHO: "Sounds odd to me, but there is no way I am going to let you and a scissor come close to my curly locks."

QUIXOTE: "It's true your locks don't stand a chance, Sancho. Okay here is the truth: My friends are trying to head off some bad press on climate change."

SANCHO: "A good cause, perhaps not. Head off--I don't like the sound of that. Though I am fascinated. How is brushing up on your coiffeur skills going to make a change in the climate spin. Planning to aerosol me?"

QUIXOTE: "We haven't captured the spray can market yet--so no. I think not. You know, this time I don't get it. I'll tell you what happened. Seems the other day some babe named Dawn was on a cruise ship. I guess someone was working her hair and using too much oil. She just about lost it. "

SANCHO: "You're losing me on this one, Quixote. I thought your friends loved oil. "

QUIXOTE: "Sancho--I told you I don't get it either. Sit in the chair."

SANCHO: "No. Look at with those dopey scissors. They look like kindergarten scissors. The edges are blunt."

QUIXOTE: "That's all they sent me. Look, Sancho, here is the truth."

SANCHO: "Quixote, you and the truth aren't even on speaking terms."

QUIXOTE: "Sancho, will you listen? Good. Some buffoons decided that they could do anything they wanted with this Dawn thing. Seems they were cutting through a storm and something slipped in the storm. Seems she hit the tipping point of the scissors. It was nothing very deep, just the point and it made a mess."

SANCHO: "That would explain the scissors without a tip. Sounds like your friends' idea of a solution."

QUIXOTE: "Anyway, just between you and I, Sancho, my friends are acting odd--even for them. Somehow they think there is a problem with the scissors if someone gets jabbed in a storm by the tipping point? I'm so confused."

SANCHO: "Perhaps Dawn was hurt and that bothered your friends."

QUIXOTE: "Don't be ridiculous, Sancho. They don't care if someone is hurt. That's what insurance is for."

SANCHO: "Of course. So they believe the tipping point refers to the end of a pair of scissors--and you are trying to do what?"

QUIXOTE: "Stop grinning like that. I need to help them with a problem."

SANCHO: "Quixote, my liege. I shall not sit in your chair but I will be my effervescent self. How exactly did this rogue wave come about? Do they know?"

QUIXOTE: "I know something about the tipping point--but they're not being clear. I think because they have been trying to cover it up. Do you think that's why I don't get it?"

SANCHO: "Or perhaps the rogue waves are getting a little more vicious and random every year? And they think blunt scissors will stop it?"

QUIXOTE: "That's idiotic. But that might be it. After all there is carbon intensity. Anyway, to cover it all up they used oil of some sort. I think Dawn really went nuts after that, screaming they had created a rogue wave."

SANCHO: "So let me see if I have this right. You are taking up haircutting to help your friends spin the story on rogue waves--which you want people to believe is a coiffure indiscretion--so they will ignore what happened to a cruise ship?"

QUIXOTE: "Plural. Do you think it will work?"

SANCHO:	"Bad hair days as a solution to climate change?"
QUIXOTE:	"That must be it. Oh this is terrible. I thought they called me in because all the haircutters on the ships were having problems with the rogue waves in storms. But we want people to link rogue waves, bad hair days, and global warming. That explains why they asked me to take up haircutting and try and make rogue waves popular. Now I get it. You've been a lot of help. Sancho, are rogue waves really that awful?"
SANCHO:	"From what I hear New York is in an uproar."
QUIXOTE:	"Oh this is terrible. Some of the wives shop there. They are very conscious about how they look, Sancho. But if they started wearing rogue waves..."
SANCHO:	"Ah huh, run with it Quixote."
QUIXOTE:	"Okay, so I need to get you, and everyone else, to believe that rogue waves are just the newest hairstyle. I'm on it now."
SANCHO:	"You might even try saying a rogue wave is like a close shave--for a while. Or even a warning."
QUIXOTE:	"Okay, great, Sancho, let me write that down. Super--I got it now. Here's what I will do: First I'll say there's no big deal with rogue waves. A few rogue waves here, a few there. Maybe I get a reality show going on hairstyling. I'll call it "Short Hair Survivors." In the mean time I am a hair cutting fool. Let's see should there be bangs in front? Maybe I can ask a few of my broadcasting buddies to play the rogue wave thing down for now by asking them to suggest recycling might cause it."
SANCHO:	"Not oil usage and the tipping point?"
QUIXOTE:	"We'll need is time to change that view."
SANCHO:	"You may not have that much time left."
QUIXOTE:	"I know. Okay, so here's my spin: 'Rogue waves were always there. You know that, right?' Sancho, I am going to make rogue waves commonplace. Then people will ignore them."
SANCHO:	"Sure, Quixote, commonplace. Good idea."

May 2, 2005
Sancho, Quixote, and Gumshoes

SANCHO: "Nice trench coat, Quixote. Have you joined the Phillip Marlow fan club?"

QUIXOTE: "Sancho, I'm on a case. Hand me that magnifying glass will you?"

SANCHO: "Of course. Is a snapshot of an ocean wave part of your current investigation, Mr. PI?"

QUIXOTE: "I'm investigating whether a lit match held to paper will burn the snapshot or, will the match go out because the ocean is wet."

SANCHO: "Is that a joke?"

QUIXOTE: "Too hard to believe isn't it?"

SANCHO: "Nonsense uber alles."

QUIXOTE: "You like that phrase don't you, Sancho."

SANCHO: "I do. What are you really looking for?"

QUIXOTE: "Sancho, I'm looking for a fingerprint."

SANCHO: "A fingerprint of what?"

QUIXOTE: "I'm looking for the Prep's fingerprint."

SANCHO: "I think that word is perp as in perpetrator not prep as in preppy, Quixote."

QUIXOTE: "Are you sure?"

SANCHO: "Certain."

QUIXOTE: "Anyway, I'm looking to get the facts, just the facts, Sancho. I'm looking for a smoking gun. And that's where you come in. I think you'd be good at detective work. You have a natural aptitude for research."

SANCHO:	"Quixote, forget about it. What happens if a gumshoe, finds something out your friends don't like?"
QUIXOTE:	"We've been working on that recently. First, we rip into it and say it's not valid by getting a few of our shills to discredit it while we have the think tank goons attack through respectable sounding publications. Second, we adjust our investments-- just in case there is the potential for any negative impacts. Third, when we are ready to reveal what everyone already knows--we make sure that my friends get the credit thereby rewriting history and expunging our mistakes."
SANCHO:	"Sounds like what you are doing with global warming."
QUIXOTE:	"Ya' think so?"
SANCHO:	"Oh, of course--now we are getting somewhere. So, Quixote, what is the core of your Kafkaesque investigation? Are you identifying a problem, a culprit, a solution, or merely trampling the Constitution into compost again?"
QUIXOTE:	"The Constitution is a piece of paper without a serial number. Therefore, we can trample on it any day we like. But, turn it into compost, never. I, and my friends, have a problem with compost. It releases methane--a major greenhouse gas--and that concerns us deeply."
SANCHO:	"Very funny, Quixote."
QUIXOTE:	"See we can be funny too. Besides, do you have any idea how much revenue the Constitution and the Bill of Rights bring in as tourist attractions?"
SANCHO:	"You're a true patriot, Quixote. So what's the problem? I need to get back to mending the greenhouse."
QUIXOTE:	"No no, you don't understand. The issue isn't the problem. The issue isn't the culprit, and crime certainly isn't the issue."
SANCHO:	"So what is it your less-than-decent friends long for?"
QUIXOTE:	"Crimes happen all the time to people. The issue is whether my friends want to make a media event of any given happening, and whether we wish to label it a crime, a discovery, a breakthrough, a reality TV show, or a sport."
SANCHO:	"But a crime is a crime."

QUIXOTE: "Not if we say it isn't. There are issues to be considered, national security for one."

SANCHO: "Translation, your oil holdings matters more than the law."

QUIXOTE: "There's lots of oil, Sancho. More than we will need. Billions and billions of barrels--I swear the reserves will go on for eons. We haven't hit the peak, we will never hit the peak and I have never been, nor have I ever participated in, a study that says we have lots less oil than we are saying. Besides, I don't want to talk about it anymore."

SANCHO: "Okeydokey. So do you have suspects in your investigation?"

QUIXOTE: "A nefarious fugitive from the beauty salon business who will stop at nothing to continue his dastardly do."

SANCHO: "Oh, nasty pun, Quixote. So what is the name of this Perp?"

QUIXOTE: "The name is Rogue Wave."

SANCHO: "As in commonplace? Rogue Wave: As in Permanent Wave?"

QUIXOTE: "An accomplice we think."

SANCHO: "Rogue Wave, that's one goofy name for a perp."

QUIXOTE: "Hey talk to the E.P., I don't make these things up."

SANCHO: "Encouraging. So you're looking for Rogue Wave's fingerprints?"

QUIXOTE: "Absolutely not."

SANCHO: "Silly me, imagine a rational conversation with you, Quixote."

QUIXOTE: "We know all about Rogue Wave. Problem is he has been seen with a Norwegian doll named Dawn. Word is she is a Princess so therefore we can't finger either of them. Gosh, I love that film noir talk."

SANCHO: "Why not pinch da' Wave?"

QUIXOTE: "We can't. Rogue's got friends in high places."

SANCHO: "About 80 feet up from what I hear, Quixote."

QUIXOTE: "So you understand that we don't want to make a media event out of the investigation."

SANCHO:	"So what will you do?"
QUIXOTE:	"Sancho, my job is to make sure the fingerprint belongs elsewhere. That's why I am using these snap shots of the ocean trying to make basic thermodynamics seem beyond the reach of an ordinary person."
SANCHO:	"You're using pseudoscience to hide something?"
QUIXOTE:	"It's not the first time, Sancho."
SANCHO:	"What's so special about Rogue Wave? What are you hiding, Quixote?"
QUIXOTE:	"Truth is Rogue Wave is like a gang. There's more and more of them every year and we need to make sure no one knows this--at the same time we need to stop them."
SANCHO:	"Because they're criminals?"
QUIXOTE:	"You should know that working with criminals doesn't bother my friends."
SANCHO:	"So then what's the problem? Did the 'make them common' strategy fail for you?"
QUIXOTE:	"The more Rogue Waves there are, the more foolish we look saying we can control the situation."
SANCHO:	"Quixote, I don't think you and your friends need to worry about looking foolish."
QUIXOTE:	"Really?"
SANCHO:	"Trust me, Quixote, there is no way your friends and you could look any more foolish."

May 10, 2005
Sancho, Quixote, and Wax Paper

SANCHO: "Quixote, that has got to be the largest roll of gift wrapping I have ever seen. Did that airship just bring it in?"

QUIXOTE: "Yup. Can you imagine how much energy we will save by doing heavy lift that takes advantage of elemental properties?"

SANCHO: "I agree. It's a great idea to use the natural properties of items to solve problems. So what are you going to do with that huge roll of gift wrap?"

QUIXOTE: "Come here and take a look at the design on the wrapping paper, Sancho."

SANCHO: "Those are pictures. I see: trees, a pond, wow, nice field. It looks so real. Wait. Why do the cows have diapers on?"

QUIXOTE: "Cow flatulence. We are doing our part for global warming. We couldn't do anymore than that. The farm lobby is huge."

SANCHO: "The diapers are real plastic, I see. Nice touch, Quixote. So what is this huge roll of wrapping paper for?"

QUIXOTE: "I got the idea from our friends in Switzerland. They are covering glaciers in plastic you know. The Swiss want to keep the glaciers from melting by wrapping them in insulation."

SANCHO: "For what? To ski an extra few years or so? Quixote, are you sure you didn't think of that solution?"

QUIXOTE: "Honest, it wasn't me. Though I must say, it does seem to be a classic Quixote answer to a global warming problem."

SANCHO: "So why the gift-wrap? Are you and your friends planning on wrapping the Arctic wilderness in paper, or just the dead fauna floating in the Arctic sea?"

QUIXOTE: "Close. The gift-wrap is for the national forests. Now that the forests are open for mineral and oil exploration we can legally violate the pristine environment, rape the land, and generally log the stuffing out of it. Afterwards, we lay this printed gift wrapping down and quick as you can say petroleum--instant bucolic meadow."

SANCHO: "I see. Then you can charge the tax-payer for maintenance, get some cash for your buddies, and claim the government is too large."

QUIXOTE: "You're getting there, Sancho. Could an MBA be next?"

SANCHO: "I'm just getting to see how you work, Quixote. So what happens once you lay the paper down and some natural event like an animal or a storm tears it to shreds?"

"QUIXOTE: "We upgrade to Kevlar; or kill all the animals who can't read the 'Please do not step on the gift wrapping' signs."

SANCHO: "Most animals cannot read, Quixote, and what about people wanting to visit the lands?"

QUIXOTE: "Now that is the best part. We are going to take the ever-expanding prison population, add in the ever-increasing poor population, add the destitute elderly, and post them around the edges of the gift-wrap. Then, anyone who even comes close to our paper landscape will be seen by our citizen-sentinels and arrested by our security arm: The Terminators."

SANCHO: "So why have the wrapping down there if no one can see it or use it? Why not just let the scarred lands heal?"

QUIXOTE: "It's a national forest, Sancho. We owe it to our children to keep it pristine once we rape the lands for them."

SANCHO: "You're destroying the land for them, Quixote?"

QUIXOTE: "Of course not, but that doesn't matter. You ninnies bought that bull about global warming hurting the economy, so now we figure anything goes. Hand me that depleted uranium rod please. It's the one glowing in the corner by the dead bugs. The lead gloves are on the shelf."

SANCHO: "Hmm--GlowBoys Manufacturing, San Jose, California-- what are you going to do with this, Quixote?"

QUIXOTE: "We will use the rods to keep the corners of the wrapping paper down so it doesn't blow away in the wacky winds."

SANCHO: "You're going to put the rods into the ground to keep a myth in place? That's going to take a lot of uranium."

QUIXOTE: "Exactly, Sancho, word is, we will have quite a bunch of these nice depleted uranium rods soon."

SANCHO: "I see, Quixote, another degenerate present from you and your friends, to our children's children."

QUIXOTE: "Try and stop us."

June 12, 2005
Sancho, Quixote, and the Science Spinners

SANCHO:	"Hi, Quixote, what's that big envelope for?"
QUIXOTE:	"Scientific reports, I am supposed to look them over and see if my friends approve them, Sancho."
SANCHO:	"You, what for? I thought you hired media lackeys for that."
QUIXOTE:	"It seems the scientific community is trying to do research without official guidance."
SANCHO:	"You can't be serious--unfettered researchers seeking scientific truth? Non-political answers, knowledge flowing?"
QUIXOTE:	"Horrible isn't it, Sancho?"
SANCHO:	"I bet it keeps your friends up at night. So how come you're doing this grunt work, Quixote?"
QUIXOTE:	"I'm covering the bases. Someone screwed up and information got out to the public."
SANCHO:	"Not pap, but real information? What is this country coming to?"
QUIXOTE:	"The worst: Information has gotten out that the federal government is editing scientific reports to suit industry requirements."
SANCHO:	"Wow, no kidding? That's a real shock, Quixote."
QUIXOTE:	"Stop laughing. Worse than that, the public has been told the government was using an industry guy to muzzle scientists on global warming."
SANCHO:	"Oh, you got caught with your hand in the peer-review-jar. Time to get into your pew and make amends."
QUIXOTE:	"Are you making fun of us, Sancho?"
SANCHO:	"Me, heavens no. But seriously, Quixote, I am appalled your friends could be so dumb."
QUIXOTE:	"You are making fun of us."

SANCHO: "So, ah, you're a commissar now, Quixote?"

QUIXOTE: "What's that?"

SANCHO: "In the old USSR that was the guy who made sure nothing was disseminated that those in power didn't approve."

QUIXOTE: "Oh we call them media-outlet CEOs. That's not me, Sancho. I'm just helping out in a crunch."

SANCHO: "Quixote, you always were a team player. And rest assured your government appreciates your efforts."

QUIXOTE: "Government? My friends don't care what the government approves of, or doesn't approve of, Sancho."

SANCHO: "No need to get hot under the collar, my lord and master."

QUIXOTE: "These damn scientists think they have a right to speak freely about important topics--that's the government's fault along with their revolutionary writings."

SANCHO: "How's that, Quixote?"

QUIXOTE: "The Bill of Rights, The Constitution. Because of those outdated documents these scientists think they have the right to unfettered free speech."

SANCHO: "They do have that right, Quixote."

QUIXOTE: "Not for much longer, Sancho."

SANCHO: "What's wrong with free speech?"

QUIXOTE: "Too much information goes to the wrong people."

SANCHO: "Who, other scientists?"

QUIXOTE: "Exactly--also the general public."

SANCHO: "And they don't even have a country club membership?"

QUIXOTE: "How else can you tell who the right people are?"

SANCHO: "A government has the responsibility to protect its citizens."

QUIXOTE: "So you see why we want less government. I bet you probably also believe that corporations shouldn't run our country."

SANCHO: "That thought had crossed my mind, Quixote."

QUIXOTE: "Sancho, we run the country because we buy the government of this country every few years by upping the price of campaigns. We own the media outlets: print, television, cable, radio, satellite, the whole schmere. If we like someone we donate the money so that politician can give the money right back to us as a campaign spot."

SANCHO: "Why, Quixote?"

QUIXOTE: "Because we say so, Sancho."

SANCHO: "Don't you think that's a bit dictatorial?"

QUIXOTE: "Sancho, we need to make sure unnecessary information does not get out to the public."

SANCHO: "On what?"

QUIXOTE: "On anything, Sancho. Under-funded pension funds, global warming, nuclear energy, corporate corruption, we have a country to run and the only thing worse than dissent is an informed population."

SANCHO: "Do you believe that, Quixote, really?"

QUIXOTE: "Why else would my friends have bought up the media outlets?"

SANCHO: "I see. But the scientists are still running wild."

QUIXOTE: "I gotta' tell ya'. Look at this: This one guy has proof we humans have forced climate change."

SANCHO: "And your job is to keep the lid on that, Quixote."

QUIXOTE: "And it is easy as long as we stay out of the light: just a few red marks, a note that his or her's next year's funding is possibly drying out, and a quick note to the researcher's boss. That will make the ninny of a post-doc tow the line."

SANCHO: "I thought your friends were agreeing to the reality of global warming, Quixote?"

QUIXOTE: "We will sell no information before we have milked it dry."

SANCHO: "Even if people will die believing your lies?"

QUIXOTE: "It's their problem if they believe us. They have enough information to the contrary."

SANCHO: "So the government is impotent to stop your friends."

QUIXOTE: "Not really. This may surprise you but some of my friends have relatives in government who aren't too smart."

SANCHO: "Do tell."

QUIXOTE: "Sancho, the way we see it, if they are too stupid to make it in industry, or oil, we put them into the government--they make great lackeys. But the really dumb ones can cause a problem."

SANCHO: "Because of a lack of morality, Quixote?"

QUIXOTE: "Mixed with a healthy does of just-plain-dumb."

SANCHO: "Boy, I'll say, Quixote."

QUIXOTE: "So now we have to go underground, Sancho."

SANCHO: "Seems the right place for you and your friends, Quixote."

QUIXOTE: "Makes you wonder what this county is coming to."

SANCHO: "Not at all, Quixote. Your friends believe power means privilege without responsibility."

QUIXOTE: "Kind of brings a tear to your eye, doesn't it?"

August 1, 2005
Sancho, Quixote, and Fascists

QUIXOTE: "Well are you happy now, Sancho?"

SANCHO: "About what, Quixote?"

QUIXOTE: "You and your friends, and that global warming mess you've gotten us into."

SANCHO: "Me, Quixote? Little old me? What did I do?"

QUIXOTE: "Global warming is the fault of the environmentalists. If we had just left it alone everything would have been fine. But no. You environmentalists had to step in and now we have to deal with global warming. It's all your responsibility."

SANCHO: "Quixote, don't you think that's a bit absurd?"

QUIXOTE: "You think so, Sancho? Damn, I was hoping that spin might work. We were hoping to focus the coming pain and anger on you environmentalists. We've been working hard targeting the F.O.E. Gosh, that's the best name for an environmental group I ever heard. Friends of the Earth F.O.E. I just love it."

SANCHO: "Seems a bit stupid as a name to me, Quixote. So dumb in fact you could have thought of the name. What are you grinning about, Quixote?"

QUIXOTE: "Nothing Sancho. Anyway from what I hear the wheels are really beginning to get in motion on global warming. The congress is arguing who owns the money and the senate is beginning to cover its posterior."

SANCHO: "The surest signs that the government is finally taking something seriously."

QUIXOTE: "I'll say. Then--courtesy of United States ingenuity--we have that big computer modeling program that everyone is claiming credit for and which will no doubt show there is global warming--caused by no one. Science marches on, Sancho. Our search for truth never ends."

SANCHO: "Ain't pseudoscience grand, Quixote?"

QUIXOTE: "It tickles me. It really does, Sancho."

SANCHO: "You worry me, Quixote."

QUIXOTE: "Don't let it bother you. Just relax. We'll spend the next few years doing all this stuff that looks like we're doing something. We'll get the media whores on it and everyone will be saying how hard we are working to fix global warming. There will be solar, there will be wind. There will be funding!"

SANCHO: "You mean nothing will be done, Quixote."

QUIXOTE: "Sancho, don't be stupid. Of course we are doing something, but we are taking care of our priorities; global warming has a time frame, remember? First, we deny global warming for a few decades. Then we say it might be happening for a few years. This year we began to open the debate on possibilities so our less important associates can bid on projects. That will take a few years. Once we've got the revenues stream nailed down we say global warming is happening, but there is nothing to worry about because it's natural. I'm thinking we can get mileage out of that--maybe an additional 24 months. After that, the public outcry begins and the public debate on what to do. The incremental revenues there will be huge at that point."

SANCHO: "So years and years of delay to increase profits, Quixote?"

QUIXOTE: "It couldn't be more obvious once you pay attention, could it Sancho? By the time it gets to the point where the population sees the problem and gets up in arms, my friends can show a decade of working the problem--maybe more. Then we all march arm and arm to meet the foe: Mother Earth and the wicked global warming. The whole idea brings a tear to my eye."

SANCHO: "Anything for the people, aye, Quixote?"

QUIXOTE: "Cynicism looks good on you, Sancho."

SANCHO: "Thanks, Quixote. Every wasted year adds decades of misery."

QUIXOTE: "Of course, but my friends don't care about that, Sancho. What good is saving the planet if you don't own it?"

SANCHO: "Is that a joke?"

QUIXOTE: "You still think like a servant, Sancho. Who is going to save something when they don't own it?"

SANCHO: "A caring person?"

QUIXOTE: "That person is just another target for my friends Caring is foolish: it's tied to soul. We trade in caring."

SANCHO: "Well put, Mephistopheles."

QUIXOTE: "Who?"

SANCHO: "Quixote, what you really mean is the effects of global warming don't matter. What matters for you and your friends is keeping control."

QUIXOTE: "Now you finally understand the global warming debate."

SANCHO: "So, again, it was never about whether global warming was happening or not."

QUIXOTE: "Of course not--any idiot could recognize the atmosphere acts as a blanket. More blanket means more kept heat energy, duh."

SANCHO: "It was never a scientific debate, Quixote?"

QUIXOTE: "Exactly."

SANCHO: "So then who gets control, Quixote? Your friends?"

QUIXOTE: "Sancho, if we had control of the circumstance then we would deal with global warming."

SANCHO: "But, your friends don't know how to fix global warming."

QUIXOTE: "You're confusing us with people who care. It isn't fixable anymore. Grief and pain are unavoidable now."

SANCHO: "What? You admit to that, Quixote?"

QUIXOTE: "Sancho, to make any real difference at this point we will have to cut our energy usage by 90% in the next five years-- you want reality? That's reality."

SANCHO: "So your friends have set us on track to worldwide tragedy. You blew it."

QUIXOTE: "Another reason to keep control."

SANCHO: "People will suffer."

QUIXOTE:	"They suffer all the time, Sancho. We're just helping the process along. Think of us as efficient."
SANCHO:	"Aren't you concerned about the chaotic nature of the climate? What if we get to the phase shift and you can't turn it all around? Which by the way, you cannot."
QUIXOTE:	"We'll pick up the pieces. We'll fix what we can, those things we can't fix we will make someone else's fault."
SANCHO:	"Your friends are devils and their minions are the uncaring stockholders of large corporations who sit silently by."
QUIXOTE:	"Sancho…I can work with that. Do you think we can tie the environmental movement to Muslim underpinnings?"
SANCHO:	"I doubt it. And you know, Quixote, there are other planets."
QUIXOTE:	"Meaning what, Sancho?"
SANCHO:	"You don't control them."
QUIXOTE:	"That's a sore point, Sancho. Try not to say that too loud."
SANCHO:	"Quixote, once you control everything what will your friends do?"
QUIXOTE:	"We'll make it all a better place."
SANCHO:	"Hahahaha--"
QUIXOTE:	"What are you laughing at? What's so funny. Sancho? Get off the floor. Quit laughing! As your master I command you to stop laughing. I didn't authorize this laughter. Stop it, Sancho--or else!"

September 22, 2005
Sancho, Quixote, and Conscience

QUIXOTE: "Sancho, I'm getting worried about these storms."

SANCHO: "Why Quixote? You have all that wealth to guard you, giggle."

QUIXOTE: "Do you think it will make any difference?"

SANCHO: "Well your lunatic friends believe they are insulated from global warming, right?"

QUIXOTE: "Of course. We can ride out any storm."

SANCHO: "Quixote, what if a few hundred thousand or a few hundred million of your neighbors cannot?"

QUIXOTE: "We have the military."

SANCHO: "So you'll tell them to fire on their family to protect your friends and you think they will do it?"

QUIXOTE: "Sancho, that's what smart weapons are for. We make it look like a video game and they won't know they are killing their children."

SANCHO: "Not such a stretch, Quixote. I'll say that. But it is insane."

QUIXOTE: "Sancho, some of my friends are not rational."

SANCHO: "Do tell, really? Naw, you must be mistaken."

QUIXOTE: "Seriously. They think economics will somehow keep the climate from following it's natural path."

SANCHO: "There are many paths, Quixote."

QUIXOTE: "Very funny, Sancho. I'm serious."

SANCHO: "I can tell, Quixote, so what do you want me to do?"

QUIXOTE: "I don't know. I think we've messed it all up."

SANCHO: "This is a crisis. Is that conscience I see rearing its ugly head?"

QUIXOTE: "Worse. My friends think it's getting away from them. They are insulating themselves now against future turmoil."

SANCHO: "Thinking their wealth and power will keep them safe. Haven't we been here before?"

QUIXOTE: "Exactly. I think they're cuckoo. Look at New Orleans. They aren't trying to fix the problem, they are trying to fix blame. They're perfectly happy to bring all those people back into an area so polluted labs cannot even publish their test results-- just so they can say there is nothing to fear."

SANCHO: "So people don't see a crisis."

QUIXOTE: "They're trying to fix a problem by ignoring it. Do you think that's madness?

SANCHO: "Could be. You know sometimes the problems mount."

QUIXOTE: "Maybe we should have fixed the smaller problems so they wouldn't multiply into big ones."

SANCHO: "Could be, Quixote."

QUIXOTE: "So what do we do?"

SANCHO: "Seems they either gut the economy or kiss our civilization good bye."

QUIXOTE: "It can't be that bad."

SANCHO: "Picture New Orleans over more cities. Then picture that happening every year and accelerating. Grim isn't it?"

QUIXOTE: "We need to do something--but not harm the economy."

SANCHO: "That's stupid--and impossible at this point. You and your friends had the chance earlier to fix things with contained economic damage. Now no matter what they do the economy will be in shambles--and people will suffer. Tell your friends congratulations: They brought forth the very worst scenario."

QUIXOTE: "But we listened to the recommendations from the White Star Competitive Institute and the Marie Antoinette Enterprise Institute. The boys at the Nero Research Facility also agreed. They said we were okay. They are our best and brightest."

SANCHO: "Wake up Quixote. The best and the brightest said up yours to your friends. The best and the brightest also said they are too decent to support your idiotic regime. And I think someone wrote: I will not work for morons."

QUIXOTE: "That could be."

SANCHO: "Don't you get it, Quixote? Atlas shrugged."

QUIXOTE: "Do you know someone suggested things might get so bad that there will be no written history of our time?"

SANCHO: "And they got a promotion, I bet."

QUIXOTE: "How did you know?"

SANCHO: "An easy guess. So the new plan is...Hoping no one remembers your friends as the greatest mass murders in history?"

QUIXOTE: "For a start."

SANCHO: "That's what I like about you and your friends--always finding the slimiest solution to every problem."

September 24, 2005
Sancho, Quixote, Max, and Bill

QUIXOTE: "Sancho, I'm beginning to think some of my friends are not rational. Have you seen my latest project?"

SANCHO: "Not rational, unwise, cuckoo? Do tell, really? Naw, you must be mistaken."

QUIXOTE: "Look at this."

SANCHO: "Oh, another movie script, hmm 'Bill and Max's Excellent Adventure'. What's it about?"

QUIXOTE: "It's a story about slavery. You see there are these two cotton-pickers in the South standing up for slavery during the abolitionist period saying how good slavery is for the slaves."

SANCHO: "You're joking?"

QUIXOTE: "Wait, there's more. So these two slaves, Bill and Max, are freed from slavery and told all they need to do is go around to the other plantations telling the slaves that freedom is slavery. They are to point to themselves and say: 'You can be free like us!'"

SANCHO: "Happy New Year, 1984."

QUIXOTE: "No, Sancho, it's actually set in 1850, though I like the sound of that."

SANCHO: "Got it. Tell me more."

QUIXOTE: "Anyway there are these big storms and a bunch of the slaves get killed because they are chained inside these huts and can't get away. Some drown, a few get sick, old people die, it's really a mess. The bad guy in the script is a doctor because he cannot pick locks and free the slaves before the storm."

SANCHO: "Sort of like a leading edge environmentalist?"

QUIXOTE: "We prefer the term eco-nut, Sancho."

SANCHO: "Who's the author, Santayana?"

QUIXOTE: "Huh?"

SANCHO: Never mind, Quixote, go on."

QUIXOTE: "Anyway Bill and Max go out to the plantations and stand on soapboxes. They tell the slaves that slavery has kept the slaves all together so they can help each other."

SANCHO: "What about the chains?"

QUIXOTE: "That's the beautiful part of the story. Both Max and Bill tell the slaves they have no chains--that the chains are not shackles--but links of love."

SANCHO: "You must be kidding."

QUIXOTE: "Not going to fly, is it? I didn't think so either. Maybe we'll have them go from plantation to plantation and just tell the other slaves the storms will only happen once every hundred years."

SANCHO: "People remember storms, Quixote."

QUIXOTE: "Hmm. You're right. Well how about telling them the storms come because the slaves weren't working hard enough and God was punishing them?"

SANCHO: "Slaves were worked awfully hard. I don't think that will work either, Quixote."

QUIXOTE: "Perhaps, Sancho. Were there environmentalists back then?"

SANCHO: "Probably, Quixote, but I believe there wasn't much media in 1850, so how could you blame the environmentalists for storms? Why are your friends worried about storms anyway?"

QUIXOTE: "My friends know the hurricanes are getting more intense due to climate change. And I think they want to promote slavery as a way of life."

SANCHO: "Which explains Max and Bill."

QUIXOTE: "Exactly. Look, here at the script, Sancho, they even have a part here where Bill and Max talk to the slaves about recommendations from think tanks."

SANCHO: "In 1850? What do they say?"

QUIXOTE: "Slavery is a natural condition."

SANCHO: "How stupid. Oh look here on manuscript. Someone scratched out plantations and put in corporation."

QUIXOTE: "One of our bright young MBA's got a little too zealous with the truth. We had him canned."

SANCHO: "What about all the years of freedom before the plantations?"

QUIXOTE: "Bill and Max ignore anything that doesn't prove their point. In fact I have a newspaper shill that follows them saying the last 100 years of data is the only information that matters."

SANCHO: "Why, Quixote?"

QUIXOTE: "The plantation owners had firm control on a hundred years of slavery by that point."

SANCHO: "That's insignificant given the amount of time humanity has been on the planet."

QUIXOTE: "Of course, but remember they're trying to chain up people's minds and souls, not just their body."

SANCHO: "And it sounds like Max and Bill are just the guys to do it. On the other hand, there are many paths, Quixote."

QUIXOTE: "I think my friends are afraid."

SANCHO: "Fear among the well insulated? I'm shocked. Why?"

QUIXOTE: "Sancho, picture New Orleans, then picture that happening to other cities every year. Grim isn't it?"

SANCHO: "Sounds familiar for some reason. You're unusually realistic, today."

QUIXOTE: "My friends should have done something."

SANCHO: "But that may harm the economy, remember? What did you call that strategy? Oh, a 'No Regrets Policy'. How'd that work out for you?"

QUIXOTE: "Not too well. We had the chance to fix things earlier with contained economic damage. Now no matter we do the economy will be in shambles--and lots of people will die. My friends are afraid they have brought forth the very worst scenario."

SANCHO: "Do I hear an echo? So what will they do now?"

QUIXOTE: "Now they have to deny the effects of global warming, again."

SANCHO: "Which explains 'Bill and Max's Excellent Adventure'."

QUIXOTE: "Precisely, Sancho, my friends believe it is every man for themselves from now on."

SANCHO: "How odd. So now there is no leadership working for the good of the people?"

QUIXOTE: "Of course there are people doing that--as you said there are many paths--but don't worry we have them muzzled and chained. The media corporations have strict orders to keep other viewpoints marginalized, ignored, or otherwise labeled as witch doctors."

SANCHO: "And you're hoping maybe a storm will get them anyway."

QUIXOTE: "Exactly, Sancho, then all we do is trot out Bill, Max, and others like them and make sure they say exactly as we wish."

SANCHO: "Slavery is freedom! An excellent adventure, Quixote."

September 28, 2005
Sancho, Quixote, and Shame

SANCHO: "Quixote, do you and your friends have any idea what the word shame means?"

QUIXOTE: "Hang, on Sancho, can you give me a hand with this real estate listing agreement."

SANCHO: "Are you selling your home?"

QUIXOTE: "No, my friends are selling some of the national parks and I have been asked to help them with the last parts of the disclosure form. If a park no longer has any glaciers in it, is that a material defect in the park, or a water feature?"

SANCHO: "Selling a few of the national parks? Is that a joke? Just whom are you selling the national parks to, the oil companies?"

QUIXOTE: "How did you know? No one is supposed to know about that. Seems kind of unfair doesn't it? Boo-hoo."

SANCHO: "You're kidding. Your friends are really planning on selling some of the national parks to the oil companies?"

QUIXOTE: "Sancho, you have been complaining that my friends are not proactive on global warming. Now we're proactive and positive on it and you act like we're a bunch of mass murders."

SANCHO: "So how is looting the national parks a positive event?"

QUIXOTE: "Looting isn't black or white. We're not really looting the national parks we're acquiring resources. We need more oil."

SANCHO: "If a grizzly bear bites one of the oil guys in the woods will you label the grizzly an insurgent?"

QUIXOTE: "We might. The news teams like the word insurgent."

SANCHO: "Why loot the national parks? You're not running out of things to loot are you?"

QUIXOTE: "Hurricanes have been a real boom for us. We're also suspending regulations on offshore drilling."

SANCHO: "For what reason?"

QUIXOTE: "The hurricanes are a great excuse to steal. My friends are terrified of global warming and the monster storms; the heat waves, the whole deal is scaring them. They feel the need to own more of the planet. It's a security-blanket thing."

SANCHO: "Quixote, what are going tell the citizens?"

QUIXOTE: "First we are going to raise gas prices again. Then we are going to say hurricane damage is cutting into oil production."

SANCHO: "That's idiotic. Global warming causes the more intense storms that did the damage. The use of petrochemicals is a major contributor to global warming. Anything that cuts our dependency on oil and forces us to conserve is a blessing."

QUIXOTE: "Not if my friends have anything to say about it. Besides, we are not in the blessing business. We're leaders. So we get to take what we want."

SANCHO: "Nonsense. Leadership is all about responsibility. You and your friends are bullies and nothing else."

QUIXOTE: "As someone once said of the British--you are a nation of shopkeepers."

SANCHO: "Yes, but look what happened to Hitler."

QUIXOTE: "Is that where it came from? Damn, I need to make sure Junior doesn't use that quote this weekend. Well anyway, no one is willing to give up their comfort to stop us."

SANCHO: "You're blind, Quixote."

QUIXOTE: "Sancho, that's why you environmentalists keep losing on this issue, you ask for sacrifice. We tell the public we will insure their way of life if they ignore global warming."

SANCHO: "But the Gulf Coast is proof that's a lie."

QUIXOTE: "Not so long as we keep that clarity off the airwaves and out of the print media."

SANCHO: "So your friends will use every event to loot public lands and insulate themselves from the coming damage of global warming by putting out the Big Lie. Well I guess the word shame really does not have meaning to your friends, Quixote."

QUIXOTE: "Of course, Sancho, if it did we'd have it removed from
             the dictionaries. Remember--we know what you read--it's a
             matter of national security. Now will you give me a hand
             with listing agreement? Does a flood count as running water?
             What about toilets, do you think we should list an outhouse
             as a full bath or a ¾ bath?"

September 29, 2005
Sancho, Quixote, and the Investigation

QUIXOTE: "Well Sancho, we finally have a probe underway for that disaster that was such a horrific mess of ineptitude and finger pointing. Aren't you proud of us? This probe will be run at the highest levels of government."

SANCHO: "Exxon, Quixote?"

QUIXOTE: "Very funny. We have to show the American people we are serious about disasters and this probe will do it."

SANCHO: "A probe into what, Quixote?"

QUIXOTE: "The disaster. That horrible event of national importance that has been swept under the rug. You know the one where all those people died."

SANCHO: "Which one, Quixote?"

QUIXOTE: "Can't you guess? I'll give you a hint. Remember a movie a few years ago showing all those people dying because they didn't head the warnings? Because they decided to ignore what they knew to be true?"

SANCHO: "Nope, too easy. Which movie, what disaster?"

QUIXOTE: "My friends have finally started the probe into the White Star Lines. It's a British company but we think we can have some impact on policy there."

SANCHO: "Who is White Star Lines?"

QUIXOTE: "Sancho, I thought you knew about current events."

SANCHO: "I do. What does that have to do with White Star Lines?"

QUIXOTE: "They are the cruise ship company that owned the Titanic and my friends are going to let no stone go unturned until they find out the truth of the disaster. One thing we do know though is that ice berg was not caused by global warming."

SANCHO: "The Titanic? Your friends are launching a probe on the Titanic?"

QUIXOTE: "Of course. This is big, really big, Sancho. Besides we have a bone to pick with the Brits."

SANCHO: "That ship sunk almost ninety years ago, Quixote."

QUIXOTE: "Just goes to show you how important uncovering the truth is to my friends. We just keep digging for the facts."

SANCHO: "What about more current disasters, like Katrina, Rita, or Mike? Why all the delay?"

QUIXOTE: "One at a time, Sancho. I bet you can't wait until we get up to speed on investigating the United Nations. It might take a while, but you need to remember, Rome wasn't built in a day. So stop worrying."

SANCHO: "Said Nero--and why should I care?"

QUIXOTE: "By the time I and my friends are done, we will have America caring about things they never even considered caring about, Sancho."

SANCHO: "To deflect people from current events like monster hurricanes caused by global warming, Quixote?"

QUIXOTE: "Exactly. The Titanic was human error. Hurricanes are, ah, intelligent design, or Castro, or locusts, or who cares."

SANCHO: "So then we agree, Quixote. You are saying denial of global warming is simple stupidity."

QUIXOTE: "We're not going to acknowledge the link. We are guarding our interests."

SANCHO: "National interests, like the interests of the United States?"

QUIXOTE: "Don't be silly, Sancho. Good joke, though."

October 16, 2005
Sancho, Quixote, and Aid

SANCHO: "Quixote, here are those smelly hotel blankets. I washed them and washed them but they still stink. Wow, those are really big boxes. What are they for?"

QUIXOTE: "My friends are putting together relief packages for Portugal, Spain, Brazil, New Hampshire, New Jersey, Massachusetts, Pakistan, India, China, Japan, Taiwan, Vietnam, Costa Rica, Mexico, and some other places. I just can't keep track of them all anymore."

SANCHO: "Oh, because of the...What do you call it, Quixote? Ah yes, cyclical weather."

QUIXOTE: "No single event can be directly tied to global warming. Sancho, help me get those pecan pies in the cooler. I want to make sure the frozen shrimp gets out there as soon as possible too, whew what a stink. Where are those hospital sheets? Oh, right here next to the bloody walkers and wheelchairs. We need to clean those again."

SANCHO: "Okay, Pontius, ah Quixote. There sure is a lot of bad weather."

QUIXOTE: "No single event can be tied to global warming, Sancho."

SANCHO: "How about a dozen or so? Oh yeah, disasters doesn't count."

QUIXOTE: "Especially earthquakes."

SANCHO: "Oh heavens, yes. And of course moving water has no mass—so there is no way that mass shifts on tectonic plates and earthquakes can be connected to ice melting."

QUIXOTE: "So see you understand. No single event can be tied to global warming."

SANCHO: "I think all this rain has made you a bit foggy, Quixote. Isn't it most likely the increase in the severity of certain events is an indicator of a new climate regime? You already admit the driver of the new climate regime is anthropogenic forcing of the climate. So no matter what you pontificate, we can tie events directly to global warming."

QUIXOTE: "I like that term: regime."

SANCHO: "Why aren't I surprised--so when will your friends tie global warming to the increased severity of the weather?"

QUIXOTE: "No single event can be tied to global warming."

SANCHO: "You must be very proud of your team's new slogan."

QUIXOTE: "Thank you. Truth is I can't be dishonest and take credit for the phrase. My friends require total honesty from their associates. The U.N., coined that phrase. Then they dropped the ball. We picked up the fumble from them a few years ago. It was one of my best pickups."

SANCHO: "Your attention to detail is impressive."

QUIXOTE: "Plus I am a straight shooter. I am happy to give them credit."

SANCHO: "Quixote, can I get the straight jacket concession for your friends when this all collapses around them?"

QUIXOTE: "I think that contract went to Halliburton. It'll be a big one I hear. Help me seal this box of supplies."

SANCHO: "Looks more like a box of trash then supplies. Why are you sending boxes of junk labeled supplies to disaster areas?"

QUIXOTE: "The boys at the think tanks suggested it. They believe sending junk from one disaster zone to another may be a booming business in the future. We add little notes that say climate events are cyclical--and not tied to global warming. The guys think we can foster years of confusion with that."

SANCHO: "Let's see: First your friends said global warming wasn't real. Then they said global warming was not really bad for America. Then they backtracked to the nonsense that the costs of global warming would not be so bad. Now we have the newest mantra that global warming and increased storm severity is not proven. Your friends are absurd, but consistent."

QUIXOTE: "It's just the ride we're taking you on. Call it: Gullible's Travels."

SANCHO: "Very funny."

QUIXOTE: "We think it's hilarious. Now keep repeating after me: No single event can be tied to global warming. No single event can be tied to global warming. Look Toto, it's Auntie Em!"

SANCHO: "Funny. So when that mantra fails are you going to try pinning global warming on a developing nation, like Oz?"

QUIXOTE: "We are working on that...Very funny."

SANCHO: "Quixote, people are going to wake up. At this point it's just a question of how much damage the American people are willing to absorb before they respond."

QUIXOTE: "Prove it! Sorry, bad joke--look--as long as we keep shipping boxes of aid around people will think we have unlimited resources to deal with disaster. They will think things are okay-- so long as they see the security blanket--bloody or not."

SANCHO: "So then this isn't really a relief package."

QUIXOTE: "We've got tons of junk that we need to get rid of from those hurricanes. What better way--then to send it out as aid--with a few messages of hope."

SANCHO: "Propaganda, Quixote?"

QUIXOTE: "Maybe a bit."

SANCHO: "So it's kind of like marrying recycling and conservation with just the tiniest bit of self-reward, Quixote?"

QUIXOTE: "You know they are buying that conservation stuff thinking it makes a difference in global warming? How stupid. Anyway, the slower America reacts to global warming the better it is for my friends."

SANCHO: "And the worse for everyone else."

QUIXOTE: "Oh well--it's the new climate regime, Sancho."

SANCHO: "Quixote, that's not what that term means."

QUIXOTE: "Give me time."

SANCHO: "I'm doing my best not to."

QUIXOTE: "What's in that dumpster they just delivered? I was hoping to get some old MRE's but I guess those days are gone for a while."

SANCHO: "It says Dick's Toxic Gumbo--good for the whole family."

QUIXOTE: "We'll pack that in the next shipment--no way that stuff is ever going to go bad. Hand me those boxes with all the beads will you, Sancho? Oh, this will not work. We need to scratch the 'Visit New Orleans' from the beads. I really thought I would make money with that one."

SANCHO: "Quixote, all these climate tragedies don't bother you do they?"

QUIXOTE: "My friends are petrified of them. The climate tragedies point to our worst fear."

SANCHO: "And that is?"

QUIXOTE: "People realizing they need to think for themselves."

SANCHO: "Heaven forbid, not that, Quixote!"

QUIXOTE: "Think of the result, Sancho: A rapidly developing sustainable economy, a host of new technologies, decentralized power generation, new transportation paradigms, housing changes. We'll have cottage industries springing up everywhere, new markets popping up, a unified population working on a common threat. A meaning to life, and my friend's net worth not worth a damn. It's horrible, Sancho."

SANCHO: "I see. So everything that your friends have worked for all these years--blown to hell by one dumb planet and its lousy little environment. Imagine, all that planet-raping work gone with the wind."

QUIXOTE: "But we're fighting back with our new mantra: 'We don't care about the wind--renewables are unreliable' program. Then there is the 'Some times the sun don't shine' program but that's going a little slow."

SANCHO: "Quixote, the stress must be awful on you and your friends. How do they cope?"

QUIXOTE: "You don't know the half of it. Why, if you even bring up the notion of uncontrolled progress in some boardrooms they'll send you packing. You know some of those board members believe they own progress: Like it's one of their most important products."

SANCHO: "So you are not even close to being the craziest of them?"

QUIXOTE: "Sancho, I'm not even a front runner. Grab that sack of rags will you? Oh and grab those busted up 2x4's and label them kindling. Then check on the cigarettes we've got drying in the sun. Oh, and unpack the galoshes for Brazil. I think we will need them for a shipment to New Jersey. Hmm, do you think, the gas credit cards should go on the top or the bottom of the pension cancellation notices…"

October 28, 2005
Sancho, Quixote, and the Bird

QUIXOTE: "Sancho, did you break that new oar I bought?"

SANCHO: "Sorry, Quixote, I was filling the sandbags. What oar?"

QUIXOTE: "The oars for the boat--the one I use for hunting birds in the park. Do you know how it got broken?"

SANCHO: "I don't know. Are they the same oars you bought in that garage sale a few months ago?"

QUIXOTE: "Yes, the left oar is toast. Darn that report. It said those oars were good for rowing about in the water."

SANCHO: "Quixote, that article was written in 1978. And I have been meaning to ask you--why would you buy old oars based on a report from so far back?"

QUIXOTE: "I didn't think the technology of an oar could change that much. Seems kinda' stupid now doesn't it?"

SANCHO: "Quixote, buddy, that oar had dry rot. The handles had a spindle-top and they were held together with cellophane tape. The blades were checked at the ends. The deep carving that said: 'Scooter is here' was rotten I don't see why you bought it."

QUIXOTE: "My friends said spindle-top oars or tea-pot domed oars were the way to go."

SANCHO: "Now I see, it is your masters' voices calling--seems ironic that as a result of listening to them, you don't have all your oars in the water."

QUIXOTE: "Very funny. So how the heck am I going to row with just the right-side oar in the water?"

SANCHO: "Think of it as a conservative viewpoint to roving the pond--you'll go around in circles."

QUIXOTE: "Circles are good. I am sure I can get somewhere by going in circles. In fact I read a report from 1997 that said that."

SANCHO: "You're joking right?"

QUIXOTE: "No."

SANCHO: "I suppose it's too much of a stretch to assume you might take an empirical viewpoint to this problem?"

QUIXOTE: "Meaning?"

SANCHO: "Well what will you do when the sun arcs across the sky and you've gotten nowhere because you are going in circles?"

QUIXOTE: "You're right. Sancho, I could do that all day long and then it would be too late to get anything done when the sun sets on us. Do you think that's what they wanted? Do you think maybe they wanted to limit my options?"

SANCHO: "Deceit, from your friends? That's possible, Quixote."

QUIXOTE: "Or maybe they didn't want me to kill animals?"

SANCHO: "I doubt it. They gave you the machine gun to hunt birds."

QUIXOTE: "Good point. What could it mean?"

SANCHO: "At every turn, your friends seem to be fostering inaction, ineptitude, and inefficiency for their own gain."

QUIXOTE: "I am a corporate knight, Sancho. They'll take care of me."

SANCHO: "Of course, Quixote, forgive me--your benefactors believe in the sanctity of science and the search for truth."

QUIXOTE: "Sancho, you know I don't like it when you fall on the ground laughing at me. It's not dignified. Besides, laughter is anti-American. You do want to fly again, don't you? I can put you on a list if you don't stop laughing at us."

SANCHO: "Okay, I'll stop laughing. You know it's okay to observe what your friends are doing to you."

QUIXOTE: "Never. We are on a search for facts. No empiricism allowed!"

SANCHO: "And no wire hangers either! Quixote, you and your friends are nuts. Science is all about observation."

QUIXOTE: "Maybe they think I am too much of a water-rover?"

SANCHO: "Maybe. Perhaps you can tell them you were hungry. Did you ingest all the birds you got last year, Quixote?"

Quixote: "Only the cardinal with the X on it."

Sancho: "What about the rest of them?"

Quixote: "Too many bullets."

Sancho: "You could consider single shot instead of full automatic."

Quixote: "Never, Sancho, the gun lobby boys would have a fit."

Sancho: "Hmm, well you do have a dilemma here, Quixote. How do you best keep mobile, so you can bag a few more cardinals, without an oar, while kowtowing to your masters? Maybe you could use your outboard motor on the boat?"

Quixote: "That darn motor makes so much noise and what a stink. It's hard to bag any game with the clatter from that gas-powered behemoth. Then there are the darn environmentalists who are already angry with me for shooting birds in the park. As soon as they see me, they'll be all over me--there is no way I'll get any cardinals this year if I make a lot of noise."

Sancho: "You could cloak the engine in a tarp and soak the tarp in snake oil. Then you could say you were doing some kind of research project on technology for the cardinals, Quixote."

Quixote: "No one is that stupid. There is an answer. We need to think. Technology always supplies an answer in situations like this. Think science. Think technology. Think the way I tell you."

Sancho: "You could try walking. Then, you could maybe...Hunt bears?"

Quixote: "That might work. Bears are tasty--good idea--Sancho. We don't have any of that bear left do we?"

Sancho: "Nope, sorry. I'll go get your machine gun. Do you want the hundred round clip or the Gatling option?"

Quixote: "No. Get the flintlock. I've got a report here from 1776 in my desk that says the flintlock will make me straight shooter."

Sancho: "The report came from the same group of friends who gave you the oars, Quixote?"

Quixote: "When they sold me the flintlock--they said it was also for self-protection."

SANCHO: "Perfect. Your wish is my command, oh Master of the Universe. Once again, Quixote, your respect for risk assessment, truth, science, engineering, and innovation inspires me to action. One flintlock, coming up."

QUIXOTE: "Natty Bumpo would be proud of you, Sancho."

SANCHO: "That's for sure, Quixote."

November 2, 2005
Sancho, Quixote, and More Birds

SANCHO: "So, Quixote, how was your hunting trip?"

QUIXOTE: "I was sidetracked by a little court room drama. Then, as I was putting the boat in the water, I looked up to see what I was going to kill first...And there it was. I had an inspiration from above and I knew what needed to happen."

SANCHO: "What would that be?"

QUIXOTE: "The evil empire."

SANCHO: "The USSR?"

QUIXOTE: "Organic poultry."

SANCHO: "Beg pardon?"

QUIXOTE: "Them, the enemy, the evil one--all served up on a platter. Death from above. Pandemics, pandemonium, and pressed, paper-wrapped propaganda la' orange, birds a la Hitchcock, SARS compote, nations cordoned boo--all served up in a Grenada reduction with just a touch of mad cow memories. That little chickadee is the answer to our global problems."

SANCHO: "Birds are a cure for your friends' madness?"

QUIXOTE: "Sancho, don't you get it: Bird-terrorists. Bogey-birds. Tweetie bin laden!!!"

SANCHO: "Oh that bird flu thing? Is that really more important than global warming?"

QUIXOTE: "Check this out. I even had one of the rags say how important it is to prepare for a disaster that hasn't yet happened and may never happen. At the end, they said how wonderful we are to prepare for the worst. We are so far-sighted. I am so sure."

SANCHO: "Nice to hear you giggle again, Quixote. Won't someone say we should be preparing for climate change?"

QUIXOTE: "Not in any media outlet we control--best we'll do is bird flu."

SANCHO: "There you go again, you and your liberal media."

QUIXOTE: "Don't blaspheme. Sancho, we were on the ropes for this global warming thing, the bell was ringing, but in a flash I knew what we needed to do."

SANCHO: "Confess your sins and get out of the way before you kill more people, Quixote?"

QUIXOTE: "Do I detect a note of bitterness? We invent another crisis you dummies will buy. Sancho, I think I have some traction on this."

SANCHO: "So, Quixote, tell me, what is the danger there?"

QUIXOTE: "Well it's not poultry. People are almost completely immune to bird flu. But I think I can get a movie tie in."

SANCHO: "Oh my, that is convenient. So who is really the enemy? Are we talking the entire winged community here?"

QUIXOTE: "Oddly enough we are only worried about cash poultry: chickens, ducks, and turkeys. We need to keep them healthy you know."

SANCHO: "What about the rest of the avian community?"

QUIXOTE: "Money talks, wild birdies walk."

SANCHO: "Got it. So you are helping the poultry producers keep their livestock healthy. Seems odd your friends were busy telling the public that the environmentalists say the sky is going to fall in and then you pull this Big Bird with a cold as a national crisis."

QUIXOTE: "Don't you see the beauty? We put money into bird flu research and that makes the poultry lobby happy. Plus, we divert attention from our indiscretions. Plus there is no chance of failure on the bird project."

SANCHO: "Why, Quixote?"

QUIXOTE: "Didn't you hear me? Humans are mostly immune to bird flu. Beautiful isn't it? The poultry producers are happy and my friends have wagged the dog again. The gravy train is back on track, thanks to yours truly."

SANCHO: "It makes me proud to be an American. Quixote, what was the inspiration from above that brought you to this epiphany?"

QUIXOTE: "A bunch of bird poop."

SANCHO: "The poet speaks."

November 10, 2005
Sancho, Quixote, and the Ecosystem

SANCHO: "Where did you get that justice statue? Say, it's not holding the scales but an oil well. And what's that in her hand?"

QUIXOTE: "A checkbook, Sancho."

SANCHO: "She has blue eyes and blond hair? Where is the blindfold?"

QUIXOTE: "We got rid of that. My friends feel that if she has a blindfold, she may not see the money. Some of the guys thought we might cover her eyes with ticker tape."

SANCHO: "Why are you all doing this, Quixote?"

QUIXOTE: "My group has been given the job of redesigning some American heritage items, Sancho. Justice was first. Then we've got a copy of the Bill of Rights--and the Constitution is over there on my desk."

SANCHO: "Why is Mein Kampf written on it?"

QUIXOTE: "One of the guys had it before me and that was his working title for the project. You can see why I got it. Of course, some of them are thinking about scrapping it all and putting out a generic corporate resolution saying people really matter and having it signed by the largest stockholders of the Fortune 500. They think we should re-title the Bill of Rights and call it 'Our Struggle to be Very Right'. Or, 'Right makes Right makes Right makes Right'."

SANCHO: "Did the elections scare your friends, Quixote?"

QUIXOTE: "Well let's just say it shouldn't be too hard to figure out who wanted to use Mein Kampf as a working title. Sancho, you know it's all because of that global warming thing."

SANCHO: "What? Don't be ridiculous. The voters were upset with corruption, double dealing, war making, being ignored, and the hurricane disaster response."

QUIXOTE: "Exactly, the intense hurricanes are caused by global warming--that's where we really messed up, this global warming thing. How'd I do?"

SANCHO: "Well almost, Quixote. So how come your friends have this again-found awareness that global warming increases hurricane intensity?"

QUIXOTE: "We are listening to the scientists. We wuv' them."

SANCHO: "That's pathetic."

QUIXOTE: "Well try this one on. We care about the people, Sancho. Why else would we stop drilling in the Arctic?"

SANCHO: "Because bullies are always cowards, Quixote."

QUIXOTE: "We do have issues, with power, but we'll get better. I'm even taking that ethics class next week. Honest, we really care about American ideals."

SANCHO: "So the election did scare your friends. I think the population knows that your friends believe that the highest form of government is a banana republic. They know you invade countries because you want to. You ignore the will of the people. You put our children at risk because substantive action might impact your hold on power. You usurp freedom of the press. You co-opt the religious beliefs of decent people and use it against them. You torture people and justify it with your need to know. In simple terms, Captain America, you blow it. You and your friends stink, Quixote. That's why you were murdered in the elections."

QUIXOTE: "I know we can change, Sancho. At least I know we can look a bit more responsive to all you, ah citizens. We've got a new guy all ready to go--and he's a man of the people. He doesn't even like torture."

SANCHO: "Ooh, how special! Does the term nausea mean anything to you? Shame? Stupidity?"

QUIXOTE: "Can it. I am tired of this game. We still have the reins of power. We are just pandering to you fools. Bread and circuses for the masses, here it comes and watch my smoke."

SANCHO: "Oh, now I see why they did the rework of Justice."

QUIXOTE: "Exactly. We're more important than this country Sancho. Don't you see that?"

SANCHO: "Quixote, you know that ticker tape you were going to put on the eyes of justice?"

QUIXOTE: "Yes?"

SANCHO: "Why don't you put your ticker tape some place else?"

QUIXOTE: "Sancho, I thought you were apolitical, an enviro-nut."

SANCHO: "Quixote, politics are just another part of the human environment--that's what makes humans special. Our ecosystem transcends the trees and the sea, the flora and the fauna, the climate and the dirt. That's what climate change is really about: It isn't an eco-horror to be feared. We have extended our outlook on the word ecosystem as a result of our minds and our greatness. Why don't you?"

QUIXOTE: "We're realists. There is no way for us to control an informed population."

SANCHO: "You're dinosaurs. Awareness beat you, Quixote, the awareness that our environment is broadening into new and perplexing areas."

QUIXOTE: "Screw the climate. We run the political system. We run the country. We have the connections and the access. We have the money and the power. We have media. We are the world."

SANCHO: "Calm down, Quixote. Or, you might have a stroke."

QUIXOTE: "Sancho, we have the Bill of Rights in our pocket for God's sake."

SANCHO: "You have, you have, you have--but you own nothing-- because for you and you're your friends, it's all for sale."

QUIXOTE: "It is all for sale. That's what makes America great."

"SANCHO: "That's another reason why you lost, Quixote. You really believe in the idea that 'America Is For Sale'."

QUIXOTE: "It isn't?"

SANCHO: "That idea is the lucre of fools, Quixote."

QUIXOTE: "My friends aren't fools, they are megalomaniacs. Apologize."

SANCHO: "Quixote, relax. It's okay--the rest of us just do not need the myth of control as much as you and your cronies. Trouble is they blew it. It is just time for the next vanity-fair to move in and buckle up their beltway."

Quixote: "Sancho, what do I do if my friends are unseated? I've got a big mortgage on this place."

Sancho: "The best thing you can do for your friends, Quixote, is to tell them to be good little boys and girls, pack up their kit and let the next crew of megalomaniacs come in as soon as possible. The rest of us have work to do."

Quixote: "What about more money, Sancho?"

Sancho: "What about energy, Quixote?"

Quixote: "Energy isn't as important as money."

Sancho: "Is that so, Quixote? Like I said: It is all about awareness."

November 17, 2005
Sancho, Quixote, and 1984

SANCHO: "Quixote, it's a little bit early to get the New Year's decorations. Oh, it's for your party. Man, that's a big sign. Let's see. Oh, they made a mistake. It says, 'Happy New Year: 1984!'"

QUIXOTE: "That is no mistake Sancho,

SANCHO: "I doubt it will work out the way you want, Quixote. You can't go backwards in time."

QUIXOTE: "Says who? Prove it. Show me your proof."

SANCHO: "Now where I heard this before? Quixote, it's going to be 2006 in January, not 1984. Everyone knows that."

QUIXOTE: "My friends are a little upset that we don't hear any voices out there in the scientific community saying next year is going to be 1984."

SANCHO: "Well why should they? This year is 2005 and next year is 2006."

QUIXOTE: "See, that's what I mean about you environmentalists. You're so sure of your dogma; you don't leave any room for an opposing viewpoint. You started it with global warming and now you are commandeering the calendar. Where will it end?"

SANCHO: "Quixote, I think you have been working too hard. Would you like an aspirin or something else, perhaps some Tamiflu?"

QUIXOTE: "No, think about it. Isn't it time you eco-nuts let go of your iron grip on things like science and literature, time and calendars, and begin to let the dissident voices come forward to prove it isn't going to be 2006 next year, but 1984?"

SANCHO: "Maybe we can clean out that padded room you had built for your Detroit friends and you can sleep this off tonight?"

QUIXOTE: "Sancho, it's like your stance on global warming. Just because the mass of scientific reports say we humans are forcing the climate, and the mass of respected scientists agree, and the facts prove them out, why can't you give equal weight to the idea there might not be global warming?"

SANCHO: "Because it is incorrect."

QUIXOTE: "Who cares!"

SANCHO: "I see your point. Perhaps, instead of aspirin, or a padded room, maybe a nice long rest might suit you and your friends?"

QUIXOTE: "Sancho, don't you see we are fighting to ignore the facts while adhering to a dead economic model and at the same time disregarding the planet and its populations?"

SANCHO: "So many problems running a junta, and yes the notion crossed my mind--Quixote. But for the sake of cross-class harmony, why, come January, is it going to be 1984?"

QUIXOTE: "Reagan's on my Christmas card."

SANCHO: "It just keeps getting better and better, Quixote. Why is sentiment designed by the mad hatter proof of the date?"

QUIXOTE: "Because E-cards are so impersonal, Sancho. And unreliable."

SANCHO: "Nice, parry."

QUIXOTE: "You know once we've cleaned out the nasty local forests by using paper for greeting cards, we can build a small nuclear power plant for my next party."

SANCHO: "You're planning to have your own nuclear power plant, Quixote?"

QUIXOTE: "It's the coming thing. Global warming you know--but there are so many groups fighting the radioactive storage issue."

SANCHO: "And so many regulations--is that why you want it to be 1984?"

QUIXOTE: "It's not just that, Sancho. We believe the lack of calendars saying it's 1983 are the very proof that next year is 1984 and since my friends hold the facts to be sacred, we demand a thorough investigation into the possibility that next year might really be 1984. Science demands it. Truth demands it."

SANCHO: "How do you keep a straight face saying that stuff? You're not just rewriting history about little things like wars anymore--you're ignoring time."

QUIXOTE: "See, that's what I mean. If we let in the slightest question of our governance, the first thing you all do is bring up a little faux pas like an unwinable war."

SANCHO: "Little sensitive to that one, are you, Quixote?"

QUIXOTE: "Not a bit. We are bringing peace to the Mideast."

SANCHO: "Hmmm, I'm beginning to suspect you might have a point with that 1984 stuff. You already have the 'War is Peace' thing down pat."

QUIXOTE: "You've seen what we did to the word 'truth'."

SANCHO: "So what's the real reason for this idiotic campaign to disprove what we all know as true?"

QUIXOTE: "I didn't say anything about global warming."

SANCHO: "I was talking about your perverse desire to ignore the calendar."

QUIXOTE: "We're not ignoring the calendar. We're just making sure it doesn't mean anything more than we want it to--like science."

SANCHO: "Now we are getting somewhere. Why?"

QUIXOTE: "Sancho, if the calendar matters to anyone, then sooner or later one of you eco-nuts is going to realize we are running out of time to deal with global warming. If it's 1984 again we have bought ourselves another 20 years to solve the problem and we're back at trickle-down-heaven."

SANCHO: "Then you know we don't have 20 years to debate, do R&D, propose pointless legislation, and then marginally reduce our carbon footprint all so your media pundits can claim we are addressing global warming and your friends can retain power?"

QUIXOTE: "Sancho, any idiot knows that--so have I convinced you to get on board with our program of claiming the upcoming year is 1984? If you do join us, then I can guarantee mounds of research dollars for you and your environmentalist friends. Plus fat government contracts that would make even a Halliburton CEO blush."

SANCHO: "You make it sound like the global warming lobby is the up and coming DC lobby group. Do they really understand the climate issue?"

QUIXOTE: "They haven't a clue."

SANCHO: "Why is that, Quixote?"

QUIXOTE: "A lobbyist is not just any idiot, Sancho. They are a breed apart. Have you seen my Madonna cassettes?"

November 24, 2005
Sancho, Quixote, and the Internet

QUIXOTE:	"Sancho, get me some more envelopes will you?"
SANCHO:	"Here you go, Quixote. Wow, that's a lot of letters. What are you doing? Starting another letter writing campaign claiming we have lots of oil?"
QUIXOTE:	"No. Nothing like that--some of my friends have made some progress with the judicial system and I have been asked to capitalize on it."
SANCHO:	"Judicial system--as in the Supreme Court--Quixote?"
QUIXOTE:	"Of course, Sancho."
SANCHO:	"I used to respect the courts."
QUIXOTE:	"Well now you're finally in step with my friends."
SANCHO:	"Oh joy. I too can be a vampire."
QUIXOTE:	"Not funny, Sancho. We're working on a plan to take the words climate change and global warming out of the dictionary. We think we can claim the words inhibit economic growth. So through eminent domain we are going to take ownership of the words and remove them from the public voice."
SANCHO:	"Quixote, you're joking?"
QUIXOTE:	"Not about this, Sancho. We think we have a shot at it. In fact, even if we can't get any traction here, we are going to make the words global warming and climate change illegal-- without also saying 'mankind had nothing to do with it'."
SANCHO:	"Kind of like a mantra, Quixote?"
QUIXOTE:	"Kind of like Adwords or the rule of law, Sancho. I hear we already have four Supreme Court justices on board."
SANCHO:	"So your friends have bought the courts now as well as Congress and the Presidency?"

QUIXOTE: "The founding fathers were careful splitting power like that--but they could never have foreseen that truth could be rendered unimportant."

SANCHO: "The constitution has been supplanted by TV, mass media, and mega-corporations."

QUIXOTE: "Exactly. It took a couple of hundred years to screw them good and eviscerate freedom. We now own your home, your land, everything. "

SANCHO: "That's terrible."

QUIXOTE: "Come on get over it. My friends aren't that bad. Did you hear the joke about flag burning? "

SANCHO: "Yes, the one about making free speech illegal."

QUIXOTE: "Funny wasn't it?"

SANCHO: "I'm all a-giggles."

QUIXOTE: "Sancho, here are the new facts: We can take anything we want. We own this country--in fact the world."

SANCHO: "The world--never."

QUIXOTE: "I'll prove it. Did you read our report that said there was a fifty/fifty chance of a WMD event in the next few years?"

SANCHO: "WMD? Weapons of Mass Destruction."

QUIXOTE: "Precisely."

SANCHO: "So?"

QUIXOTE: "Let me try again. Our people told everyone we had discovered the likelihood that WMD would be used soon."

SANCHO: "So? What's wrong with intelligence gathering?"

QUIXOTE: "Quit being a slave will you? Sorry, I mean servant."

SANCHO: "Are you saying the report was a threat? That your friends are saying if they don't get their way they are going to blow things up and kill people?"

QUIXOTE: "Who else besides my friends have the WMD, the logistics, and the delivery systems?"

SANCHO: "So it was a threat."

QUIXOTE: "Now you understand that little bit of news, Sancho."

SANCHO: "I can't believe it. Did it really come from the American military?"

QUIXOTE: "Of course not. This doesn't involve them. They're too patriotic--too decent. Do you know they die for this country and its people--in droves?"

SANCHO: "Yes, Quixote, I did know that."

QUIXOTE: "My friends laugh about that one, Sancho, frequently. But all kidding aside, my friends have made some prudent purchases. We don't need the military. By the way--don't tell my friends but I admire those soldiers."

SANCHO: "My lips are sealed, Quixote. So are those envelopes being sent out to the Senators and Congress-people to make sure they continue to support your friends in the elimination of free speech and our freedoms?"

QUIXOTE: "Don't be silly, Sancho. These letters are going out to the people who count. Corporate boards, large stockholders in oil companies, the wealthy and the powerful--the decision to tighten our grip needs their support. We aren't fascists after all. What are you laughing at?"

SANCHO: "So the rest of them: congress, the executive branch, the judicial branch, the people--they no longer matter."

QUIXOTE: "Exactly, but look there is something important I need to say. I hope you are not upset with me calling you a slave instead of a servant. Honest--it was just a slip of the tongue."

SANCHO: "Servant? Slavery? They are just words, Quixote. How important could they be? Like ah, global warming...Or freedom....Or...Dirty bastard megalomaniac."

QUIXOTE: "Well good, Sancho. It would be difficult for my friends and me if you slaves were too upset. Oops, there I go again calling you a slave, silly me."

November 30, 2005
Sancho, Quixote, and the Greeks

QUIXOTE: "Alpha, beta, gamma, delta, and now epsilon? Sancho!"

SANCHO: "Yes, oh befuddled one. How can I help you?"

QUIXOTE: "I've got a huge problem."

SANCHO: "Ya' think, Quixote?"

QUIXOTE: "Stop that. I have real troubles, Sancho."

SANCHO: "I saw you were counting on your fingers and toes so I did have a clue there was a problem."

QUIXOTE: "That's not it. I was counting that way because I have to tutor Junior next week on counting storms and I am trying to understand mathematics from his perspective."

SANCHO: "Looks like you are well on the way to seeing his view point, Quixote. So what's the issue?"

QUIXOTE: "Sancho, I was given an assignment a few weeks ago to help spin a new TV pilot called My Three Greeks. It's a situation comedy about a family living in the Caribbean. They have these three sons named Alpha, Beta and Gamma--God knows how many there will be now. Anyway, it's the hilarious story of how the boys grow up, an update to 'My Three Sons'."

SANCHO: "Quixote, it looks to me like that original title is shot to Hades."

QUIXOTE: "Exactly. I need a new name for my comedy show. Sancho, six is too many kids."

SANCHO: "You could try 'The Brady Bunch Goes Greek'?"

QUIXOTE: "Not bad. No, I don't think that will work, sounds a little kinky."

SANCHO: "Oedipus Wrecks?"

QUIXOTE: "You are not helping. They're snickering at us. I need something with impact."

SANCHO: "Are things bad in Montreal?"

QUIXOTE: "Are you kidding me? No country will meet their Kyoto targets. My friends have the phantom menace all lined up in Asia. That puts us well on the way to scuttling any agreements on carbon reduction for the future, plus there is no country leadership. Everyone is either a consultant on carbon trading or looking for money to build a power generator from waste products. The deals are coming in by the boat-load and the boys in nuclear look like the white knight. The band is blaring technology to the rescue! With any luck at all my friends think they can turn the whole conference into a total shambles before the week is out."

SANCHO: "Sounds like quite a coup for America. I want to thank you and your friends for conscripting me and my fellow Americans into your mayhem."

QUIXOTE: "We're pleased to enlighten the masses."

SANCHO: "So what's the problem, Quixote?"

QUIXOTE: "Sancho, I've got too many storms."

SANCHO: "Have you considered counting in Latin?"

QUIXOTE: "Sancho."

SANCHO: "All right. Maybe it will help if you tell me more about the TV show."

QUIXOTE: "Eventually we are going to have the boys marry three girls who work for FEMA. Guess what their names are?"

SANCHO: "Katrina, Wilma, and Rita?"

QUIXOTE: "That's supposed to be a secret. How did you know?"

SANCHO: "Just a wild guess. Don't know if I can help here, Quixote. Just title the show: Greek American style--no then it would have to be an episode on COPS."

QUIXOTE: "Besides it sounds too foreign."

SANCHO: "The Locusts?"

QUIXOTE: "Is that Greek, Sancho?"

Sancho: "Seems like it to me."

Quixote: "No. Never--too revealing."

Sancho: "How about: Oil Wells Greasing Gaia?"

Quixote: "Nope, we have to leave oil and gas out of this."

Sancho: "Sadam, not Sodomy?"

Quixote: "Stop it, Sancho."

Sancho: "Kyoto, Quo Vadis?"

Quixote: "Sancho, quit it. Besides, that's Latin again and there is no way they are going to go through all the Greek letters and start using Latin letters."

Sancho: "Why is that, Quixote?"

Quixote: "They are officially closing hurricane season this week."

Sancho: "Sort of like a sports league after a bad gambling scandal, Quixote."

Quixote: "Exactly. My friends have had enough of this storm stuff-- and by making a big deal out of ending the season they think maybe--with the right spin--they can get an action figure tie-in or maybe trading cards tied to the hurricanes."

Sancho: "Your friends are a bunch of Muppets."

Quixote: "That's for sure. Did you know they believe they are taking a proactive stance on the storms? They say by declaring the hurricane season over and taking control of the spin we are taking control our environment."

Sancho: "Quixote, hurricanes may become a year-round event."

Quixote: "Prove it. Hah, got you again with that."

Sancho: "Now I have a name for your TV sitcom, Quixote."

Quixote: "Hit me with it, Sancho."

Sancho: "Truth or Consequences."

Quixote: "I don't see the humor, Sancho."

SANCHO: "How odd--oh and Quixote--I don't believe your fingers and toes are enough appendages to count all the storms."

QUIXOTE: "That's okay, Sancho, Junior will never make the leap anyway."

December 15, 2005
Sancho, Quixote, San Francisco and U.S. Patent #5,003,186

QUIXOTE: "Look, Up in the Sky! It's a cat! It's a hat! It's, oh nuts. When you're done unpacking the suitcase would you come out here?"

SANCHO: "I'm done, my liege. I still don't understand why you decided to accompany me to San Francisco. What's up, Quixote?"

QUIXOTE: "Sancho, what do you call those white lines in the middle of a roadway?"

SANCHO: "White lines, I think."

QUIXOTE: "That won't work. What's a good word for something that's up in the air and all powerful?"

SANCHO: "The climate?"

QUIXOTE: "Not funny. We're beginning to go forward with some extensive aerosol work and we need to brand white lines as everyone's friend--or something else."

SANCHO: "If you breathe in too much of the paint spray they put on the streets it will kill you."

QUIXOTE: "No, in the sky."

SANCHO: "You're painting the sky with deadly white lines?"

QUIXOTE: "Us? Never. Look outside, Sancho."

SANCHO: "San Francisco is a beautiful city, Quixote."

QUIXOTE: "Not that, the sky."

SANCHO: "Do you mean the jet contrails, Quixote?"

QUIXOTE: "Contrails, yes that's part of it. My basic plan is to tie them into a huge mythological creature flying around, but what?"

SANCHO: "Quixote, this one sounds like a set up. Why don't you take your concept and land on Coit Tower."

QUIXOTE:	"What soured you?"
SANCHO:	"I know a set-up when I hear one."
QUIXOTE:	"I need help here."
SANCHO:	"That I know, how about a flying elephant?"
QUIXOTE:	"No. Think of the fallout."
SANCHO:	"How about flying donkeys?"
QUIXOTE:	"Nope. My friends hold both symbols as sacred."
SANCHO:	"You're right--they are pretty much the same thing. Hmm, how about birds, Quixote?"
QUIXOTE:	"Well, ah. I can't use them."
SANCHO:	"Ah ha, I've got it: flying chickens. Look up in the sky! It's a bird! It's a plane! It's a chicken!"
QUIXOTE:	"Pilots don't like to be called chicken. Besides, Sancho, it's too direct--we can't tie chickens into it because of the bird flu thing. At least not yet--we have friends in the poultry industry to take care of."
SANCHO:	"And Ayn Rand said there was no such thing as altruism. Yet the plot thickens."
QUIXOTE:	"Sancho. You don't trust me."
SANCHO:	"That's a fair assessment."
QUIXOTE:	"Sancho, all I'm doing here is working on a concept. I have to plant a seed of thought; just like you environmentalists plant trees. But I need something strong that flies around."
SANCHO:	"You know, Quixote, it really has gotten cloudy here quickly--reminds me of Seattle."
QUIXOTE:	"Are you impressed by the clouds, Sancho?"
SANCHO:	"Should I be? Oh I get it, your friends own the coffee franchise in this city also?"
QUIXOTE:	"No, the clouds. Was that a joke?"

SANCHO: "Your friends are going to take credit for clouds now, Quixote? Seems a bit over the top doesn't it?"

QUIXOTE: "Does it?"

SANCHO: "Oh, that's it. Are your friends using aerosols to try and offset global warming? That is it, I can see by the twitch in your weasely little eyes. You and those nasty little sociopaths are spraying the sky to add albedo so you can keep your place at the top of the spittoon."

QUIXOTE: "Forget I said anything. They are contrails, Sancho."

SANCHO: "They just seem to persist for a few hours. Does this San Francisco trip also have something to do with your bird flu scam,Quixote?"

QUIXOTE: "You mean like 'just in case people get sick from what we are spraying up there we are going to call it bird flu'?"

SANCHO: "I see. So that's what you are you doing in San Francisco."

QUIXOTE: "We need to have symbol of strength that flies around. I was tired of working on it and I decided to join you here in San Francisco."

SANCHO: "Nonsense. What are you really up to?"

QUIXOTE: "Sancho, I've got it."

SANCHO: "How coincident--lay it on me, Machiavelli, er, Quixote."

QUIXOTE: "Look up in the sky. It's a bird. It's a plane. It's, it's a Dragon!"

SANCHO: "Quixote, you can't do that. That's silly. Oh hang on, you have already linked bird flu to Asia. Then there's the huge Asian population in San Francisco. It's the largest Chinatown in North America. If you use a dragon, people in the U.S., will link the so-called bird flu with Asians instead of your aerosol program. Wait a minute...That's racism."

QUIXOTE: "No, Sancho. That's what we call concept marketing. Best part is we get away free if the aerosol project goes south: another successful Teflon marketing strategy courtesy of yours truly."

SANCHO: "There must be other cities you spray besides San Francisco? How do you know people will get sick here first?"

QUIXOTE: "It doesn't matter, Sancho. We own the media, remember? One way or the other it will all start here with the dragon. "

SANCHO: "With your racism, you mean. Quixote, you've reached a new sum of contemptibility."

QUIXOTE: "Ask me if I care, Sancho. My boogie-bird concept has left the egg."

SANCHO: "Like a vulture, Quixote."

QUIXOTE: "Sancho, I am being a patriot. Did you know an eagle was a vulture?"

SANCHO: "Especially the way you and your friends use it, Quixote."

December 18, 2005
Sancho, Quixote, and Happy Trails

QUIXOTE: "Happy Trails to you--until we meet again. Happy Trails to you, until we..."

SANCHO: "Nice song, Quixote. So what are you doing this PM, manufacturing spin for Dale Evans?"

QUIXOTE: "I have a new assignment, Sancho, 'Better Living through Chemistry'. Happy Trails to you..."

SANCHO: "So what's with the Cleopatra get-up? You're taking this San Francisco thing a bit too far. My, you do look silly in that black headdress and pantaloons. I can't even comment on your chest."

QUIXOTE: "That isn't the least of it. I need to incorporate a snake into the whole Happy Trails thing."

SANCHO: "An A.S.P."

QUIXOTE: "No jokes, please, Sancho."

SANCHO: "Okay, Quixote, but you know the EP is going to toss and turn all night with punus-interruptus. But back to your problem."

QUIXOTE: "Ozone, Sancho. Did you hear about it?"

SANCHO: "What a mess, Quixote. I thought that was getting better. You guys really blew it on that one."

QUIXOTE: "We never said we could fix it. Anyone who says we said we could fix it is in for a budget cut. Our official position was we could fix it by 2050. By the way, we've just upped that estimate to 2065."

SANCHO: "Quixote, you said it was fixed."

QUIXOTE: "We were a bit optimistic. See, this is just the kind of problem we don't want to have happen again."

SANCHO: "Then you agree re-engineering a planet's climate could be a might bit tougher than you first thought?"

QUIXOTE: "Sancho, the climate is so complex."

SANCHO: "Can I quote you on that, Quixote?"

QUIXOTE: "No."

SANCHO: "So the problem is…"

QUIXOTE: "My friends are engineering solutions to climate change."

SANCHO: "Not a thing wrong with it, Quixote. Tell your friends I approve of proactive investigation."

QUIXOTE: "Sancho, the ozone hole will take another 60 years to fix. The thermohaline system has been reduced significantly; the glaciers are not so glacial anymore. Storms are getting intense; the list goes on and on."

SANCHO: "Oh heavens, you mean there are positive feedbacks for global warming and they are already making themselves felt?"

QUIXOTE: "Yes. I mean no. I mean we need a positive spin on our remediation work for the system."

SANCHO: "Which system?"

QUIXOTE: "The use of aerosols to adjust albedo."

SANCHO: "Climate systems are too complex and too energetic for us to know how major changes like that will impact us right now."

QUIXOTE: "It would sure be nice if we had another planet to experiment on…To get things right."

SANCHO: "Heck, you could send the military in to subdue locals, and experiment to your heart's delight. Of course there would be the insurgents…"

QUIXOTE: "Ha, ha. But you see why I am worried: I am told we cannot check our remediation theories on an adequate test-bench."

SANCHO: "And you are concerned about the danger for our population and the planet?"

QUIXOTE: "Not really, we are concerned we don't have the right spin when things go wrong. This ozone issue was a terrible embarrassment--and my friends count on me to keep the TV-droids asleep."

SANCHO: "What about just fixing the problem? Wouldn't that make your task easier?"

QUIXOTE: "We'll get it right sooner, or later. In the mean time I own the yeoman's task of keeping my friends from looking like a bunch of incompetent boobs."

SANCHO: "You do have a tough job, Quixote."

QUIXOTE: "Tell me about it."

SANCHO: "So why not deal with climate change now by fixing the root cause: Cut CO_2 output by 70%."

QUIXOTE: "There will be chaos."

SANCHO: "Nonsense, you're beginning to believe your own spin."

QUIXOTE: "You blaspheme, Sancho."

SANCHO: "We can deal with the economy, Quixote. The population is not inept."

QUIXOTE: "My friends do not like that option, Sancho."

SANCHO: "Oh, I see. So your friends are telling us we will have a strong economy while the climate heaves and they are performing planetary wide science experiments without proper controls or proper testing."

QUIXOTE: "We haven't the time for proper control or tests. That would take decades and we have a crisis."

SANCHO: "I was wrong about your friends, Quixote; they aren't Muppets. They are psychotic. Quixote, they recognize the problem is growing to crisis proportions yet rather than addressing the root cause, they choose re-engineering the entire climate?"

QUIXOTE: "And I need to spin it; because it might hurt our economy and cause bad, bad, icky, things."

SANCHO: "They ignore the root problem because--they say--it may hurt the economy. Yet they insist it is okay for mistakes to happen on a planetary level--which by the way would be much, much worse than a ruptured economy--because it could make the climate chaos worse."

QUIXOTE: "That's about the size of it."

SANCHO: "How insane is that, Quixote?"

QUIXOTE: "Truthfully--off the charts, Sancho--but my friends don't care. They believe the planet is their game-ball, and if they don't own the game, they will just take their ball home."

SANCHO: "Change my words psychotic friends to sociopath friends, Quixote."

QUIXOTE: "Duly noted, so what do you think? Can't you just see it? Cleopatra lies on her divan and there is her A.S.P., hanging overhead. It slithers around and belts out Happy Trails."

SANCHO: "It falls on her and...."

QUIXOTE: "The snake kills Cleopatra with its poison--no--bad spin."

SANCHO: "So why not train the snake not to bite her, or change the history books to say she died of something else? Look, you doctored information about the ozone hole---what's one more fib? Let's try this: An A.S.P., hangs overhead singing Happy Trails--and the A.S.P., never bites anyone."

QUIXOTE: "Seems unbelievable doesn't it, Sancho?"

SANCHO: "Well, yes, Quixote."

QUIXOTE: "You know, Sancho, if we are going to be rewriting history anyway, instead of saying Cleopatra died from the snake-- maybe we can call her death the first recorded case of bird flu?"

SANCHO: "Perfect, Quixote, then Cleopatra, the snakes, truth, and science can all march arm in arm out the door--into a wildly chromatic sunset."

December 27, 2005
Sancho, Quixote, and War

QUIXOTE: "Sancho, if I say there might be terrorists in the Sahel, no, in ah, West Africa--would you believe me?"

SANCHO: "I don't know, Quixote, have your friends invaded the Sahel?"

QUIXOTE: "Do locusts count? Sancho, we haven't invaded, but we do have advisors on the ground."

SANCHO: "Quixote, your friends have invaded West Africa?"

QUIXOTE: "Let's say we have them bugged. Missed the joke? Let's try this: What if I say by invading the Sahel we can cut down on the hurricanes hitting the American South?"

SANCHO: "So instead of cutting back on carbon dioxide you want to invade other countries? Is this a joke, Quixote?"

QUIXOTE: "Sancho, this is definitely not a joke. I know it is not as important as oil, but let's just hypothesize that by invasion we might be able to cut down on hurricanes that hit the U.S."

SANCHO: "What gives you the right? Regardless, I would call you and your friends Fascists."

QUIXOTE: "Then there is nothing I can say to make you think we're just civilized humanitarians who think it is okay to invade a country or two to make things safer in Atlanta?"

SANCHO: "Of course not, Quixote, why would you expect me to support the bullying of other nations--you mean because of global warming?"

QUIXOTE: "Yes, Sancho-- and because it benefits us."

SANCHO: "So what?"

QUIXOTE: "Sancho, global warming is a huge crisis. We need to take extraordinary measures or things will get bad, fast."

SANCHO: "No kidding. Cut your CO_2 emissions."

QUIXOTE: "We have an economy to protect."

SANCHO: "Quixote, in the past that might have made a difference, but you have waited too long. The damage from global warming will be worse than a bad economy, no matter what you do. The tundra is about to burp methane."

QUIXOTE: "We know. So should we invade for political gain?"

SANCHO: "We are Americans. We do not invade countries for political or economic gain."

QUIXOTE: "Mistakes of the past cannot be rectified, Sancho."

SANCHO: "The citizens of this country are not savages. They will never support evil."

QUIXOTE: "Sancho, we need to reduce the vegetation in the Sahel to limit the moisture. That way we can cut down on the hurricanes. It's as simple as that."

SANCHO: "Does that mean the vegetation in Central and South America will have the same fate?"

QUIXOTE: "Well…yes, Sancho."

SANCHO: "So we might invade our neighbors to cut down on how global warming affects the US?"

QUIXOTE: "We're considering using the Monroe Doctrine on that one."

SANCHO: "And whom is your culprit: Gaia? Atmospheric capacity for carrying humidity goes up as the planet warms."

QUIXOTE: "That might make Gaia's approval rating vulnerable. On the other hand, we could claim one of the South American leaders is a communist--or a wacko. Sancho, I don't like it either. What should I do?"

SANCHO: "Remember, Quixote, only bad little boys and girls invade and kill people because it is convenient."

QUIXOTE: "And the hurricanes will get worse anyway."

SANCHO: "The hurricanes are just a symptom of global warming, you ninny. They are a pressure relief valve at this point. In limiting their formation, you will just speed up the formation of other chaotic events--like more intense storms, tornadoes, or U.S., West Coast hurricanes. What are you going to do then, drain the Pacific?"

QUIXOTE: "No such things as West Coast hurricanes, yet. On the other hand if we drain the Pacific, drilling might be more profitable. Of course then the fishing would be different."

SANCHO: "Sure, you could claim Osama bin Ahi caused the hurricanes. Quixote, global warming is a zero sum game. That makes the U.S., a pariah--no better than the Nazi's of World War II. The removal of national self determination from your neighbor is aggression--regardless of the reasons--including global warming's effects."

QUIXOTE: But America will acquire increasing damage from hurricanes."

SANCHO: So cut your CO_2 output. You're going to do it sooner or later anyway and the more countries you anger now the worse it will be later. Don't you see that?"

QUIXOTE: "Sancho, my friends are sometimes a bit short sighted."

SANCHO: "Quixote, your friends couldn't navigate a bicycle, let alone a country."

QUIXOTE: "They don't see it that way."

SANCHO: "Your friends are swine who don't have a civil bone in their body."

QUIXOTE: "Well, yes, I know. Hmm, this is going to be tougher than I thought. Then I guess we'll go with the terrorist angle. Sancho, I know the spin is asinine because nothing is going to cover up our plans--so let's see--I'll just reach into my baloney-bag and pull out something saying we are going to defeat ideological entrepreneurs trying to gain a foothold by reaching out to the disaffected, disenfranchised, or just the misinformed and disillusioned'."

SANCHO: "You do have a sense of humor, Quixote, that was very funny. On the other hand, if the jackboot fits…"

CHAPTER 10
2006

January 9, 2006
Sancho, Quixote, and Down Under

SANCHO: "Okay, Quixote, you are all packed and ready to go. Do you have your shark repellent?

QUIXOTE: "Yup. We like coal."

SANCHO: "Your drought repellent?"

QUIXOTE: "Yup. We love coal."

SANCHO: "Your sunscreen?"

QUIXOTE: "Yup. Coal good!"

SANCHO: 'Bug repellent?"

QUIXOTE: "Yup. Coal is good for the economy."

SANCHO: "Lightening repellent?"

QUIXOTE: "Yup. Me like coal."

SANCHO: "Wind breaker?"

QUIXOTE: "Yup. Coal is my friend."

SANCHO: "Your rice cooker? I see you already have your shipping container full of bull crap."

QUIXOTE: "Very funny, Sancho."

SANCHO: "Oh c'mon, Quixote, you said the meeting you are going to is a frame up job."

QUIXOTE: "That doesn't mean I will not take my work seriously."

SANCHO: "Shifting blame is demanding work, Quixote. I have seen that."

QUIXOTE: "You can't imagine. First, there is setting up the shill."

"SANCHO: "Oh don't forget your rice paddle."

QUIXOTE: "Got it, then there are the meetings themselves."

SANCHO: "Oh, do you have your illustrated history of the 1938 Munich talks, Quixote?"

QUIXOTE: "I have that as well. I think you will be surprised just how important it is to shift the blame on global warming."

SANCHO: "Not in the least. On the other hand, Quixote, if your friends are able to convince the world that the developing nations are the real cause of global warming by entering into negotiations with them and then stabbing them in the back--I assure you--nothing will surprise me."

QUIXOTE: "You underestimate my friends, Sancho."

SANCHO: "My inability to see your friends' deceit is not underestimation--it's called decency. Some of us just can't plumb the same depths of treachery as your friends."

QUIXOTE: "That's why the world is ours, Sancho."

SANCHO: "And thanks to your friends the planet is getting nastier by the moment. Quixote, I don't suppose there is any chance your shill will push for a reduction in carbon dioxide emissions?"

QUIXOTE: "Not a chance."

SANCHO:	"So what will your shill do if someone asks how the U.S., feels about its 20% share of the 150,000 deaths attributed to global warming this year? That's 30,000 dead."
QUIXOTE:	"We will say prove it--then impeach the source--what else?"
SANCHO:	"Well your friends are consistent."
QUIXOTE:	"Sancho, we have just invaded two countries. We're planning to invade another one within the year; we've destroyed an American city by ignoring years of warnings. We poison the air our citizens breathe so we can keep control of the economy--do you really think the death of a few thousand people is going to bother us?"
SANCHO:	"A few hundred thousand is just the beginning--global warming is going to get a lot worse. What will you do with the new storm damage?"
QUIXOTE:	"We control the media, Sancho, and we have an economy to profit from, so don't bother me with minutia."
SANCHO:	"It's a great time to be an American, Quixote."
QUIXOTE:	"See, you're becoming a cynic. They like that, Sancho."
SANCHO:	"The notion of a national heart attack pleases your friends?"
QUIXOTE:	"One of them in particular."
SANCHO:	"But you don't understand, Quixote. I wasn't being cynical."
QUIXOTE:	"Meaning?"
SANCHO:	"It is a great time to be an American. We have the opportunity to stand for core American values."
QUIXOTE:	"Violence, greed, jingoism, an insatiable lust for power, the Simpsons, those things?"
SANCHO:	"No Quixote, the real values: Truth, justice, freedom and the rights of people everywhere to self-determination. We Americans will soon bind the covenant with past Americans by standing for our country and the planet. We have no choice."
QUIXOTE:	"You're a fool, Sancho, and those who died for this country were fools also."

SANCHO: "Why?"

QUIXOTE: "Because they believed in words from the Constitution and the Bill of Rights--so quit throwing them in my face. They are just pieces of paper stuck to the boot of a controlled media."

SANCHO: "Only to you and your thug friends, Quixote."

January 16, 2006
Sancho, Quixote, and the Five Dwarfs

SANCHO: "So, Quixote, how was your trip down under?"

QUIXOTE: "Sancho, it was great--there wasn't an environmentalist in sight. Everyone considered peer review as nothing more than a consumer testimonial. Five times a day we bowed east to the birthplace of the term carbon intensity, and before we got in our boat we all received a souvenir book."

SANCHO: "What was the souvenir?"

QUIXOTE: "Snow White and the Five Dwarfs."

SANCHO: "You mean seven?"

QUIXOTE: "Nope--there are only five dwarfs, Sancho."

SANCHO: "Where are the other two, Quixote, please don't say they were down-sized."

QUIXOTE: "There never was a sixth or seventh dwarf."

SANCHO: "Of course there was--the story is Snow White and the Seven Dwarfs."

QUIXOTE: "Prove it, Sancho."

SANCHO: "Quixote, you're making a joke."

QUIXOTE: "Snow White and Seven Dwarfs is an old world notion."

SANCHO: "I thought your friends identified with Europe?"

QUIXOTE: "Regardless, Sancho, there are only five dwarfs now--along with Snow White--of course."

SANCHO: "Your friends' mania for control seems a bit overdone."

QUIXOTE: "Sancho, wait until you see what we do with the Arabian Nights."

SANCHO:	"From what I have seen, Quixote, the writing is on the walls. So then Snow White and her Dwarfs aren't going to do anything about global warming?"
QUIXOTE:	"We like coal. We love coal. Coal good!"
SANCHO:	"Meaning what, Quixote?"
QUIXOTE:	"We are married to coal. I like to think of coal as the bride of carbon intensity."
SANCHO:	"Frankenstein will have a better rep."
QUIXOTE:	"Meaning what, Sancho? Are you and your eco-nuts going to fight us on the seductive beauty of coal?"
SANCHO:	"What for?"
QUIXOTE:	"We do not expect you to give up so easily."
SANCHO:	"Quixote, you don't get it. You're not fighting scientists, environmentalists, or me. You and your band of buffoons have decided to wage war against the planet by forcing the climate. Some of us are trying to keep as many people alive as possible while you and your nitwit friends work through your control issues."
QUIXOTE:	"So you admit we've won."
SANCHO:	"Your friends are humanity's foolishness encased in flesh--the by-product of civilization--ego dragging the species to the edge of extinction. The information dearth your friends have erected grows by leaps and bounds. Soon the planet will wash your friends away as if they were maggots in a torrent."
QUIXOTE:	"Do you think your viewpoint matters?"
SANCHO:	"You and your friends want to make sure nothing is going to change so fossil fuels are the core of your energy future. In doing so you'll ignore science."
QUIXOTE:	"We wuv technology; we wuv science--as long as they behave. We are pushing for a technological solution to global warming."
SANCHO:	"While your friends paint the population into a corner."
QUIXOTE:	"We sacrifice only the willing. That from the tobacco guys."

SANCHO:	"Quixote, 150,000 people died last year from global warming. Were they willing?"
QUIXOTE:	"Give me ten minutes of network news time and an op-ed in the Journal and I'll convince the consumers out there in TV land and the vanity-fair elite that the dead begged for the opportunity to be wasted."
SANCHO:	"That's what you have done with the technology, spun it into propaganda for the uninformed?"
QUIXOTE:	"And I can do it whether you guess my name or not. Pretty grim, isn't it, Sancho?"
SANCHO:	"Very funny. 150,000 people dead--and that number will take off like a rocket in the near future. Just how fast do you think new technology will impact the CO_2 footprint?"
QUIXOTE:	"Sancho, don't you get it? My friends don't care about that. With more deaths, we have less energy usage. Therefore, we have less CO_2 output. We have it all figured."
SANCHO:	"Your friends are pushing a 23% reduction in CO_2 output by 2030 --does that mean you expect a 23% reduction in the population of the planet by then?"
QUIXOTE:	"I'd never admit it if we did."
SANCHO:	"Quixote, what about a billion dead from global warming?"
QUIXOTE:	"Prove it. Hah, see you can't prove it, Sancho. Coal is the color of my friends' souls, and so what if a few people die in the future keeping our economy strong."
SANCHO:	"Oh now I see: The output of your meeting down under was to sacrifice children for coal."
QUIXOTE:	"Exactly. Kind of a 'Coal for Kids' program. I wish we could use that term, it's awfully catchy."
SANCHO:	"But a bit morose--you might also rename the five dwarfs."
QUIXOTE:	"To what?"
SANCHO:	"How about Ugly, Dopey, Greedy, Greasy, and Sleazy?"
QUIXOTE:	"Sancho, call them what you want, just so long as Snow White looks snow white. My friends don't care."

January 21, 2006
Sancho, Quixote, and Junior

QUIXOTE: "Sancho, I need a hand here."

SANCHO: "Quixote, you look worn out. Did your math lesson with Junior not go well again?"

QUIXOTE: "I swear I have never met a more strident man."

SANCHO: "You're joking, Quixote. He has the fortitude of a limp noodle."

QUIXOTE: "Sancho, when I first began working with him, I wrote down two plus two equals four. He brought in a team of shills from Cato, Pew, and Heritage. They lectured me on how they were right because they all agreed they were right. So the following day I tried again, showing him two plus two equals four with manipulatives. Next thing I know he orders this spook to start tapping our phone and reading our emails. Today, he tells me he will cut funding to the local university and have the local government condemn my house for a new gambling casino unless I relent. Then, he said if I insist two and two equals four the next time we meet, he will call for a Department of Justice investigation and have an article planted in the media claiming I have been spending government money for meals."

SANCHO: "Quixote, how's that feel for you? Ah, have you been doing that?"

QUIXOTE: "It was my tax refund for god's sake, but CMM will never print that part of the story."

SANCHO: "Quixote, who is CMM?"

QUIXOTE: "The Corporate Media Machine."

SANCHO: "So you do as he says, or else."

QUIXOTE: "And that's a fact. How am I supposed to get any education into him?"

SANCHO: "Now you know how I feel about explaining the absurdity of carbon intensity."

QUIXOTE: "That's more than stupidity, Sancho, but I am getting the idea. Too bad it has traction."

SANCHO: "So maybe you should just let him go on being a moron."

QUIXOTE: "Trust me, you needn't worry about that. I just don't understand why he refuses to believe two plus two equals four."

SANCHO: "You mean like why he can't understand there is too much CO_2 in the atmosphere so therefore we need to immediately reduce to CO_2 to pre-industrial levels?"

QUIXOTE: "Sancho, truth has no place in scientific debate unless it supports an accepted economic model. I think he has a private agenda."

SANCHO: "Quixote, Junior and his friends' refusal to face climate change is turning anthropogenic forcing of the climate into a multi-generation disaster. The population doesn't matter to them--except as a herd of consumers. Of course, they have an agenda."

QUIXOTE: "Shhh."

SANCHO: "What's wrong, Quixote?"

QUIXOTE: "Be careful what you say, Sancho."

SANCHO: "Do you think they are bugging us out here in the middle of this pigeon coop? What about freedom of speech?"

QUIXOTE: "Freedom of speech? Sancho, do you have any idea how angry he was today when I tried to explain that some math problems yielded answer that are over twenty?"

SANCHO: "A fingers and toes issue?"

QUIXOTE: "Precisely."

SANCHO: "What about Dick? He can he count on him."

QUIXOTE: "That's not funny, Sancho."

SANCHO: "Quixote, does he think two and two equals twenty-two?"

QUIXOTE: "The leap over twenty on his fingers and toes is just too much for him. And when he gets frustrated--watch out."

SANCHO: "No wonder carbon intensity makes sense to him..."

QUIXOTE: "Just before I left, Junior told me this two plus two thing is un-American."

SANCHO: "So will he label you a terrorist? Quixote? Quixote? You have got to be kidding me. You're the most un-terrorist corporate shill I know."

QUIXOTE: "That's corporate knight, but thank you, Sancho."

SANCHO: "You are most welcome."

QUIXOTE: "But Sancho, he doesn't negotiate with terrorists so he is threatening to stop talking to me. Then he threatened me with a trip to Guantanamo or a cruise missile at dinner time."

SANCHO: "Junior is a bully. What will you do?"

QUIXOTE: "Sancho, I think I will just agree to anything he says."

SANCHO: "Quixote, spinelessness as a way of life has some major disadvantages. On the other hand you may have a new slogan to spin:' Fascism and Fear: As American as Apple Pie'."

QUIXOTE: "It's not Fascism, Sancho; we're calling it executive privilege in the face of terrorism."

SANCHO: "And fear?"

QUIXOTE: "Enlightened self-interest."

SANCHO: "But, Quixote, Junior and his friends label who is a terrorist and who is not a terrorist--regardless of the whole story. They ignore truth and justice for their own goals."

QUIXOTE: "I know. But if I push the truth something terrible might happen."

SANCHO: "And there you are, Quixote: America 2006. You see, two and two does equal four--nothing like mathematics to ferret out the facts."

January 26, 2006
Sancho, Quixote, and Ecoterrorists

SANCHO: "I have an idea: How about instead of your friends battling the environmental community we find some common ground and begin working together on global warming?"

QUIXOTE: "My friends are always willing to look at new ideas, Sancho, and if there is money to be made, all the better."

SANCHO: "So you think they might listen to us?"

QUIXOTE: "Run your ideas past me and we can examine the options."

SANCHO: "Okay, Quixote, so how about if we suggest to the population they grow something in their homes? It doesn't matter how much, just something people can use."

QUIXOTE: "Such as?"

SANCHO: "Oh, I suppose any plant that isn't a house plant--say a spice, or a fruit, or a vegetable--perhaps a healing herb. Then the items can be a local resource and a carbon sink, the energy cost to produce them will be minimal, people can trade these items among their neighbors and a local economic model might grow and strengthen."

QUIXOTE: "Might work, Sancho, but some of the large grocers will object. Then there are the credit cards. How will people pay for those homegrown products?"

SANCHO: "Cash or barter, I suppose."

QUIXOTE: "The banks and the IRS will also have kittens. What other ideas do you have for addressing global warming?"

SANCHO: "Well, people might not drive their cars one day a week."

QUIXOTE: "Whoa, Sancho, are you insane?"

SANCHO: Huh?"

QUIXOTE: "Do you have any idea what a 1/7 reduction in auto usage would do to the steel, rubber, aluminum, gas and our already ailing auto industry?"

SANCHO: "Quixote, do you have any idea how much energy we might save and then there is an immediate reduction in CO_2."

QUIXOTE: "The economic impacts will be horrific, Sancho."

SANCHO: "The human benefits and climate impacts outweigh that, Quixote. What if we have local markets on those days and maybe some local sports?"

QUIXOTE: "You mean like flea markets, garage sales, non-mall events? My friends don't like those--they cut into inventory turns. And a local sports franchise is out of the question. Those are cash cows."

SANCHO: "I hadn't thought of it that way, Quixote. How about if the population buys items that are less processed?"

QUIXOTE: "Such as?"

SANCHO: "Well some cleansers, health products, and cosmetics could be put together at home from base ingredients. That will cut CO_2 and the huge energy expenditures for processing and lord knows the natural products work just as well."

QUIXOTE: "Sancho, this is why my friends call you eco-nuts, terrorists. Do you have any idea the number of industries that will suffer? Fragrances, cosmetics, some of the largest home products manufacturers could suffer significant stock losses. Billions in equity might be wiped out. You are talking madness."

SANCHO: "I see, Quixote, maybe we foster more cottage industry? You know where local companies make products from local materials. We could set up small power generators. Then there will be new jobs. These will be new industries that take into account CO_2. Your friends can invest in them, and the energy costs for transportation wouldn't be a factor."

QUIXOTE: "Do you have any idea how that might impact the rail and trucking industry?"

SANCHO: "Oh, of course. Well then, maybe, we can move some of the manufacturing back onshore and the truckers and rail lines can move some of those goods around. Then the huge energy and CO_2 shipping costs will go away. Innovation will follow a return of the manufacturing base."

QUIXOTE: "Sancho, then you are hitting the shipping industry right where it hurts. You just don't understand the way the global economy works. If you start building these regional economies inside industrialized nations then you disperse control to the populace. The large multinationals become extraneous. The whole economy transforms from a consumption base to a sustainable base. The economies of scale are lost, quality will go down, and prices will rise."

SANCHO: "Quality is a function of understanding your process. The economies of scale only work if the market and wages are in harmony, otherwise we mortgage our future by too much debt. And prices will find their own level based on sustainable economics--that's what a free market economy does. In this case a free market economy based on support for the environment."

QUIXOTE: "It will never work, Sancho."

SANCHO: "Why not, Quixote?"

QUIXOTE: "Where are my friends in all this?"

SANCHO: "They have the inside track--they should do fine."

QUIXOTE: "Fine isn't good enough, they will lose control once the systems become flexible. Two, my friends don't understand a sustainable economic system based on human dignity. Three, corporations don't function well unless they are integrated top to bottom. Four, we own the pie, why split it up to help the great unwashed masses? We don't even like you guys."

SANCHO: "Because, Quixote, there is no place to hide from global warming. All of this is going to happen anyway."

QUIXOTE: "They believe they can hide from global warming."

SANCHO: "So your friends still believe in the New Orleans Gambit."

QUIXOTE: "Hiding from the facts, drowning truth with money, deceit, and intimidation are my friends' way of life, Sancho, you know that."

SANCHO: "But the other way the environment heals. People take control of their lives. Work becomes meaningful. The family is strengthened and communities are built."

QUIXOTE: "Sancho, my friends already have that."

SANCHO: "What about the rest of humanity?"

QUIXOTE: "They will never accept that argument--and they will never support your proposals. Until you come up with a plan that benefits my friends first or gets them more power, so you might as well forget it. My friends will fight you shill and think tank."

SANCHO: "So you are saying the economy is at war with the environment and the population."

QUIXOTE: "Not all the population, just 99% of it. The other 1% is fine. And you need to know my friends are working diligently to double that number."

SANCHO: "To 2%? That's awfully white of them, Quixote."

QUIXOTE: "Yes, rather, but it spins well. And anyway, aren't you the one who believes people and the environment are one cohesive entity, Sancho?"

SANCHO: "Yes, but what does that have to do with adjusting to the climate?"

QUIXOTE: "From your standpoint, nothing, but from our standpoint the longer we keep the people out there in TV-Land from realizing a healthy environment is a healthy population the longer we stay in control. Don't you see, this is a game of desperation for my friends?"

SANCHO: "For many people it's not a game, Quixote, but survival, and caring for their loved ones."

QUIXOTE: "And that's we call you and your kind eco-terrorists."

SANCHO: "You mean those who work for a healthy environment are terrorists because they work to transition from a dead economic model to vibrant model?"

QUIXOTE: "My friends' do not believe their economic model is dead."

SANCHO: "Look around you. Of course it is."

QUIXOTE: "Prove it."

SANCHO: "We have been here before, Quixote. You were wrong the last ten times you said that and you are wrong now."

QUIXOTE: "So what, Sancho? Trust me, if you pursue cooperation and rationality on global warming I'll have a dozen op-eds waiting by morning. The academics from certain universities will be all over the place like vacuum cleaners explaining why our economic system of consumption and corruption is the best that ever was--or could be. Three networks will announce a link between environmentalists and Al Quida and Junior will bumble out a few sentences when some lackey asks him a scripted question about sustainable economies in a news conference."

SANCHO: "Do you really believe people are that gullible, Quixote, even after your friends' failures on the economy and global warming? The word is getting out your friends are making it all worse by curtailing an effective response to global warming."

QUIXOTE: "Sancho, truth is my friends are just not creative enough to change the economic model. They do understand the tools of controlling the population: They do know how to politicize issues, start wars, and spread terror. If they could just figure out how to intimidate Gaia, they'd have it all solved."

SANCHO: "But then isn't the consumption based economy the real terrorist here--by telling us all we have no hope?"

QUIXOTE: "Only the way my friends run it, Sancho."

SANCHO: "Amen to that, Quixote."

January 31, 2006
Sancho, Quixote, and Gags

QUIXOTE: "Sancho, I don't have time to talk now. I am working inside. This land is your land. This land is my land."

SANCHO: "Gardening? That's awfully green of you, Quixote."

QUIXOTE: "What's so strange about that? I am concerned about the state of our onions."

SANCHO: "That's great, Quixote. What is that greasy mark on the onion? Is that an "X" on it?"

QUIXOTE: "That's so everyone knows who owns the onion--it's like a brand. My brand."

SANCHO: "Why not use your name?"

QUIXOTE: "Truth is I have an "X" on my posterior."

SANCHO: "I don't need to know more on that. You know that claiming the onion is yours doesn't necessarily mean the onion will grow better. It is not a stock certificate."

QUIXOTE: "No I cannot manipulate it. And since I have taken over the onion patch the onions have grown so sickly; even though I keep bringing in more and more resources."

SANCHO: "That's quite a pile of soil you have in the corner."

QUIXOTE: "More soil means more growth--simple economics. And I am all about growth."

SANCHO: "So you are concerned about the growth of the onion?"

QUIXOTE: "Does a bear scratch in the woods? Does a duck quack? Did Sadaam have weapons of mass destruction? Should this black stuff on the inside of the onion concern me?"

SANCHO: "Looks like the onion is rotting, Quixote."

QUIXOTE: "Oh, rot's all right. I have an affinity for decay and maggots-- it is part of the natural world and I am so green! On the other hand, I wouldn't want my X marker to go away."

SANCHO: "So you really don't care about the onion. You just do not want your name tied to the rot, Quixote."

QUIXOTE: "Sancho, I am so green. I queried my think tank people to tell me how to make the onion grow better."

SANCHO: "And they said?"

QUIXOTE: "Add corn."

SANCHO: "You better not say anything like that in front of a real researcher."

QUIXOTE: "As long as the researcher is on the payroll it will not matter. Look, we have too much dependence on foreign soil and it is no good for our onion; therefore I am thinking we can create more soil from American corn, or grass, or wood chips."

SANCHO: "We have lots of soil outside the greenhouse, Quixote. Truth is the greenhouse is just too warm and that's hurting the state of the onions. We need a functional window for cooling."

QUIXOTE: "So you are suggesting I am not dealing with the greenhouse heat if I cut down our dependence on foreign soil to make the onion healthy?"

SANCHO: "Well, yes. But more importantly why not just make the greenhouse work for you instead of making it your enemy?"

QUIXOTE: "Now that is interesting: Are you saying the onion is rotting because of a greenhouse effect?"

SANCHO: "You are truly hopeless. Do you care about facts at all?"

QUIXOTE: "Not a bit. But, Sancho, if the real problem is the greenhouse effect then the real fault lays with you gardeners and not me. If they hadn't brought the notion of a greenhouse to me I'd never have built it and put the onion inside it--so the rot is not my fault."

SANCHO: "The greenhouse was here long before we arrived. The gardeners told us how it works and what its function is."

QUIXOTE: "I liked Chance, Sancho. He was my kinda' guy."

SANCHO: "Right, then he said it's an important tool for growing things but we needed to respect it. Then you took another vacation."

QUIXOTE: "Did I make money off that conversation? Did my friends?"

SANCHO: "Not a penny--but the costs in keeping a too-warm greenhouse are mounting every day."

QUIXOTE: "That is not my fault. I think it is the fault of the glass. Or maybe science is all together wrong about the glass. Maybe glass is deadly?"

SANCHO: "Like some aerosols?"

QUIXOTE: "The glass. Do I have a study from a think tanks on it?"

SANCHO: "You did. Enterprise said it leads to a fragile economy and Pew said glass was of little consequence because it is transparent."

QUIXOTE: "So, Sancho, we have quite a quandary. What do you say is the problem with the rotting onion?"

SANCHO: "I think your inability to deal with the greenhouse effect, is helping the onion rot, but I suspect the real problem is the humidity from the water and manure mixture around the onion."

QUIXOTE: "Do you really think a medium full of manure will rot the onion?"

SANCHO: "Quixote, I am sure the rotting state of our onion is a direct result of the media being full of manure."

QUIXOTE: "So then I should add more crap to the media?"

SANCHO: "You have it all wrong--less manure is better--not more."

QUIXOTE: "Oh I can't do that--especially on this greenhouse issue."

SANCHO: "Quixote, you are quite mad."

QUIXOTE: "The greenhouse effect and all the manure I use for the onion are innately tied. My researchers told me so. You'll be impressed by my scientific acumen. Check this out: The warmer it gets, the more it rots. So we add more manure to the onion to help it grow. You see the manure adds nutrition and that helps the plant heal."

SANCHO: "Quixote, now I think the onion is rotting because of stupidity."

QUIXOTE:	"Wait I have an idea. I've got a case of corn hooch in the back. Perhaps I can add some white lightning to the onion--better yet, I can talk to the onion about adding the hooch. You're supposed to talk to plants, you know. No wait, I can add the hooch to the media full of manure first. By golly, that might work."
SANCHO:	"Quixote, hooch is poison. First, you wanted to add too much manure to the problem and now you are going to pickle the poor onion by saying a little booze will make everything all right."
QUIXOTE:	"Sancho, I think the hooch will cut down on our use of foreign soil also."
SANCHO:	"It sounds like a still-born idea to me."
QUIXOTE:	"Bad pun."
SANCHO:	"Quixote, what about if we really deal with the basic science of it all. Why not cut down on the crap in the media and let some fresh air into the greenhouse?"
QUIXOTE:	"I've got it Sancho. We could put a small nuclear power plant uphill and then we could use the extra power in the greenhouse to increase the humidity. I know, we let the effluent flow around the plants, and keep the plants warm. Plants like warmth, so we add more warmth, then a little more manure and an extra dose of booze--just to keep the onion happy-- and think we have this state of the onion issue licked."
SANCHO:	"This is not a martini, you moron. Alcohol will not help. Hot irradiated water will not help. More humidity will not help. More manure is pure death. Quixote, more is not necessarily better."
QUIXOTE:	"Well I could substitute some material from the peat bogs. I own some land in the tundra that I am making available for drilling--wait I have it! This environmental stuff is fun, Sancho. Listen: If you don't like nuclear power how about methane to power the greenhouse?"
SANCHO:	"That will not help the onions. Quixote, listen to me--"

QUIXOTE: "Sancho, The discussion is over. Thank you for your inputs. Besides, I have a friend with some hooch to sell. I have another friend who wants to push small nuclear generators. I have another friend who needs me to ignore the greenhouse for some reason. A few other friends who have some excess drill rigs that needs to be leased."

SANCHO: "And the peat bog?"

QUIXOTE: "Oh that's not for anyone--it's just my contribution to the environment. I like being green. Truth is, this all tires me out and if I can find a way to keep the onions' rot below the surface while placate my friends I am going to do it. Therefore I am going to add more manure to the media."

SANCHO: "Quixote, why not remove the rot, plant the onion in the right location, feed it prudently, then add water based on rational practices and nurse the onion back to health? While it gets healthy you can help your friends find something to do that doesn't kill things."

QUIXOTE: "Sancho I have a solution--mine. I like it and I am going with it. I am so glad we had this talk about the state of the onion. It is a proud night to be an American. Good night and God bless. I'm ready for a drink. How about you, Sancho?"

February 7, 2006
Sancho, Quixote, and Krill

SANCHO: "Quixote, I have a great idea for global warming--something your friends can help with--and something environmentalists will support."

QUIXOTE: "Sancho that would be splendid. How much money do my friends make on it?"

SANCHO: "I'm not sure if they will make any money on it, Quixote."

QUIXOTE: "Well, I'll listen anyway, go ahead."

SANCHO: "Okay. Krill can have a significant positive impact on the uptake of CO_2 by the oceans."

QUIXOTE: "Krill, they are what the whales eat, right?"

SANCHO: "Krill can be an important negative feedback system for global warming. They have the capacity to take CO_2 and efficiently send it to the bottom of the ocean. The problem is the Antarctic oceans have warmed and as a result the number of krill has decreased by as much as 80%."

QUIXOTE: "So we need to tell everyone there are lots of krill and they help in global warming. I like it."

SANCHO: "No Quixote. We need to increase the number of krill in the ocean."

QUIXOTE: "So we genetically engineer a new..."

SANCHO: "Quixote, please listen."

QUIXOTE: "We get some chemical fertilizers..."

SANCHO: "Quixote--we need to find a natural way of increasing the number of krill. It will not solve the problem of global warming but it will add another negative feedback loop to the process. It's a small step but it is a good step."

QUIXOTE: "I got it. Sorry--we can't help with that right now."

SANCHO: "What? How come?"

QUIXOTE: "Well on second thought maybe we can help--if your friends will help my friends?"

SANCHO: "Quixote, climate change is not a negotiation--it is a circumstance."

QUIXOTE: "What's the difference, Sancho?"

SANCHO: "A circumstance is non-negotiable. It just is."

QUIXOTE: "Well then you will appreciate this, Sancho. My friends at the Big Logging Machine, otherwise known as BLM, are having a problem. Research has turned up in the journals that contradict what logging companies wish to see published."

SANCHO: "Perish the thought."

QUIXOTE: "Sancho, my friends have decided to eliminate funding for any research that doesn't meet the requirements of the Big Logging Machine."

SANCHO: "Didn't BLM used to stand for The Bureau of Land Management--and wasn't it a part of the government?"

QUIXOTE: "Once, but now it is a front for logging and mining interests."

SANCHO: "How can that be?"

QUIXOTE: "Sancho, remember you said a negotiation and a circumstance were different?"

SANCHO: "Yes."

QUIXOTE: "Well the circumstance of BLM, and many other agencies related to research, how shall I put it are now in a circumstance that could be considered, ah, friendly to industry."

SANCHO: "But U.S., agencies are responsible to the people. It is still the government of the United States of America."

QUIXOTE: "Any government is bad government, Sancho."

SANCHO: "That platitude has wrecked a nation. What do you want?"

QUIXOTE: "I think we can support your krill idea if your environmental friends will just accept that parts of the federal government of the United States are to be owned by industry."

SANCHO: "I think they can agree to that."

QUIXOTE: "That was too easy. Why?"

SANCHO: "Because, unless we recognize the facts of our lives and deal with them there is nothing the people of this country can do to fix their problems. It's true about the physical environment; it's true about the social environment. To solve a problem you need to understand the severity of the problem."

QUIXOTE: "So then you eco-nuts have no problem accepting that BLM is being used as a Big Logging Machine? And that it is the result of capable lobbying."

SANCHO: "None whatsoever--it's the truth--as unpleasant as it may be. But I have a truth for you, Quixote."

QUIXOTE: "What's that, Sancho?"

SANCHO: "Unless we cut CO_2 emissions by 70% within the next few years our economy is going to go belly up--regardless of how much graft your friends pump into the system. The benign climate we now enjoy, which would have facilitated economic recovery, will be gone--making economic recovery almost impossible. Your friends don't realize it but their time is over, Quixote. You blew it, Captain America. Stick that in your lobby."

QUIXOTE: "Prove it, Sancho."

SANCHO: "The damage on the Gulf Coast is an ongoing economic event, Quixote. Extreme weather is also a future feature of the American fiscal landscape."

QUIXOTE: "New Orleans is a blemish."

SANCHO: "New Orleans is the most obvious example of global warming's highly negative impact on our economy, Quixote. You know it and I know it. Now how about we go grow some krill?"

February 13, 2006
Sancho, Quixote, and Hunting

SANCHO: "Whoa, Quixote, what the heck is all this stuff? Looks like you are planning another war."

QUIXOTE: "What? Not yet, oh, this stuff--it's body armor, Sancho. I've been invited to go on a hunting trip."

SANCHO: "And the bottles?"

QUIXOTE: "People get shot all the time when they are hunting--those are antiseptics-- Sancho."

SANCHO: "Is that so--gin, vermouth, and scotch? Now I see why hunting is such a dangerous thing to do."

QUIXOTE: "Don't let the NRA hear that. Actually, the danger depends on whom you are hunting with, Sancho. Guns don't kill people, politicians do."

SANCHO: "And whom are you going hunting with, Quixote?"

QUIXOTE: "The National Weather Service."

SANCHO: "That's like 4,700 people?"

QUIXOTE: "No, I'm actually going hunting with one or two of the top guys--and some of their friends from Commerce."

SANCHO: "What are you hunting for?"

QUIXOTE: "Meteorologists, scientists, researchers--a few guys from other parts of NOAA, a NASA scientist or two thrown in just for fun--I'm pretty sure hunting season has just closed on lawyers."

SANCHO: "This weekend from what I hear. So you're planning on... shooting your prey?"

QUIXOTE: "We like to call it retirement, Sancho."

SANCHO: "Where are you planning on doing this?"

QUIXOTE: "There's a large fenced ranch in the south. We will invite the scientists down there and let them loose in the fields. After a few minutes we'll go out and find the most experienced of our prey and retire them."

SANCHO: "Seems like too much fun."

QUIXOTE: "I gotta' tell ya'. We have a small funding kiosk set up with solicitations for research. As the scientists come in for dollars, my friends and I wait for them. The ones that know the most are our targets."

SANCHO: "How do know which ones are which?"

QUIXOTE: "The experienced ones move slower and they to recognize the landscape. You know I also think they believe scientific fact and the search for knowledge will protect them. Regardless, they are always quick to support the truth. We hide in the committee-blind waiting for them."

SANCHO: "So in fact the researchers are probably the ones who need body armor around your friends."

QUIXOTE: "I'm here to tell you."

SANCHO: "Don't we need experienced meteorologists and scientists, Quixote?"

QUIXOTE: "What for? They are a drain on our federal budget just like energy conservation, oil drilling regulations, educational programs, election oversight, and federal forests."

SANCHO: "I see. So what happens when we have weather problems related to global warming--won't we need their expertise?"

QUIXOTE: "Junior and Dead-eye are hoping no one notices."

SANCHO: "The retirement of so many capable scientists?"

QUIXOTE: "The storms."

SANCHO: "Smart plan--exactly what I have come to expect from your friends."

QUIXOTE: "Sancho, we are unwavering in our quest for legitimacy."

SANCHO: "Which has nothing to do with the truth--like say our need to immediately cut carbon dioxide."

QUIXOTE: Don't be naïve, Sancho, of course not."

SANCHO: "So crippling the country's ability to cope with global
             warming is still what your friends are aiming for these days?"

QUIXOTE: "That's incorrect, Sancho. We want the population to be able
             to cope with global warming. We need them. We need them
             sightless of course, but we need them. Think of it this way.
             My friends and I are like ranchers--and what good is a ranch
             without sheep and cattle?"

SANCHO: "To say nothing of targets. Once again the unwavering
             commitment to your own welfare peppers my landscape of
             awareness."

QUIXOTE: "Sometimes we do hit what we are aiming at--and that's why
             I am getting this new body armor."

SANCHO: "There are the antiseptics, Quixote, oh that explains the
             scatter-gun reports of your media flunkies."

QUIXOTE: "For legitimacy the right gauge always matters."

SANCHO: "Of course. Quixote, your body armor looks brand new."

QUIXOTE: "Nice stuff too."

SANCHO: "How'd you get it, Quixote?"

QUIXOTE: "It seems a shipment for the Mideast got sent over to the club
             this weekend by mistake."

SANCHO: "One of your friends jacked a shipment of body armor so
             they could go hunting?"

QUIXOTE: "Lobbyists are always looking to seek favor. They know we
             expect the best graft possible. We're leaders Sancho, not
             quail. Though I understand there can be confusion."

SANCHO: "Quixote, I have never seen a six foot tall quail."

QUIXOTE: "I know a VP who would take umbrage at that statement."

SANCHO: "Of course. So the quality of your graft matters."

QUIXOTE: "More than you could ever imagine. It is too bad scientists
             don't have a PAC. Some good old palm-grease might reduce
             their termination numbers."

SANCHO: "How many government scientists are you planning to, ah, retire?"

QUIXOTE: "A thousand minimum, Sancho."

SANCHO: "That's a lot isn't it considering there are only 4,700 people in the whole weather service."

QUIXOTE: "We have breeding facilities all over the country Sancho. In a few years time we'll have ranch-raised researchers coming out of our ears--and they will understand the landscape, the flexibility of truth, and more importantly, the worth of a buck."

SANCHO: "I understand you have shot that all to hell as well, Quixote?"

QUIXOTE: "Sancho, my friends have made such a mess of the bucks you wouldn't believe it. That's another reason we are retiring so many researchers."

SANCHO: "The budget scam, Quixote?"

QUIXOTE: "Economists get retired as well, you know. From now on--in America--it is bullets not books, Sancho."

SANCHO: "And the truth will set you free."

QUIXOTE: "Especially now that my friends control the budget, Sancho."

February 16, 2006
Sancho, Quixote, and Peace

QUIXOTE: "Peace, Sancho."

SANCHO: "Quixote, say you look like the hippie from hell with that scruffy wig. Those pink pants are a bit long, especially with tire tread sandals, and the flag shirt--how tacky. I do like the bright orange vest though."

QUIXOTE: "You can never be too careful, Sancho."

SANCHO: "So why the getup?"

QUIXOTE: "The outfit is our way of showing support for peace, Sancho. You know for too long my friends and I have been seen as warring, monopolistic, megalomaniac crooks."

SANCHO: "You know Quixote, if it walks like a quail, flies like a quail, and stands six inches high, it probably is a quail."

QUIXOTE: "That's not funny, Sancho. I am talking about peace here."

SANCHO: "A piece of what?"

QUIXOTE: "Peace, you know, like this with my two fingers."

SANCHO: "Quixote, you need to turn your hand around--two fingers up like that are hardly saying peace."

QUIXOTE: "Oh, damn. I told Junior he had it wrong."

SANCHO: "What kind of peace are you looking for, Quixote? Iraq, Iran, China, Gitmo, what?"

QUIXOTE: "Not these, Sancho, we must remain ever vigilant--besides we have a huge budget to burn through."

SANCHO: "So what's the scam?"

QUIXOTE: "We are hearing rumblings about people comparing global warming to a war."

SANCHO: "So your friends are going to invade planet Earth because it harbors weapons of mass destruction?"

QUIXOTE: "No."

SANCHO: "Global warming is forcing people to reconsider the odious event of nuclear power, so you want sanctions against the Earth because those with nuclear power might make nuclear weapons?"

QUIXOTE: "That's ridiculous, Sancho."

SANCHO: "You're telling me."

QUIXOTE: "Sancho, we think it's time we faced the enemy: Planet Earth."

SANCHO: "Of course. Your friends have decided to take the gloves off and attack Earth with chemicals, pollution, over-population, deplete the oceans, foul the skies, rape the forests, and then poison the farmlands?"

QUIXOTE: "No."

SANCHO: "You're right that eco-terrorism seems to have backfired on you."

QUIXOTE: "Sancho, do you understand global warming at all?"

SANCHO: "Gaia is adjusting for human ego and we call it global warming."

QUIXOTE: "Sancho, we are not going to be able to control the planet. It is too big and it is going to do what it wants."

SANCHO: "No kidding? How radical. Quixote, you sound like an eco-nut."

QUIXOTE: "Sancho, the planet is waging war on humanity."

SANCHO: "Don't be a boob, Quixote. We are a flea. We bit the 'big dog on the block' with our greenhouse gases and Gaia is proceeding to scratch itself to remove the irritation. It is no war--it isn't even a sneeze."

QUIXOTE: "Sancho, I think global warming is a war we cannot win."

SANCHO: "Do tell."

QUIXOTE: "Sancho, it means so much to us humans and so little to the planet."

SANCHO: "Now you have it, Quixote."

QUIXOTE: "Sancho, global warming is at least as important as a regional war. We should defend ourselves."

SANCHO: "Quixote, your frames of reference are becoming so humanistic."

QUIXOTE: "Sancho, we are not preparing for this conflict. Don't you realize our strategy for global warming is like saying that when the enemy starts shooting we need to absorb the losses--and then everything else will be okay? Where are our missiles, our planes, our smart bombs to deal with the conflict?"

SANCHO: "Buried under fossil fuels contracts, lobbyist junkets, and faux corporate profits?"

QUIXOTE: "That's not funny."

SANCHO: "Well maybe you are saying carbon intensity, moronic platitudes about our economy, Fascist oppression of truth, and more oil, are not an effective response to the threat of global warming?"

QUIXOTE: "Sancho, they may not be."

SANCHO: "Global warming is the real weapon of mass destruction."

QUIXOTE: "So I say give peace a chance, Sancho."

SANCHO: "You are impressive in your lack of shame. Doesn't suing for peace with the planet seem like weakness to your friends?"

QUIXOTE: "On a good day. On a bad day we sell more oil leases, or go hunting."

SANCHO: "It's a losing battle, Quixote."

QUIXOTE: "We know that, Sancho. That's why my friends will spin it to the planet's fault."

SANCHO: "Fault--the planet? Is that a joke?"

QUIXOTE: "No. We figure there is nothing that takes place that we can't somehow tie into the planet."

SANCHO: "I hear the faintest rumblings of environmental awareness, Quixote."

QUIXOTE: "We still have horrific consequences to cope with--do you have any idea how this might impact our ability to raise campaign funds?"

SANCHO: "To say nothing of storms, disease, and sea level rise--why don't they just cut CO_2 emissions by 70%?"

QUIXOTE: "You do not understand the concept of plausible deniability. If we respond then my friends can't say it wasn't their fault when it all goes to hell. And we are sure that's coming in the near future."

SANCHO: "Quixote, when your friends were genuinely unconvinced they might have been cut some slack. But now everyone knows we are in for a horrible time from global warming--and your friends are still preaching their defeatist mantra: 'Oh we can't adjust our economy. Woe is us'."

QUIXOTE: "But it isn't their fault. The planet is waging war against us. All we want is peace with the planet."

SANCHO: "And your friends are willing to prove that by cutting the forests, poisoning the air with particulate matter, and fighting wars for the last drop of oil."

QUIXOTE: "We just need to show the planet who is boss by turning public opinion against it. Now, how do you make those peace symbols? It looks like a jet aircraft, doesn't it? You think if I spell Exxon down the center anyone will notice?"

SANCHO: "Gee maybe, Quixote. But by showing the planet that we are the boss--how is that peace?"

QUIXOTE: "Sancho, you just don't understand peace."

SANCHO: "Quixote, for your friends, peace is a graveyard."

QUIXOTE: "And that's why we don't care to look beyond the spin."

February 22, 2006
Sancho, Quixote, and FOB

QUIXOTE: "...And Sancho, just make sure you don't lock the shipping containers."

SANCHO: "You don't mean that. Is this a gag?"

QUIXOTE: "No."

SANCHO: "But Quixote, those are your best vintages of port. We have to keep them safe. The items might get lost--or worse."

QUIXOTE: "Quit whining. No one is going to steal the port, Sancho."

SANCHO: "Quixote, of course they will."

QUIXOTE: "Not from what I hear. Junior says we should trust strangers with our port. He says he is very close to an epiphany on policy here."

SANCHO: "He is very close to a drunk-tank."

QUIXOTE: "Sancho, relax--Junior has plans to guard our port."

SANCHO: "I'm listening."

QUIXOTE: "Convicted felons, con men, and uncaring thugs--they will keep the bad guys away. Junior says no one will mess with his shotgun wielding cronies."

SANCHO: "Quixote, why doesn't he just use terrorists?"

QUIXOTE: "I can't talk about that."

SANCHO: "Now that's a gag. Quixote, nut-cases and terrorists are the ones who are going to do the stealing. Your friends are just giving them the port."

QUIXOTE: "Sancho, what gives you the idea this is up for discussion?"

SANCHO: "We are a free and open country."

QUIXOTE: "One of our favorite gags, Sancho."

SANCHO: "Quixote, what is this gag thing you have going?"

QUIXOTE: "Think of it as a maturing national focus."

SANCHO: "Overall or just on our port?"

QUIXOTE: "Sancho, there will be a huge number of unlocked shipping containers with some very valuable items as well as some highly dangerous weapons. Our port is safe. Oh, and all the nuclear weapons will be plainly marked."

SANCHO: "Quixote, how is that going to deter the theft of our port--though I agree that after those kinds of heists, the port concerns will be moot."

QUIXOTE: "First there will be so much to loot; Junior says the chances of losing our port are small. Second, with so much to steal he thinks they will get confused. Though that may be a projection on his part."

SANCHO: "The truth does hurt some times, go on, Quixote."

QUIXOTE: "Plus they are putting up a big sign saying 'please don't steal the port--or any items that will make you rich, dangerous, or powerful. No one is watching'."

SANCHO: "I'm beginning to gag on this whole plan--you really think a sign will deter anyone, Quixote?"

QUIXOTE: "In fact, Junior thinks I should tape a sign to the exterior of the shipping container that says: 'Don't wine'--"

SANCHO: "Puns are not gags, Quixote."

QUIXOTE: "Gags have many uses. My friends use them in science all the time."

SANCHO: "Why are we giving away the port?"

QUIXOTE: "Oh, then there is our bird-flu...in the hand. Oh, also the moment they steal the port they will have to sell it through my friends."

SANCHO: "And how is that good?"

QUIXOTE: "We make money on it. Also, a port shortage will raise the price of port. Do you remember when we had that oil embargo? It didn't work very well and I think this whole thing comes from that. Consider this: With this shipping scheme, we can have embargoes on everything. My friends will haul away huge profits."

SANCHO: "A gaggle of green--so then the port doesn't really matter to you, Quixote?"

QUIXOTE: "Think if it as a change in the American spirit."

SANCHO: "From right to wrong?"

QUIXOTE: "The truth is, Junior has a debt to pay."

SANCHO: "Blackmail, bad math skills, or did someone threaten him with a quail hunt?"

QUIXOTE: "I can't discuss that."

SANCHO: "Another gag, hmm... So this port thing is all a new con, Quixote."

QUIXOTE: "Why would you say that?"

SANCHO: "Junior is the biggest terrorist around."

QUIXOTE: "He gets confused--that's all. He's very concerned for the welfare of the common man."

SANCHO: "You mean the common-consumer. Quixote, what would you call Junior's policy on global warming? Concern for the environment and humanity?"

QUIXOTE: "Think of it as an oil portrait of reality."

SANCHO: "Now that's the truth."

QUIXOTE: "Must be time for a gag, Sancho. Over all, I think sending valuable items and dangerous material in unlocked containers is a sound, workable plan. I am not the least bit worried about the port, even the really pricey, out-of-this-world, stuff."

SANCHO: "So then the stratospheric port is no concern to you or your friends."

QUIXOTE:	"A good exit strategy counts, Sancho. But that said--Junior says I am to trust anyone he says."
SANCHO:	"Now I know this whole thing is a gag."
QUIXOTE:	"Precisely, Sancho, and here is the punch-line: Sometimes a gag is all that a once-free people can count on."
SANCHO:	"There is even a gag on global warming truth in America, Quixote."
QUIXOTE:	"Sancho, do you believe telling people they need to cut CO_2 emissions by 70% within the next few years is acceptable to my friends?"
SANCHO:	"Which is why we have satiric gags, Quixote."
QUIXOTE:	"Naturally Sancho. So you understand why we have gags on scientists going public with facts we corporate lackeys don't approve of."
SANCHO:	"To say nothing of entrenched interests who are so mired in a dead end economic system they can't get out of their own way, Quixote."
QUIXOTE:	"Sancho, they like a good joke."
SANCHO:	"For instance: carbon intensity."
QUIXOTE:	"You can't say things like that, Sancho."
SANCHO:	"Which leads us to the gags on journalists and the media."
QUIXOTE:	"My favorite gags are the racist jokes about foreign cultures and researchers, Sancho--especially the ones that lead to war."
SANCHO:	"You'd have to be a fool to laugh at that one, Quixote. On the other hand, I suppose as our culture continues spinning into a repressive society the gags change."
QUIXOTE:	"Like everything else in our society, boldly moving from freedom to suppression."

February 25, 2006
Sancho, Quixote, and Critical Mass

QUIXOTE: "Sancho, what do you know about the bicycle insurgents?"

SANCHO: "Beg pardon, Quixote, I haven't heard about that one. What do they do, ring their bells too loud in front of a gas station? Thumb their noses at refineries? Sell their oil stock?"

QUIXOTE: "This isn't funny."

SANCHO: "Oh this does sound critical, Quixote. Tell me, has Al Quaeda stopped using jets and moved onto Schwinn as a weapons platform? Imagine the destruction of a fully loaded Schwinn crashing headlong into an Escalade. The steel frame would melt within minutes."

QUIXOTE: "Stop it. Sancho, I have just gotten a rush assignment to deal with these terrorists. I am told these bicyclists have no respect for traffic."

SANCHO: "Lord knows we all love traffic jams, Quixote."

QUIXOTE: "There are groups of bicyclists roaming the cities in large numbers."

SANCHO: "Has Homeland Security looked into this?"

QUIXOTE: "Junior has tried to contact them, but every time he calls them they break out into gales of laughter and send him into their voice-mail system."

SANCHO: "That port thing I guess. A loss of credibility can be an ugly event. So what's the problem with people riding bicycles?"

QUIXOTE: "There are too many of them."

SANCHO: "So let me see if I understand. People ride their bicycles in cities and that is a problem."

QUIXOTE: "Yes, Sancho."

SANCHO: "Why? Do they threaten anyone?"

QUIXOTE: "No."

SANCHO: "Do they break things, litter, cause a commotion, pollute the air, or shoot guns at each other, Quixote?"

QUIXOTE: "No, but they make it hard for people to drive their cars."

SANCHO: "Well then send in Blackwater."

QUIXOTE: "Sancho, this isn't funny."

SANCHO: "Oh, Quixote, you have no idea how funny this is. Not only does the emperor have no clothes but he is impotent against a group of citizens on bicycles."

QUIXOTE: "What does that mean?"

SANCHO: "Are you saying that at certain times of the day there are so many bicyclists on the road the manifest destiny of the automobile to choke our lungs, spew greenhouse gases, spread consternation, anger, kill pedestrians, and promote classism is not only under siege, it is trumped?"

QUIXOTE: "My friends can't have that kind of behavior in the populace."

SANCHO: "So that's the beauty of this. No one gives a damn what your friends want."

QUIXOTE: "Sancho, that's what scares them."

SANCHO: "They need to get over it. The automobile has had a long run, but it's days as the dominant carrier, frustration provider, and pollution system have come to an end. Hold a mass for it and pass the air pump."

QUIXOTE: "Sancho, how can you say that? Do you have any idea about the economic impact of people driving less?"

SANCHO: "Do you have any idea of the huge impact large scale bicycle ridership might have on climate change?"

QUIXOTE: "What about jobs?"

SANCHO: "What about economic evolution, Quixote?"

QUIXOTE: "Nothing changes unless my friends bless it."

SANCHO: "Oh the economic boogeymen returns. The days of an economic system consuming all it encounters are gone. Consumption jobs are over. Sustainability jobs are growing."

QUIXOTE: "We're not going to give up without a fight."

SANCHO: "Whom are you going to fight? The game is over: F=MA, my liege"

QUIXOTE: "My friends will lose control."

SANCHO: "And this is all it will take to wrest control from them?"

QUIXOTE: "We can't have this."

SANCHO: "Your friends' position seems ah…Tenuous. To say nothing of absurd."

QUIXOTE: "Stop laughing."

SANCHO: "No problem. So what are you going to do?"

QUIXOTE: "I've got a media clamp on the events already, so far as the general public knows, Critical Mass as just a group of kooks who tie up traffic driving their anti-American bicycle."

SANCHO: "That's the terrorist group? You must be very proud of yourself for this one. So what are they really, Quixote?"

QUIXOTE: "A projection of force by the people of this country demanding what is rightfully theirs."

SANCHO: "As I said, you can't argue with F=MA. No wonder your friends are crazed about bicycles and Critical Mass. It's the Boston Tea Party all over again."

QUIXOTE: "Don't say that out loud, Sancho."

SANCHO: "Sorry, Quixote, no one will ever hear me say Critical Mass is America's 21st Century Boston Tea Party: Citizens standing for their right to be recognized. So what are you going to do?"

QUIXOTE: "Keep a lid on it--try to marginalize them. Spew venom. Buyout the manufacturers of bicycles, get an 18 speed bike to hurt someone. I don't know."

SANCHO: "They are doing so much good by showing how easy it is to take the streets back from cars. Imagine all that clean air."

QUIXOTE: "I know what I can do: We'll start a campaign that Critical Mass causes traffic jams."

SANCHO: "Unlike poor planning and useless public transport."

QUIXOTE: "You are right. Bird flu? Cancer? I know, bicycles are the number one cause of Teflon."

SANCHO: "Huh?"

QUIXOTE: "Too weak--I know. We can blast them as anarchists in a media barrage for the commuter: Four wheeled freedom vs. the godless bicyclists. Just give me a few months on the boob tube and by the time I am done I will frame bicycles as the number one cause of global warming."

SANCHO: "Like that cow flatulence thing you tried a few years ago."

QUIXOTE: "We're gonna' get that one to fly, you'll see. But right now, the two wheeled scourge is at our doorstep--hide your women and children. Praise the Cord and pass the gas."

SANCHO: "King George is rolling in his grave with laughter. Quixote, commuters hate their commute, now you going to try and get them to fight for it?"

QUIXOTE: "You bet your saddle bags, Sancho."

SANCHO: "So let me get this straight. We have a movement called Critical Mass that exists in many cities in the U.S., and around the world. Every so often, they take the streets back from the cars and ride together. They don't pollute. They don't hurt anyone. They just put cars in second position."

QUIXOTE: "Right and those who drive cars aren't going to take it anymore. We will demand our right to cause our own traffic snarls. What good is a traffic snarl without pollution anyway? Fourith by land, twoith ain't tea. Bicycles suck, take it, from me.' No that's a little harsh. Don't you love the creative process?"

SANCHO: "You are delirious--commuters are stuck in traffic every day of their working lives. Why would they get angry at people trying to show them a better way--rather than those who cause traffic?"

QUIXOTE: "Why do they smoke cigarettes again? I'll tell you why: Advertising is their friend."

SANCHO: "So I see. Do you mind if I introduce a bit of sanity--you have started to foam at the mouth."

QUIXOTE: "That's the froth of righteous indignation at the bicycle insurgency. I wonder if checkpoints would help?"

SANCHO: "Does Critical Mass announce their rides?"

QUIXOTE: "Yes."

SANCHO: "So what kind of idiot goes out when people are riding en masse?"

QUIXOTE: "A belligerent idiot we think. But truthfully, we're not sure what kind of idiot, but we're hoping to clone them."

SANCHO: "Quixote, I'd say anyone and everyone should join the rides so they can see alternative ways to move food, supplies, and their bodies. With this kind of progress we can really start to cut CO_2 emission by 70% in a few years."

QUIXOTE: "Just had to get that in didn't you, Sancho?"

SANCHO: "I just can't say it enough. Critical Mass is a wonderful idea."

QUIXOTE: "Sancho--how do my friends make money off it?"

SANCHO: "They cannot. These people are about freedom, Quixote."

QUIXOTE: "My friends cannot control a free person or a free people."

SANCHO: "Have you considered referring this to the Security Council?"

QUIXOTE: "That's an idea, Sancho. The bicycle of mass destruction--say isn't critical mass a nuclear thing? Maybe I could say bicycles are a potential source of weapons grade plutonium?"

SANCHO: "Or your friends could cause a riot about a bicycle cartoon?"

QUIXOTE: "We just did that one, too soon to do it again. I think we shall stick with either the nuclear angle or the economic angle."

SANCHO: "The economy doesn't really matter does it, Quixote?"

QUIXOTE: "Never did--just so long as we run the show."

SANCHO: "You've convinced me to join Critical Mass. Thank you."

QUIXOTE: "We will fight you, and all you'll get is a nice ride on a bicycle."

SANCHO: "For some of us, Quixote, that's all we ask."

February 26, 2006
Sancho, Quixote, and Hurricanopoly

QUIXOTE:	"Sancho, have you ever played Monopoly?"
SANCHO:	"Of course Quixote, that's the game where you buy urban real estate and try to make the other players go broke."
QUIXOTE:	"Exactly--well my friends and I have a new game; we call it Hurricanopoly."
SANCHO:	"How do you play Hurricanopoly, Quixote?"
QUIXOTE:	"Well the basic idea is everyone draws a city card. If your city is devastated by a climate event you do everything you can to buy the city and privatize it."
SANCHO:	"You can't buy a city, Quixote."
QUIXOTE:	"New Orleans can't pay its bills anymore and the future looks…Murky."
SANCHO:	"Odd, New Orleans did everything Junior and your friends said it should do."
QUIXOTE:	"Exactly: It ignored the facts of global warming--like we told them to."
SANCHO:	"It didn't take precautions against global warming because your friends said that was an economic black hole."
QUIXOTE:	"And so the city fathers figured the economic impacts of adapting to global warming would be worse than the event."
SANCHO:	"And now the city is broke."
QUIXOTE:	"Worse than that, Sancho, it has almost no economic life and a flood of government service bills like police protection, fire protection, road maintenance."
SANCHO:	"Then there are the repair bills and the infrastructure work, Quixote, seems like they should have paid more attention to preparation."
QUIXOTE:	"Did you know half the population has not returned?"

SANCHO:	"Quixote, how many of those not returning are living in other parts of the country?"
QUIXOTE:	"The real question, Sancho, is how many of those not returning are living anywhere."
SANCHO:	"Oh, I see, so is population reduction a part of Hurricanopoly?"
QUIXOTE:	"It can be."
SANCHO:	"Was it on purpose?"
QUIXOTE:	"No, it just happened. But it has a nice ring to it."
SANCHO:	"So what happens next in Huricanopoly?"
QUIXOTE:	"Here is where the game gets interesting. The same people who told the cities to ignore the warnings."
SANCHO:	"Shills, hacks, oil companies and investment bankers?"
QUIXOTE:	"Right. They step in and arrange loans--or help the federal government to arrange loans."
SANCHO:	"That's awfully darn decent of them and so civic-minded. But isn't that financing expensive for everyone in the city?"
QUIXOTE:	"Well, yes, but that's the path to winning the game, Sancho. One way or the other, the city is in your pocket once that happens."
SANCHO:	"Sounds like feudalism."
QUIXOTE:	"My friends love that game, Sancho."
SANCHO:	"Wouldn't it be better if we were preparing for global warming?"
QUIXOTE:	"Not from my friends' perspective."
SANCHO:	"Quixote, what if there is regional devastation?"
QUIXOTE:	"I like the way you think, Sancho--so you think we have other games to play like Toronadopoly, and Diseaseopoly, and Seariseopoly?"
SANCHO:	"All thanks to global warming."

QUIXOTE: "You might have been right all along, Sancho. There does seem to be money to be made in this climate change thing."

SANCHO: "Imagine the fun if two or three major cities are hit at the same time. The strain on resources and available funds to rebuild will devastate areas as they compete for funding. Imagine the fun your friends will have hoarding resources and profiteering."

QUIXOTE: "This environment thing is sounding better and better to them, Sancho. This global warming mess almost guarantees us prime urban properties--if not entire regions--for pennies on the dollar. Heck, why buy Boardwalk and Park Place when in a few years you can buy all of Atlantic City? And I thought the game pieces were just in the Southeast."

SANCHO: "Ah, Quixote, just one question: What will you do when a major climate event hits your city?"

QUIXOTE: "I will not live in a city."

"SANCHO: "What will you do when it hits your region?"

QUIXOTE: "What's that supposed to mean?"

SANCHO: "What happens to your Monopoly games when a serious climate events blows through your major assets and instead of being a player in the game of Hurricanopoly you are a game piece?"

QUIXOTE: "Can that happen, Sancho?"

SANCHO: "You might even have other problems."

QUIXOTE: "Like what?"

SANCHO: "Feeding your family. Housing them. Finding food."

QUIXOTE: "I'm rich--that's ridiculous. I have too much money for global warming to impact me."

SANCHO: "Quixote, to a large extent the impact has already happened--you haven't felt the pain side of it yet."

QUIXOTE: "Prove it, Sancho."

Sancho: "We've been here before, Quixote. When I said, there was global warming you said prove it. When I said global warming was an event of the present, not the future you said prove it. When I said, the hurricanes and the storms would get more intense, you said prove it. Now I say preparing for global warming is better than taking the economic hit and you again say prove it. But in the future there will be no place for you to mess up. Aren't you tired of being wrong, yet?"

Quixote: "You are saying New Orleans isn't an economic game but the harbinger of what's to come with global warming."

Sancho: "Exactly--Katrina's landfall wiped out the economic base of a city and the region. The devastation has ramifications for years into the future--and there are more Katrinas on the way. Plus they will be bigger and more intense. As a result, recovery will be far harder than now. Is it really so hard to recognize that the economic game has changed?"

Quixote: "You are saying the economic system is not as important as the climate."

Sancho: "I am saying the fingerprint of global warming has firmly ensconced itself in the seat of humanity's economic systems and I am surprised you and your friends cannot see it--given your vantage point."

Quixote: "So what is that fingerprint?"

Sancho: "You can't have business as usual after multiple major weather events. So as climate events increase in intensity and frequency--economic resiliency decreases to zero."

Quixote: "Economics is cyclical."

Sancho: "As long as you have a benign arena in which to function. And that is your vulnerability."

Quixote: "I refuse to believe this."

Sancho: "It doesn't matter if you believe it or not. The climate system does not care. At some point, you will pass the place of effective proactive preparation and enter triage. Soon after that our outmoded economic system will collapse. This is what happened in New Orleans. Quixote--this is the real game of Hurricanopoly--only the planet always wins."

QUIXOTE: "And I am to believe events like a devastated New Orleans will populate the world wiping out our investments in the medium term?"

SANCHO: "Quixote, take off your rose-colored glasses; the only reason New Orleans may survive long enough to be pummeled again by another weather event is there are other entities not apparently damaged by climate events who are there to help it rebuild."

QUIXOTE: "Like my friends, the Hurricanopoly players?"

SANCHO: "Correct. But Quixote, what happens when their support systems are devastated?"

QUIXOTE: "The federal government will step in."

SANCHO: "I thought there was too much government in our society?"

QUIXOTE: "The facts change when the media supports it--er when we tell them to support something. Grow up."

SANCHO: "It doesn't matter--no help will be available when we have a series of cities hit, or entire regions. Start dealing with global warming, Quixote. Cut your CO_2 emission by 70% and begin an orderly transition--you have less than half a decade to get it going."

QUIXOTE: "Prove it, Sancho."

SANCHO: "New Orleans, Louisiana, oh blind one--that's our future--unless you and your friends can relocate your heads out of your misplaced economic seat and into the daylight."

March 7, 2006
Sancho, Quixote, and the Blogs

Quixote: "Sancho, would you blog for us?"

Sancho: "Meaning?"

Quixote: "You have an affinity for the environment and an in-depth, thoughtful sense of complex climate change issues. We enjoy the way you write and we'd like you to write for us."

Sancho: "Doing what, Quixote?"

Quixote: "We want you to promote our programs by posting comments to different parts of the web and then claiming the pieces as your point of view."

Sancho: "So we are talking about propaganda?"

Quixote: "Propaganda is such an ugly word, Sancho. We consider this type of work 'extending the truth'--but yes--we want you to advance our agenda."

Sancho: "You want me to promote the plans of Junior and his friends by prostituting my name and my work?"

Quixote: "Sancho, we have group medical and dental--plus--we pay quite well."

Sancho: "How much?"

Quixote: "More than a living wage, Sancho."

Sancho: "That all seems like a generous offer, Quixote, especially for just a few words on the internet every so often."

Quixote: "It is a full time job. We'd even help you with some topics."

Sancho: "Meaning...You have someone who writes the copy for me to post, Quixote?"

Quixote: "Some of it, Sancho--not all of it. We would give you complete artistic freedom to put it into your own style--so long as you do not contradict the objectives of our corporate partners."

SANCHO: "Quixote, I am insulted you would eveneven asked me to do this kind of work. I could never consider writing for you and your gaggle of megalomaniacs."

QUIXOTE: "We respect your ability to communicate, Sancho. This is a compliment."

SANCHO: "Your friends are immoral, duplicitous, and evil. Plus, I find your agenda ridiculous and shameful, Quixote."

QUIXOTE: "Well then why don't we blog our conversations? That would make our conversations more of a forum. I think a fair, impartial discussion has merit. Don't you want our debate to have a balanced point of view on the environment?"

SANCHO: "Quixote, blogs are nothing more than a set-up--a system to mute an honest viewpoint by diluting the web site through paid propagandists--as you have just proven."

QUIXOTE: "But Sancho, for years we've been corrupting truth with shills on the news groups, list-servers, radio, TV, and every other media we can find. We want your help to quell truth on the Internet. Name your price. Legitimacy hurts my friends."

SANCHO: "Well, Quixote, sooner or later there had to be light into your activities."

QUIXOTE: "We work in the dark, in the background. It's our vocation."

SANCHO: "Like snakes."

QUIXOTE: "Only, we don't need the sunshine to work."

SANCHO: "Then you will understand this next statement, Quixote."

QUIXOTE: "Which is?"

SANCHO: "Quixote, take your money, take your viewpoint, take your corruption, and stick it where the sun will not shine."

March 9, 2006
Sancho, Quixote, and CVs
(Previously Unpublished)

QUIXOTE: "Sancho, we need to talk. Have you ever considered getting a PhD?"

SANCHO: "Quixote, I am disinclined to personify the Perils of Pauline strapped down to a tenure track waiting for the corporate Orpheus in a blue suit and a white hat to rescue me from publish or perish hell with a fat salary and a house in Palo Alto."

QUIXOTE: "Because you had all that, Sancho?"

SANCHO: "That and more, Quixote, but more because none of that is my goal. I am a servant plain and simple."

QUIXOTE: "With a PhD, the media would know who you are and respect you. The government would seek your advice. Leaders of industry might hire you as a consultant."

SANCHO: "So what?"

QUIXOTE: "It's tough to get funding without a PhD, Sancho. Of course, then you'd have to worry about your reputation."

SANCHO: "Ah the fool's game. You want me to play by your rules."

QUIXOTE: "Why don't you?"

SANCHO: "No thanks."

QUIXOTE: "Without a PhD you seem one dimensional to the media."

SANCHO: "Actually Quixote, I am five dimensional. Length, Width, Breadth, Time, and Scale."

QUIXOTE: "You are saying Scale is the fifth dimension."

SANCHO: "I'd never say that. I don't have a PhD. Go ask a topologist."

QUIXOTE: "So is that your real interest?"

SANCHO: "My real interest is time dilation."

QUIXOTE:　　"Hard to believe any of this is true. Don't you see how much money there is for you in the climate game?"

SANCHO:　　"Let's just say there are many paths, Quixote."

QUIXOTE:　　"You are a new renaissance man, Sancho. But just because they want you to wear their labels doesn't mean they are going to mistake who you are."

SANCHO:　　"And so I remain your humble servant, Quixote."

March 13, 2006
Sancho, Quixote, and Servers

SANCHO: "That restaurant down the street is closed, Quixote."

QUIXOTE: "Really, how puzzling? What happened, Sancho?"

SANCHO: "I thought you might know something about it."

QUIXOTE: "It did seem like a lot of undesirable waiters and waitresses."

SANCHO: "What are you talking about?"

QUIXOTE: "Sancho, what do you say we go out and plant that spring field? I believe it has been well tilled at this point."

SANCHO: "Did you have something to do with that restaurant closing?"

QUIXOTE: "Have you ever noticed how wait staff are un-American?"

SANCHO: "You had a problem with the waiters and waitresses and so you closed the neighborhood restaurant down?"

QUIXOTE: "You're twisting my words. All I know is watching the wait people wasn't enough for my friends. We needed to do more."

SANCHO: "Meaning?"

QUIXOTE: "It is important for us to control the servers."

SANCHO: "Why do your friends care about waiters and waitresses in a small town?"

QUIXOTE: "Seems my friends invested heavily in a Cuban Bar and Grill. After they opened it, the servers gave them problems."

SANCHO: "The food servers? Oh my, servers are waiters--now I see."

QUIXOTE: "The servers passed information about our grilling techniques and we couldn't have that--especially because we needed to be coy about our grilling."

SANCHO: And so you concluded acting loyal to your friends meant closing down a restaurant--because they had a grill I bet?"

QUIXOTE: "Sancho, all I know is to be a loyal American I had to put an end to another group of vicious, insidious waiters."

SANCHO: "I marvel at your grip on reality. Where should people eat?"

QUIXOTE: "They can go to the bakery for food, Sancho. The Madam Antoinette Bakery just opened. It is one of our franchises."

SANCHO: "This I knew. So did you close down the restaurant to drum up business for your franchise?"

QUIXOTE: "No I believe in free trade. We were just going to listen to the waiters and waitresses-but when my friends heard the servers weren't putting out information we approved, I was told to shut down as many of them as possible--and that restaurant in our neighborhood was the perfect place to start."

SANCHO: "So you are against waiters and waitresses because they may not support, or they might steal, the grilling techniques of your friends?"

QUIXOTE: "I never knew a bistro could be a hot bed of insurgency."

SANCHO: "Only in the Elmer Fudd theory of hospitality, could one conclude servers are the enemy of freedom. By any chance did your friends talk about a denial of service attack?"

QUIXOTE: "How did you know?"

SANCHO: "I used to watch Delusions of the 'Rich and Insular' on TV."

QUIXOTE: "Did you know we have the right to close down any restaurant that is not serving the best Interests of our country?"

SANCHO: "You mean like serving rice in the wrong way?"

QUIXOTE: "Thank goodness--and with the Patriot Act we are now safe from insurgent waiters trying to steal our freedom."

SANCHO: "You mean servers."

QUIXOTE: "Whatever. Let's say one day you are at an eatery and you mention that unless we cut emissions we are in for economic collapse--and one of the servers picks it up and relays it to another. Do you see what might happen?"

SANCHO: "A denial of service attack served up by one of your local patriots?"

QUIXOTE: "We remove the server thereby making menu-surfing once again safe for all Americans."

SANCHO: "Of course that will not stop tornadoes from tearing apart mid-western cities."

QUIXOTE: "Who cares, Sancho? You need to understand my friends define grief as: information shared without our approval."

SANCHO: "Wildfires burning thousands of acres matters how much?"

QUIXOTE: "We cannot lose control of the servers. Freedom must resume its march."

SANCHO: "Under the watchful eye of Darth Vader on Quaaludes. Quixote, how can a neighborhood wait person, have any social impact?"

QUIXOTE: "I'm not sure but we mean to keep it minimal. Food insurgency is underway. Do you think there are tofu terrorists?"

SANCHO: "No."

QUIXOTE: "A whole wheat waffle conspiracy?"

SANCHO: "No."

QUIXOTE: "Béchamel bombers?"

SANCHO: "No."

QUIXOTE: "The boogey-bird?"

SANCHO: "That's one of yours, Quixote."

QUIXOTE: "I told you we had traction with that one, Sancho."

SANCHO: "Quixote, are you sure your friends were talking about wait staff and not, say Internet Servers?"

QUIXOTE: "Computer food orders are not in my footprint, Sancho. So what if people phone in food orders and bypass the waiters. This is America--land of free choice."

SANCHO: "Calm down. Why are you shouting? What's that in your hand? Oh my, it looks like a small microphone. I think your friends are trying to establish an information bottleneck on anything they don't like."

QUIXOTE: "Sommeliers are exempt I think. Sancho, in truth I do not understand the elaborate plans to guard our grilling techniques."

SANCHO: "Did they say...how?"

QUIXOTE: "This has nothing to do with Native American servers Sancho. I think it is waiters everywhere, regardless of race, creed, or color. America is once again a shining light of liberty."

SANCHO: "Do you know how they will guard their grilling techniques?"

QUIXOTE: "They just told me to keep an eye on the servers. The world is a dangerous place, Sancho. Loose lips cause censure."

SANCHO: "Then there is the minor matter of global warming--obviously nowhere near as important as rabid waiters."

QUIXOTE: "Roger that. One question: Do aerosols tenderize meat?"

SANCHO: "Just in the lungs, Quixote."

QUIXOTE: "Oh that might be--one of the guys said something about never mentioning asbestos in the sentence as aerosols. What is this thing? Oh no, it is another listening device. Sancho, you do know I am loyal to oil, don't you?"

SANCHO: "Feeling a little paranoid? Quixote. Maybe a little rust in that corporate armor, oh, corporate knight?"

QUIXOTE: "Junior has that global warming thing solved with aerosols."

SANCHO: "You both seem to share the same grip on reality--I'll say that--Quixote."

QUIXOTE: "Ban the busboys! Scuttle the Sous Chef! Savants to servers! Waste the waiters. Remember the Maine!"

SANCHO: "How about this quote, Quixote? Those who deny freedom to others, deserve it not for themselves; and, under a just God, can not long retain it."

March 17, 2006
Sancho, Quixote, and Life-blood

QUIXOTE:	"Sancho, did you hear the one about the cosmic star-waves causing global warming?"
SANCHO:	"I heard that one, Quixote."
QUIXOTE:	"I love a good laugh, don't you? Did you hear the one about the asteroid that crashed into the Earth a hundred years ago as the cause of global warming?"
SANCHO:	"I heard that one as well, Quixote. Were those yours?"
QUIXOTE:	"I wish they were. Truth is we have had a shake-up and some new kids are setting the spin."
SANCHO:	"Quixote, did you hear the one about the hurricane season that will be worse than last year's hurricane season? Oops, you stopped laughing."
QUIXOTE:	"Sancho, it hasn't happened yet and you have no proof."
SANCHO:	"Quixote, scientific reports are coming in by the cart-load. Many are about rising sea surface temperatures in the ocean and their tie to global warming. Many also then link global warming to increased hurricane intensity."
QUIXOTE:	"So what, Sancho? As long as we control the popular media, your scientist friends are whistling in a vacuum. We control the information flowing to the masses. We own truth."
SANCHO:	"Soon we are going to have another shocking hurricane season. We need to make some course adjustments."
QUIXOTE:	"My friends will not do that."
SANCHO:	"Why not, Quixote?"
QUIXOTE:	"It might hurt the stock market and cause a recession by giving people a sense of vulnerability to the climate."
SANCHO:	"Why is that bad? We are all vulnerable to our climate."
QUIXOTE:	"You miss the point."

SANCHO: "You are willing to sacrifice human lives to keep your equities investments safe, Quixote."

QUIXOTE: "They are my friends' life-blood."

SANCHO: "What about the La Nina? In good times, it is a contributing factor to hurricane intensity. Now, coupled with increased sea surface temperatures in the Atlantic it will spell disaster. Think about the people in Florida and Cape Cod."

QUIXOTE: "Sancho, if we start dealing with a problem before it occurs and it does not transpire we have wasted time and money."

SANCHO: "Your friends work at being stupid, don't they, Quixote?"

QUIXOTE: "Plausible deniability and the economy are our ways out of this mess, Sancho."

SANCHO: "Quixote, the blight that was Katrina will soon spread over the Gulf. How much it will spread this year--I do not know. But I do know that the climate's impact on economic activity will soon render our wealth useless unless the financial system is tuned to our new environment."

QUIXOTE: "You mean like carbon trading?"

SANCHO: "No I don't mean carbon trading. Carbon trading is a cherry in a shit storm, Quixote."

QUIXOTE: "Sancho, I have never heard language like that from you."

SANCHO: "With carbon trading you are telling us we are doing something about global warming by doing nothing. In the end, that delays a substantitive response to global warming---thereby condemning people to death and misery while wasting time, energy, and money on obsolete models."

QUIXOTE: "You've called our efforts on global warming 'Death by Newbies'."

SANCHO: "I hadn't realized that the death of others was an acceptable way for you and your friends to feed your money-for-blood-portfolios. Perhaps the term 'Economic Vampires' might have been a better term."

QUIXOTE: "It does give the phrase 'blood bank' a new spin. Regardless--the economy must be taken care of at all costs."

SANCHO: "Quixote, the economic system of our planet is fragile. By refusing to make the hard decisions, hiding from facts on global warming, and micro-managing the popular response to global warming, your friends have proven the U.S., markets are not up to the task of coping with climate change."

QUIXOTE: "Maybe the economy is a little fragile in these difficult times."

SANCHO: "If it is that fragile, Quixote, why would we depend on it to help us? It will certainly collapse under the climate barrage because it cannot to cope with non-linear changes. You have proven that with your fear."

QUIXOTE: "Logic will not be tolerated. Think carbon intensity."

SANCHO: "Oh, that's right, your friends need to stay out of the light."

QUIXOTE: "Don't think of us as ghastly. Think of us as chic in our habits."

SANCHO: "Think about reducing CO_2 output by 70% immediately. Enhance the structural transition to low energy usage and begin working on storm preparations as if you were fighting a war. You cannot run. You cannot hide. Sooner or later the dawn will break over you and your friends."

QUIXOTE: "We are following a no-regrets policy."

SANCHO: "You can't even do that right."

QUIXOTE: "We have made mistakes. That is true--but with increased surveillance, a police state filled with fear, ongoing propaganda on terror, and economic tyranny--my friends think they can get through the near term with only minor discomfort."

SANCHO: "Your friends have the boldness to support reports saying an asteroid 100 years ago, or electro-magnetic radiation from distant stars, causes global warming--instead of the accepted scientific viewpoint humans have altered of the radiative balance of the planet--that can only mean one thing."

QUIXOTE: "What is that?"

SANCHO: "Junior and his friends are well on their way to being remembered as the greatest mass murderers in the history of our species. And you can take that to the bank."

March 22, 2006
Sancho, Quixote, and Roller Coasters

SANCHO:	"Quixote, here is that second bottle of rum. Where do you want it?"
QUIXOTE:	"On the table, but be careful it is a bit rickety--I think those ants eat wood as well as people."
SANCHO:	"Fire ants can be dangerous, Quixote. Maybe another location would make sense for your roller coaster?"
QUIXOTE:	"Sancho, we need to stay the course."
SANCHO:	"Quixote, you're digging a ditch to hold up a roller coaster in a mound of fire ants. Why don't you move your excavation a few feet to the east?"
QUIXOTE:	"Because then someone will say I ran. And there is no way I am going to get caught again by someone saying that."
SANCHO:	"But Quixote, the support for the roller coaster is supposed to be over there anyway. The only reason you started digging here was you miscalculated."
QUIXOTE:	"Fire ants or not, miscalculation or not, the roller coaster goes here because that's where I started digging my hole."
SANCHO:	"Can't you see it is going to fall down around you?"
QUIXOTE:	"I'd rather be wrong and stay the course than, ah, damn. Oh I don't know."
SANCHO:	"It's your grave, Quixote. There was no way I am going to ride that roller coaster of yours."
QUIXOTE:	"It's not permanent. My friends asked me to build this model of the roller coaster here so we could work out the bugs."
SANCHO:	"That doesn't mean you add bugs to the system to flush out the ones you don't know about, Quixote."
QUIXOTE:	"That's what you think. We know what we are doing."
SANCHO:	"Who ever heard of a roller coaster called the Weather?"

QUIXOTE: "Hey, we got away with Banana Republic for a store--this ought to be a breeze."

SANCHO: "More like a tornado. So how come the roller coaster supports are so big?"

QUIXOTE: "Well the first big drop is called La Nina. The second one, a bit smaller is El Nino. We need to make it high enough that the cars keep moving. We would have disaster if the cars stopped moving."

SANCHO: "Bicycles are nice."

QUIXOTE: "They do not enhance the weather roller coaster, Sancho."

SANCHO: "No kidding. So what is that big circular turn going to be called?"

QUIXOTE: "We were going to call it the Carbon Trader but since it spins you around and you get nowhere, or we will call it Wacky Weather."

SANCHO: "And that smell tunnel?"

QUIXOTE: "The part where you feel your stomach turning is the Aerosol tunnel. You know I never knew building a roller coaster model was so much work, Sancho."

SANCHO: "Well if you didn't redesign it every time you saw something you didn't like--it might be easier."

QUIXOTE: "I think I am going to have to name that part where it loops around and goes down under the whirly thing on top."

SANCHO: "It looks dangerous."

QUIXOTE: "Well no one has gotten killed yet so it must be safe, Sancho. I'll call it the Distant Future part of the ride."

SANCHO: "The most dangerous part?"

QUIXOTE: "Precisely."

SANCHO: "I see. And the purpose of this is to get people used to what is going to happen in climate change?"

QUIXOTE: "Don't be silly--have you ever heard of the show called Wild Fire?"

SANCHO: "I think so."

QUIXOTE: "The more we can blunt horrific terms on the weather roller coaster the better we are at keeping you all from reacting to its danger and the reality of your circumstance."

SANCHO: "Quixote, it seems a little late for that. Even the people down at the nut-house are beginning to fathom a problem."

QUIXOTE: "Sancho, trust me, the people in Silly Valley haven't a clue. We've got them so tied up in a game called green chase they'll never see the whole problem--until they are well along the weather roller coaster."

SANCHO: "What is the green chase--the environment?"

QUIXOTE: "Dollars, marks, yen, farthings, and pounds, my boy: The pursuit of loot--in this case through green things."

SANCHO: "How could people be so...confused?"

QUIXOTE: "Sancho, I asked them if they wanted to ride my roller coaster. They all said yes. So that is all I am required to do."

SANCHO: "Why would they do that--they can see it isn't safe. Anyone can see that."

QUIXOTE: "I told them their ride would make them rich--or at least pay their mortgage."

SANCHO: "That would do it."

QUIXOTE: "Myth has its place in governance. Hand me the rum spray bottle."

SANCHO: "Thirsty?"

QUIXOTE: "I am sure this will get rid of the insurgents. Hmm, didn't work yet. We'll try again in little bit."

SANCHO: "Quixote, some of those fire ants have almost completed munching on your table. It won't be long until your rum's felled."

QUIXOTE: "It looks useless to me against these insurgents."

SANCHO: "How can they be insurgents if this is their anthill and we invaded it with our roller coaster support?"

QUIXOTE: "That's the beauty of spin, Sancho."

SANCHO: "But it seems idiotic and wasteful to fight with them when it was you who made the mistake. There goes your booze."

QUIXOTE: "You were right, the rum's failed--we need to stiffen our resolve on this roller coaster."

SANCHO: "Diagonal support might be a good idea at that, Quixote, but I don't think that's what you are talking about, is it?"

QUIXOTE: "I think we need to dig up every square inch of this yard and find every fire ant colony."

SANCHO: "Sounds like a plan to me, Quixote, but one question?"

QUIXOTE: "What's that?"

SANCHO: "What are you going to do with the rest of the calamities?"

March 24, 2006
Sancho, Quixote, and Noah

SANCHO:	"Quixote, just what is the matter now?"
QUIXOTE:	"We have a problem, Sancho: sea level rise."
SANCHO:	"Don't tell me conscience rears its ugly sound byte?"
QUIXOTE:	"Sancho, there are terrorists in our government."
SANCHO:	"Excuse me, Quixote? Try that again."
QUIXOTE:	"I just received a secret memo to begin an in-depth investigation of Noah."
SANCHO:	"What does a biblical person have to do with our government?"
QUIXOTE:	"Biblical? For a well-informed servant, Sancho, I am surprised you do not know about the National Oceanic and Atmospheric Administration."
SANCHO:	"That's NOAA. Your memo--see--it talks about the guy who built the ark because of the floods. Noah--as in the Bible?"
QUIXOTE:	"Oh, now it makes sense. I feel much better. Okay, now I can pursue this terrorist group across the globe. Let's see whom can we bomb next?"
SANCHO:	"That's the Quixote, I have come to fear and ponder. So, what do you and your friends have against Noah?"
QUIXOTE:	"I have nothing against him, Sancho. I just believe that we need to monitor this terrorist's activity in our country and abroad, so freedom can bloom."
SANCHO:	"Quixote, the guy is dead."
QUIXOTE:	"It doesn't matter, according to this other memo; it says 'his followers are everywhere.' Junior's attorney sat with me in my office and just now showed me incontrovertible evidence that large portions of the suspect population in this country can be traced back to Noah and his family--and we all know what family means to those people. Blood is thicker than water."

SANCHO: "Seems like they are both on the rise."

QUIXOTE: "Huh? Oh, look at this; remind me to talk with that lawyer about his spelling."

SANCHO: "He had Noah spelled wrong too?"

QUIXOTE: "He's a new guy--you have to give him a break."

SANCHO: "Quixote, if you take the bible literally we all come from Noah and his family."

QUIXOTE: "See, Sancho, their insidious theistic bent infects all of us-- even you. This must be why they called me in--to fight the evil propaganda of Noah and his sea rise terrorists."

SANCHO: "Quixote--this is a bit over the edge--have you been lifting Junior's meds?"

QUIXOTE: "Sancho, certain elements of our society are trying to push the eco-nut global warming agenda by saying the oceans are rising quicker and quicker."

SANCHO: "The seas are rising, Quixote. The rate of the rise is also accelerating--rapidly. That's pretty common knowledge in the scientific community."

QUIXOTE: "Good--then our programs keeping scientists mute are working perfectly--because no one else knows."

SANCHO: "I forgot the truth matters little in the face of a rising equities market, Quixote."

QUIXOTE: "Precisely, Sancho. Noah's viewpoint might impact the economy negatively. Here, on this other document--it says: 'After careful investigation we are set to announce that Al Qaeda, Saddam Hussein, and Jessica Simpson, are directly descended from the first eco-terrorist, ah, give me the pen. They spelled it wrong again. N-O-A-H, Right? Noah--"

SANCHO: "Perfect."

QUIXOTE: "--And that elements of the communist party and all the environmental organizations have a cult-like blood tie to N-O-A-H.'"

SANCHO: "Quixote."

QUIXOTE: "Then I will add: 'And that certain scientists in this country are being conscripted to follow--in lockstep--his heinous beliefs about the oceans rising."

SANCHO: "But you agree the seas are rising."

QUIXOTE: "I do."

SANCHO: "So shouldn't we do something to address the problem?"

QUIXOTE: "What problem, Sancho?"

SANCHO: "Global warming causes sea level rise. Also, the glaciers and ice sheets are not only melting, they are entering a second phase of melting and fracturing."

QUIXOTE: "Sancho, can the big pieces of ice break off into the ocean and raise sea level along with the runoff?"

SANCHO: "Without a doubt, my liege--the faster runoff rates we were seeing are just the first step, next comes the increase in glacial surge--we are starting to see that now. Then the chunks increase in size. Eventually the melt water increases and the very large ice chunks will slide into the sea. That will be followed by an almost continuous flow off the ice sheets rather than fits and starts. After that the large ice sheets on the WAIS will move because the decrease in their mass will allow for land beneath the ice sheets to rebound upwards."

QUIXOTE: "Prove it--just kidding. So, soon it will not just be water, but city-sized pieces of ice flowing off the land into the sea?"

SANCHO: "Kind like cowing, Quixote, not calving."

QUIXOTE: "Very funny."

SANCHO: "Quixote, even now the rising seas are causing damage--lots of it--they even make hurricanes more destructive."

QUIXOTE: "Prove it, Sancho."

SANCHO: "Again? The reports are everywhere. But do not worry; if your friends do something they have no exposure to the belief they are being proactive, decisive, or capable."

QUIXOTE: "Many views do scare them, Sancho. Did you know I have in my custody documents that were found in the possession of certain insurgent scientists that plainly calls out flooding in major coastal cities like Miami, New York, and San Francisco? My friends and I believe we must protect our people from these terrorist acts--science will just have to wait."

SANCHO: "Quixote, you wouldn't know reality if someone splashed you in the face with an iceberg."

QUIXOTE: "With God's help, good poll numbers, and a strong stock market my friends and I think we can make the issue go away. We may have to provide some money to social programs to do it--we really made a mess out of Medicare--but that's okay. We can tie it all together with another tax cut."

SANCHO: "You can't spin away sea level rise, Quixote."

QUIXOTE: "Sancho--we had already put so much pressure on the scientists they were nervous about even bringing up sea level rise--without a mountain of data."

SANCHO: "A victory--no doubt--for you and your friends."

QUIXOTE: "Hell, why else would they say just a three foot sea level rise in a hundred years? Sancho, I already told you slowing the public perception of global warming is job one."

SANCHO: "And I thought the scientists were just being conservative."

QUIXOTE: "Our influence is subtle because we wouldn't want anyone to stand up calling for a major reduction in greenhouse gas output."

SANCHO: "You mean like a 75% reduction of GHGs within a decade?"

QUIXOTE: "You used to say 70%, Sancho."

SANCHO: "Quixote, you may not understand the implications of the accelerating sea level rise--but I do. You should be shocked at how fast the process is proceeding. Look at it this way: Every year some new climate parameter, not just sea level rise, pops up and turns against us."

QUIXOTE: "Kind of like the planetary poll numbers turning against humanity day by day and getting worse...fast."

SANCHO: "Something along those lines, Quixote."

QUIXOTE: "So we massage the poll numbers, Sancho, with aerosols."

SANCHO: "Quixote, fifty years ago, we figured out that air pollution was bad for us. Now you are advocating using air pollution to adjust global warming. That's idiotic."

QUIXOTE: "First things first, Sancho. We hunt down and bring to justice all the terrorists in this country with ties to Noah and his family of religious zealots."

SANCHO: "You need help. You are wasting time, Quixote."

QUIXOTE: "Exactly--but nonetheless--I am going to brand sea level rise as their weapon of mass destruction. I can get traction on that, Sancho."

SANCHO: "Quixote, they are warning about sea-level rise--they aren't causing it."

QUIXOTE: "Of course they are--we are going to label them energy terrorists because they drive SUVs, they buy highly processed consumer goods. They buy big homes. Clearly Sancho, the terrorists are the cause of sea level rise--not my friends."

SANCHO: "The truth is coming out, Quixote--albeit at a glacial pace."

QUIXOTE: "I believe we can throttle even that tiny bit of truth--with the right media reports."

SANCHO: "Quixote, you do know the rising sea levels will cause disasters in the short term, don't you?"

QUIXOTE: "Of course. The evidence is everywhere. The risks are enormous. Do you know what sea level rise will do to the San Joaquin Valley? Or how much food comes out of that area?"

SANCHO: "So why not fix the problem, Quixote?"

QUIXOTE: "In due time. First the terrorists--the so-called scientists--will be exposed for their insidious connection to the environment, and Noah, and how they try to undermine freedom marching across the globe."

SANCHO: "The scientists are not trying to stop your march,they are just suggesting you turn in your jackboots for galoshes."

QUIXOTE: "By the time I am done vilifying Noah no one will ever take that radical group seriously again."

SANCHO: "You mean because they are under the jurisdiction of the Department of Commerce?"

QUIXOTE: "What--oh don't be silly, Sancho. Not that NOAA, the real problem--that terrorist insurgent, Noah, the one that is undermining our American way of life."

SANCHO: "Oh, I thought you meant the organization that muffles the truth, conscripts scientists for private interests, hampers honest scientific investigation, and keeps the facts from the public-- all to support its own objectives at the expense of the people?"

QUIXOTE: "Exactly. I can see no other term for them, other than a 'terrorist organization'. Can you, Sancho?"

April 3, 2006
Sancho, Quixote, and Hope

QUIXOTE: "Sancho, you are just so dismal about all this global warming stuff. Lighten up."

SANCHO: "I will do my best, Quixote. What brought that on?"

QUIXOTE: "Hope. We want everyone to see hope is in our future. You and your eco-nut-scientists are pushing global doom too far. Have you considered opening a 'Dystopia-Is-Us' store?"

SANCHO: "Quixote, do tell me about the beacon of light and trust."

QUIXOTE: "You are bludgeoning the public with horror stories about global warming. Junior and my friends are promoting hope, Sancho."

SANCHO: "So, by screwing in low voltage light bulbs, driving a little less, and composting veggies, the climate will be okay, Quixote?"

QUIXOTE: "For now, yes. My friends are suggesting you-all push the little things that everyday people can do, to make a difference."

SANCHO: "Like voting?"

QUIXOTE: "Oh no, never, not that. Voting gives the common person power. My friends will not allow that."

SANCHO: "So, Quixote, you want apathy, fostered by a lack of hope--as the public's reaction to global warming--promoted, in part, by scientists and legislators spewing useless ideas and ineffective solutions."

QUIXOTE: "It's policy, Sancho."

SANCHO: "How do you sleep at night, Quixote? Or do you and your friends just hang upside down waiting to feed?"

QUIXOTE: "Sancho, there is nothing we can do. The ship of economic activity cannot be turned quickly enough to cope with global warming. We must stay the course."

SANCHO: "Oh, the Exxon Valdez gambit--always useful when there is a drunk at the helm--Quixote."

QUIXOTE: "Sancho, economic disruption will not be tolerated by the public."

SANCHO: "Now that is defeatist, Quixote."

QUIXOTE: "We're realists...Why are you laughing? What's the joke, Sancho?"

SANCHO: "I'll tell you. You are so predictable, Quixote. First, you say we cannot modify our economic system."

QUIXOTE: "Precisely, Sancho."

SANCHO: "Because it is fragile."

QUIXOTE: "Very."

SANCHO: "But, Quixote, then you say that when our economic system is battered by climate change, its resiliency will carry us through the tough times."

QUIXOTE: "Exactly, Sancho."

SANCHO: "But we can't adjust the economy's course--when it is healthy?"

QUIXOTE: "Now you have it, Sancho."

SANCHO: "How absurd--that's part of my laughter. Here comes the rest: What do you do when the public wakes to your economic myth?"

QUIXOTE: "We plan to say technology makes it all right. We plan to turn the whole planet into one big Silly Valley of techno-ninnies. Worst case, Sancho, we'll start another war."

SANCHO: "Quixote, who is left to bomb?"

QUIXOTE: "We could bomb South America--this limits the vegetation there and that cuts down on the moisture coming north, which will limit hurricanes from the south. We are so proactive on global warming."

SANCHO: "Quixote, being one with the planet, does not mean we need to control the planet."

QUIXOTE: "We are in control, Sancho."

SANCHO: "Yet you pander to the notion of social responsibility, feign morality, and erect facades of caring. That doesn't seem like control to me. It looks like fear."

QUIXOTE: "The public perceives control--therefore we are in control."

SANCHO: "With apologies to Descartes. Global warming can be addressed."

QUIXOTE: "Without a doubt, Sancho--but facing the reality of global warming and dealing with it means my friends must give up their hold on power--literally. So we push technology uber alles--right after Adam Smith has left the building."

SANCHO: "So we can make a difference. You admit that, Quixote."

QUIXOTE: "Oh, my, yes. But solutions are not important. Power is."

SANCHO: "And therefore the hope you put out, whether it's in the form of science, politics, economics, or technology--they are all gambits."

QUIXOTE: "You are so naive. Children will curse our generation."

SANCHO: "And your job is to make sure they curse someone other than your friends."

QUIXOTE: "Like politicians, economists, scientists, and technologists."

SANCHO: "Your predictability is a comfort, Quixote, but you need to get your brains out of your assets."

QUIXOTE: "Corporate assets have made America the country it is today. Technology will overcome!"

SANCHO: "Quixote, this technology to the rescue routine sounds like a Star Trek episode--what will you do when that fails?"

QUIXOTE: "We are thinking of pushing the alien thing. It's not such a leap after that. I think if we tell people aliens are going to help us, we can hold power until the end. And after that, it will not matter. The slide into ignorance will be complete."

SANCHO: "So that is your end-game--you and your friends want to push an exit strategy for civilization?"

QUIXOTE: "It makes every con worth it. We have not done so good a job of civilizing humans. Why are you smiling? I'd think this would seem sad from the standpoint of an uptight environmentalist."

Sancho: "Humor is one way to deal with global warming, Quixote."

Quixote: "Or maybe you finally see the humor of it all, Sancho."

Sancho: "You mean that we get what we deserve, Quixote? That the joke is on us for trusting godless, soulless entities to govern us?"

Quixote: "It is a difficult pill, no?"

Sancho: "Quixote, I love the alien finale--it bespeaks your friends' predictability."

Quixote: "So why are you smiling, Sancho?"

Sancho: "The public's inability to recognize your friends' path has ended today. The truth stares them right in the face. Oh, and Quixote, the game is far from over. After all--there are many paths. Alien indeed!"

April 5, 2006
Sancho Quixote, and the Tipping Point

QUIXOTE: "Sancho, please hurry. Unless we get these groceries into the house, the milk will reach the tipping point."

SANCHO: "I'm on my way, my chaotic despot, at this moment."

QUIXOTE: "Oh, and Sancho, please get me more shaved ice. My Manhattan has reached the tipping point as well."

SANCHO: "You mean the ice is melting, Quixote?"

QUIXOTE: "The term melt is so arcane, Sancho."

SANCHO: "Okay…Here is your ice, in a fully post-bifurcated state."

QUIXOTE: "My knowledge hit the tipping point when you said that."

SANCHO: "Ice--scattered in a bowl…Ah…Is there something new going on, Quixote?"

QUIXOTE: "I love tipped ice in my drinks. The design is so tipping point. Going on? Whatever do you mean, Sancho?"

SANCHO: "I believe your vocabulary has mislaid some of its adjectives. Shall I ask the EP to edit you back to normal?"

QUIXOTE: "Truth is, Sancho, my friends and I are demystifying the term tipping point by overuse."

SANCHO: "Why?"

QUIXOTE: "If we start using it everywhere now--when scientists and others use tipping point--it will have less impact."

SANCHO: "Seems the impact should be heightened, not diminished."

QUIXOTE: "We are on opposite sides of the ice on this issue. But I will say we have reached the tipping point in this conversation."

SANCHO: "I'll just get the rest of the sandbags out of your limousine."

QUIXOTE: "Hold on a minute. Maybe you can help me? And don't tell anyone what I am about to tell you, okay?"

SANCHO: "You have my word as a proper noun."

QUIXOTE: "Did you know the human time-scale and the geologic time-scale are not the same?"

SANCHO: "I had that one figured out, Quixote."

QUIXOTE: "Sancho, someone told my friends that a moment in the geologic time-scale might not be a moment to us. Instead, it might be more like a decade, or more, to humans."

SANCHO: "Different scales imagine that? So you are asking if the notion of a 'tipping point' is really 'tipping years' to us--because humanity's time-scale is so much shorter than the Earth's time-scale?"

QUIXOTE: "Yes."

SANCHO: "Since a decade is a miniscule part of planetary history and therefore a moment, or a point, I'd say yes. I wonder, does this mean the human time-scale is the 'Original Spin'?"

QUIXOTE: "That was funny, Sancho. Thank you."

SANCHO: "We are in this together, Quixote."

QUIXOTE: "Sancho, I think the climate's tipping point is going to be long and unpleasant. An event we will all experience."

SANCHO: "To say nothing of the resulting climate regime that follows."

QUIXOTE: "We don't know what that will look like, do we, Sancho?"

SANCHO: "All we really know is it will be foreign to our experience."

QUIXOTE: "My understanding has reached a tipping point. This is too scary. I think we are right to keep talking about the tipping point to downplay it."

SANCHO: "Or maybe you are using the term tipping point all the time, because deep inside--as beings of this planet--we feel the event. As a result, the term has become pervasive."

QUIXOTE: "Nonsense, Sancho, I have direct orders to ignore the planet--for the sake of the economy."

SANCHO: "I do believe your friends have committed a faux pas--insofar as corporate greed is concerned--Quixote."

QUIXOTE: "The penalties are stiff for that one, Sancho. Do you really think some environmental, planetary, woo-woo thing is going on here: rather than simple megalomania and avarice leading to deceit?"

SANCHO: "I do."

QUIXOTE: "From my friends?"

SANCHO: "Quixote, they loathe admitting the heinous crime of connection to the planet, but who knows? It could be the planet has sway--even over stockholder greed."

QUIXOTE: "You blaspheme--greed is reality. Selfishness is sentience. Dominion demands dividends. There is no way the planet could have weaseled its way into my friends' consciousness."

SANCHO: "Their walls to cognition are formidable--but I believe it has happened."

QUIXOTE: "No--we are predators. We don't react. We are decision-makers. We seize the moment by the throat and own it."

SANCHO: "Well, Quixote, I'd say your seizure has met the tipping point--and it is us."

April 12, 2006
Sancho, Quixote, and the Talent Show

QUIXOTE:	"Sancho, will you have the sandbags in place by April 22?"
SANCHO:	"I believe so--expecting an Earth Day flood?"
QUIXOTE:	"No, but please make sure the bags are sturdy, Sancho."
SANCHO:	"What's the problem? Is it the rains?"
QUIXOTE:	"No, Sancho."
SANCHO:	"The funnel cloud formations propagating faster than you thought, Quixote?"
QUIXOTE:	"No."
SANCHO:	"Fear of deadly Pacific storms?"
QUIXOTE:	"No."
SANCHO:	"The dying deciduous trees collapsing down upon us?"
QUIXOTE:	"No. Oh that reminds me, Sancho, see if you can get me more wood for the fireplace."
SANCHO:	"You are a true citizen of Gaia--so why the Earth Day deadline?"
QUIXOTE:	"My friends and I are going to have a get-together here and I want the bunker walls completed in time."
SANCHO:	"You are celebrating Earth Day in a storm bunker? Sounds like you, Quixote."
QUIXOTE:	"Sancho, we're having a bit of a fete--sort of a 'Roast the Earth' get-together--all in good fun."
SANCHO:	"Who will be running the blood sucking booth? Or did you put the nix on that one for Earth Day?"
QUIXOTE:	"We are not vampires, Sancho."

SANCHO: "I see, Quixote. So this Earth Day fete is a little bit of lighthearted juke for you and your friends. And the theme spoofs global warming?"

QUIXOTE: "They've been spoofing Earth Day for years, Sancho. No reason for you to be so sanctimonious."

SANCHO: "So why did they invite you this time, Quixote? They have never invited you to one of their parties before?"

QUIXOTE: "I'm the master of ceremonies. They want to thank me for another year of inaction on global warming. We're calling the party: 'A Cap and Trade Jamboree'."

SANCHO: "So there is a lot of buffoonery, nonsense, and tall tales followed by excuses, hand-wringing, and concerned looks."

QUIXOTE: "Humor, music--that kind of thing--but the talent show will be the focus."

SANCHO: "Quixote, what kind of talent are these people going to display besides how to portray the deaf, dumb, and blind chimps dressed in Armani?"

QUIXOTE: "First we start with the Oil and Gas Soft Shoe Singers doing the tune 'Don't Worry, Be Happy'. Then we follow it with the Cyclical Pundits retelling tricky patter on climate editorials from TV news shows and Wall Street Journal."

SANCHO: "Oh that will be funny."

QUIXOTE: "Precisely--then we have the Dancing Economists on the wonders of societal rigidity sponsored by Viagra and Exxon/Mobil."

SANCHO: "Presumably the economists will climax their ditty by impaling Gaia from all sides."

QUIXOTE: "With stock certificates, junk bonds, and little oil wells."

SANCHO: "Who will cast the first coal?"

QUIXOTE: "Coal has another little skit. They will do it with the boys from nuclear. The gang will dress up like The Rolling Stones--some of them glowing of course--and sing 'Under My Thumb'."

Sancho: "So your Earth Day celebration is shaping up to be sort of a nihilist folly?"

Quixote: "Then for the teens, we have puppet show called Strings and Media. They are my favorite."

Sancho: "Why is that, Quixote?"

Quixote: "They do a very funny comedy rap routine called 'Impress, Express, Digress, Redress, and Repress'."

Sancho: "It will have 'em rolling in the aisles."

Quixote: "We tag on that with The Minstrel Trailers."

Sancho: "I shudder to ask."

Quixote: "A bunch of the guys and gals from FEMA will dress up in blackface and tap dance to an updated version of 'The Battle of New Orleans'."

Sancho: "Propriety be damned, Quixote?"

Quixote: "Oh then there is the Windup Academics--they do this wonderful act in mime--with their palms out."

Sancho: "So the whole range of social degradation caused by inept leadership, displayed for the purpose of...policy-maker dispensation?"

Quixote: "No, it's all for fun. Wait until you see the updated version of 'Waiting for Godot'. The play has been recast with some of the senior managers from NOAA, NASA, and NSF. One gal dresses in a lab coat and shows up with a report that proves global warming. They immediately send her to a park bench where she waits for funding that never arrives."

Sancho: "Your Dada would be proud, Quixote."

Quixote: "Don't be so parochial, Sancho. Oh, and then we have a group of shill-scientists doing a formation ballet with hockey sticks to the tune of 'Luck be a Lady'."

Sancho: "How about you, Quixote, what will you do besides your MC shtick?"

QUIXOTE:	"I'm working with the Cap and Trade Con men--it's a group of DC lobbyists. We're going to do a spoof on social responsibility. In it, we keep adding and subtracting numbers so nothing gets done."
SANCHO:	"So art does mimic real life."
QUIXOTE:	"What does that mean?"
SANCHO:	"Can I go back to stacking sand bags now, Quixote?"
QUIXOTE:	"Then there are the dancing girls in grass skirts."
SANCHO:	"That's a bit risqué isn't it, Quixote?"
QUIXOTE:	"They dance in a deep pool, and as they dance, we slowly fill the pool. It is going to be funny to see the look on their faces when they realize they can't swim with those heavy grass skirts."
SANCHO:	"Wit déclassé--whose idea was that one, Quixote? You?"
QUIXOTE:	"Actually, some of the guys from the think tanks came up with that one. I could never come up with something as warped as that."
SANCHO:	"Quixote, all you'd need is the funding. Are the dancers forced to disrobe so they do not drown?"
QUIXOTE:	"Well the name of the skit is 'Sink or Swim', Sancho."
SANCHO:	"Which just happens to be your friends' global warming strategy--so are there plans to throw environmentalists to the lions?"
QUIXOTE:	"My friends and I have risen well beyond that kind of Romanesque entertainment, Sancho."
SANCHO:	"Time for me to stack sand bags, Quixote."
QUIXOTE:	"Oh, Sancho, you need to hear this one: When the girls are done, we release water from the side of the pool. Anyone who can't get out of the way washes down the muddy hillside hitting the bunker. We're calling it 'Love Your Levee, or Leave It'."
SANCHO:	"Won't your friends balk at that embarrassment?"

QUIXOTE: "I'm not stupid. We're opening the sidewall where the wait staff has a break area. Can't let the servers get too comfortable."

SANCHO: "You have a remarkable hold on reality, Quixote--but isn't a mini-flood dangerous?"

QUIXOTE: "We will make sure no one gets hurt. It isn't like a real flood."

SANCHO: "How good of you."

QUIXOTE: "Then for the kids, we have the whale hunt, the seal bashing, and my favorite: the coral kill."

SANCHO: "Coral kill, Quixote?"

QUIXOTE: "The kids get balloons filled with hot water. They throw them at different colored sugar sculptures that look like coral. First one to collapse their local ecosystem wins."

SANCHO: "You are making me ill, Quixote."

QUIXOTE: "Another favorite for the kids will be the 'Aerosol Rag'."

SANCHO: "As in asthma?"

QUIXOTE: "A pianist with an air tank pounding out 'Love Is In The Air'."

SANCHO: "Why are your friends so perverse, Quixote?"

QUIXOTE: "Sancho, do you think global warming is easy for us?"

SANCHO: "You mean condemning their fellow humans to misery and death from global warming bothers them, Quixote?"

QUIXOTE: "Don't be a servant for a moment, will you, Sancho?"

SANCHO: "I get it--there's concern about cutting GHG emissions by 75% within a decade."

QUIXOTE: "You know, I could put you on as a comedian."

SANCHO: "I'll pass. So what are your friends' stressors?"

QUIXOTE: "Portfolios are at risk. Fortunes are waiting to be stolen. Resources still need to be plundered--also--it's not easy making decisions on which companies should prosper and which ones should die."

SANCHO: "To say nothing of the people."

QUIXOTE: "Exactly, Sancho."

SANCHO: "The strain on you and your friends certainly does appear to be taking a toll, Quixote. Will you be serving snacks, Thorazine, or just barbecuing the poor?"

QUIXOTE: "Wait till you hear the finale: a tribute to Junior with the tune 'Mack the Knife'."

SANCHO: "Very fitting--and it sounds like a fun time for your friends, Quixote."

QUIXOTE: "Do you really think so, Sancho?"

SANCHO: "Quixote, there is no doubt in my mind this Earth Day gala of yours is precisely their idea of fun."

April 15, 2006
Sancho, Quixote, and the Rain

SANCHO: "Look at that rain, Quixote."

QUIXOTE: "What's the big deal, Sancho? It's just rain."

SANCHO: "And those clouds, what is the thing on the horizon, under the clouds? Isn't that what they call a rain-foot?"

QUIXOTE: "It's rain, Sancho."

SANCHO: "Isn't that where tornadoes come from, thunder storms?"

QUIXOTE: "I suppose so."

SANCHO: "So then what are those whirly things that appear briefly then disappear under the clouds."

QUIXOTE: "Sancho, I don't know what you are talking about."

SANCHO: "Okay, Quixote, I'm probably just being too careful--but I'd swear I keep seeing rotation in those spindly clouds that seem to drop out of the bottom of the thunderstorms--and there are so many of them."

QUIXOTE: "Sancho, you're seeing things. It doesn't mean anything."

SANCHO: "So then, Quixote, in say five years or so, those formations will not develop further and become say funnel clouds or tornadoes?"

QUIXOTE: "Of course not, Sancho. Have you met my new friend?"

SANCHO: "I see you have a new puppy, Quixote, What's his name?"

QUIXOTE: "Toto."

SANCHO: "Of course it had to happen sooner or later. Might I also enquire of you, my wizard, if perhaps those large hailstones we saw the other day are anything to worry about?"

QUIXOTE: "Of course not. But you know I do have a concern."

SANCHO: "What would that be?"

QUIXOTE: "Did you see that scarecrow move?"

SANCHO: "Of course not, Quixote. Scarecrows are made of straw. Perhaps the winds that tore that limb from the fir tree moved the scarecrow. Whoops there it goes."

QUIXOTE: "Which way, Sancho, to the east or the west?"

SANCHO: "Is one way better than the other, Quixote."

QUIXOTE: "You mean: is one 'which way' better than the other 'which way'?"

SANCHO: "Something like that, Quixote."

QUIXOTE: "I don't know. My gosh was that a cow flying by, Sancho?"

SANCHO: "No it was a picture of a goat that was munchin' on grass."

QUIXOTE: "Kind of like a munch kin to the cow?"

SANCHO: "I guess you could say that, Quixote."

QUIXOTE: "It is so windy. This storm is a whoppa'."

SANCHO: "I marvel at your weather acumen, Quixote."

QUIXOTE: "Well I am tired of that cowardly line you keep giving me."

SANCHO: "On climate change or on cutting GHG emissions by 75%?"

QUIXOTE: "Both. I am sure it is not cowardly lying, this need to follow the gold."

SANCHO: "That road does call you, Quixote. To me it is just tin."

QUIXOTE: "Oh, the rain has stopped. Look a rainbow. What's that on the other side of it?"

SANCHO: "Which side?"

QUIXOTE: "The far side."

SANCHO: "Oh, I see. It looks a balloon."

QUIXOTE: "Funny seeing one of those out during a thunderstorm, aye Sancho?"

SANCHO: "It sure is."

QUIXOTE: "So have I convinced you we don't need to worry about cloud formations developing into tornadoes all across the country in a few years. I swear on Toto it will never happen."

SANCHO: "Of course, Quixote, it couldn't be clearer."

April 23, 2006
Sancho, Quixote, and Drake's Passage

QUIXOTE:	"Sancho, I finally understand a key problem of global warming."
SANCHO:	"Fabulous, Quixote, meanwhile, I need to find out what's wrong with the Hoover, then we can talk."
QUIXOTE:	"I'm shocked, Sancho."
SANCHO:	"Quixote, the Hoover is broken and the floor is covered with 'I'm the real Daddy Warbucks' buttons'. Plus, it's beginning to rain again…"
QUIXOTE:	"Have a seat on that sand bag under the Exxon awning and we can talk."
SANCHO:	"Fine, Quixote, dazzle me with your lucidity."
QUIXOTE:	"I was sitting down with some of the brains from the think tank yesterday."
SANCHO:	"--The gang with the lamp shades on their heads and the tee shirts that said, "Science For The Uninformed'?"
QUIXOTE:	"Right, well we were sitting around arguing how best to spin this thermohaline system and Drake's Passage to the masses…"
SANCHO:	"You were? I am impressed your friends from your intellectual chicken ranch were debating so lofty a topic, Quixote."
QUIXOTE:	"We only seem like lightweights."
SANCHO:	"Of course, Quixote, so how did this Socratic frat party lead to an environmental epiphany?"
QUIXOTE:	"It's all about spin and global warming, Sancho."
SANCHO:	"I see, Quixote, another world-shattering insight brought forth courtesy of indentured servitude--and scotch."
QUIXOTE:	"You don't get it, Sancho."

SANCHO:	"Do I have to?"
QUIXOTE:	"Global warming is causing the spin of the earth to change, Sancho."
SANCHO:	"It's so miniscule--we lose picoseconds every so often from global warming. It hardly matters--other than as a curiosity."
QUIXOTE:	"See, I knew you didn't get it."
SANCHO:	"But, Quixote, the moon has far more impact--the time lost means nothing."
QUIXOTE:	"Sancho, time has nothing to do with it. If the spin of the Earth is slowing then my spin on the news is going to be slow as well. There is no way I am going to be as effective as I once was. I think I'll have a guy from CEI writing a paper on it."
SANCHO:	"Quixote, I think you need to go lie down. You are missing…"
QUIXOTE:	"Sancho, if the planet's spin is slowing, then so is my spin."
SANCHO:	"Quixote, it doesn't work that way."
QUIXOTE:	"Prove it, Sancho. I am part of the environment, right"
SANCHO:	"You know, Quixote, you win. I think I am just going to let it be: the spinning planet, spinning infinitesimally slower, impacts news spin. Can I go back to cleaning up the mess?"
QUIXOTE:	"So, Sancho, you agree?"
SANCHO:	"Anything you say, my despotic sage."
QUIXOTE:	"Good, then I need your help on something. I need to spin--taking into account the slowing spin due to global warming--a connection between Drake's Passage and the thermohaline system."
SANCHO:	"First what do you think Drake's Passage is, Quixote?"
QUIXOTE:	"A tectonic event which modified the flow of the thermohaline system by removing a barrier to the current."
SANCHO:	"That was impressive--oh--you're reading it off your sleeve."
QUIXOTE:	"Junior taught me to remember things that way."

SANCHO: "Quixote, I'll go with what you say for the time being. What's the problem? Do you want to claim Drake's Passage does not exist?"

QUIXOTE: "We batted that around yesterday--but I think because of global warming and my reduced spin capability--we have to accept its existence."

SANCHO: "A wise notion on your part."

QUIXOTE: "Thank you, Sancho. Anyway, as you know, the thermohaline system seems to have reduced its effectiveness and so we want to tie it in Drake's passage."

SANCHO: "Why?"

QUIXOTE: "To convince people that a less effective heat transfer system."

SANCHO: "--The thermohaline system."

QUIXOTE: "--Right--is nothing to worry about."

SANCHO: "Say it is cyclical, Quixote. You're getting a lot of mileage on that with storms."

QUIXOTE: "It doesn't seem to be working this time--something I am attributing to the reduced effectiveness of spin due to global warming."

SANCHO: "Ah, maybe. The planet will do that to you, Quixote. If only Gaia had more respect for economics."

QUIXOTE: "The original eco-terrorist--Gaia--did you hear we made eco-terrorism a crime in Pennsylvania?"

SANCHO: "Let me know when you serve the summons on Gaia."

QUIXOTE: "We'll get there. America is the most powerful nation on the Earth."

SANCHO: "Quixote, what's the question?"

QUIXOTE: "Do you think it is possible that we might claim the opening of Drake's Passage was a cooling event and not a warming event? What are you laughing at?"

SANCHO: "Did your think tank boys come up with that one--as a way to lessen the concern about global warming?"

QUIXOTE: "We all did. Why are you laughing?"

SANCHO: "You give me hope, Quixote. In answer to your question--I think you might get somewhere with that hypothesis. You might even attribute a multi degree drop in temperature, in the Palocene period, to the opening of Drake's Passage."

QUIXOTE: "We could get some of our guys to do a paper on it. I think NSF has some funding that I could get my hands on. But what good is the temperature drop, Sancho?"

SANCHO: "Well, that temperature drop might mean that the current thermohaline system is more efficient in moving heat around the planet due to the opening of Drake's Passage."

QUIXOTE: "So I can say the temperature drop is the result of the opening of Drake's Passage?"

SANCHO: "Keep working, don't let that nasty planet thing get to you."

QUIXOTE: "So instead of the thermohaline system warming the planet, it might--in the long term--actually have cooled the planet?"

SANCHO: "Right, Quixote."

QUIXOTE: "So then I can say that systems change in many ways and this reduction in the thermohaline current's effectiveness is just a minor cyclical event we need not worry about."

SANCHO: "And use Drake's Passage as proof. It is perfect, Quixote."

QUIXOTE: "That will help us--but I don't understand something. If the current configuration of the thermohaline system is a cooling event--rather than a warming event--won't that mean as the thermohaline current becomes less effective, temperatures will rise?"

SANCHO: "See, Quixote, you have a new global warming theory right smack dab in your lap. A few years ago, without the impact of a slowing planetary spin, you would have been able to spin your way right past that thought. But here we see global warming slowing your spin."

QUIXOTE: "By jiminy, you're right, Sancho. Gaia is so insidious--even if the thermohaline system is a cooling system not a warming system, I can ignore it. I am no slave to Gaia. But isn't the suggestion of this enough to modify some presumptions of our climate models?"

SANCHO: "Don't worry, Quixote, it's just a bunch of data and if there is one thing you and your friends are still good at--despite the impact of global warming on your spin--it is the ability to keep science muzzled."

QUIXOTE: "Thank you, Sancho. We are rather proud of that."

SANCHO: "I know you are, Quixote. And please, consider my support on planetary cooling by Drake's Passage as my way of saying thanks to you and your friends for all they have done for science, America, and the world."

April 26, 2006
Sancho, Quixote, and the Horsemen

QUIXOTE: "Sancho, the truck is here."

SANCHO: "Here I come, Quixote. Talk about a vanity-fair, what do you want with that? It's a satellite."

QUIXOTE: "We're going to put it next to our greenhouse."

SANCHO: "For what?"

QUIXOTE: "Global warming, its effects are starting to show and I need data on the greenhouse effect."

SANCHO: "And who could doubt your commitment to scientific truth?"

QUIXOTE: "This isn't science, Sancho. Do you know that people are getting sick from seafood? Citizens are losing their home insurance on the East Coast. Water problems are mounting. Pipelines are a mess because the permafrost is melting. We've got floods and tornadoes. The Gulf is targeted again for another big hurricane. We must appear as if we are doing something. Heck, even gasoline prices are on the rise."

SANCHO: "I am touched by your concern. Obviously selling less product and making more money is a major sacrifice."

QUIXOTE: "Sancho, when we raise the price of oil people cut back on driving and the CO_2 it emits."

SANCHO: "Do you believe that will work, Quixote?"

QUIXOTE: "It might help, Sancho. You have to admit the free market system has sallied forth to rescue the planet."

SANCHO: "Enter the knights of fossil fuels to cut car use a few percentage points--and in the process gouge people for the privilege. It's a rather warped world--wouldn't you agree?"

QUIXOTE: "Bah, you eco-nuts are never satisfied, Sancho. No one is going to cut back unless we force him or her to cut back. You know I had this same discussion with some of our brethren in the northern colonies."

SANCHO: "What colonies to the north, Quixote?"

QUIXOTE: "Canada."

SANCHO: "Canada is a sovereign nation, Quixote."

QUIXOTE: "Sancho, quit being so naïve, the Arctic Ocean is about to be ice-free and my friends plan to own those waters. Our Canadian colony is the tool for owning the Arctic's riches."

SANCHO: "Insane greed is another example of global warming's effects."

QUIXOTE: "Sancho, the world is getting uglier and uglier."

SANCHO: "Thanks to your friends, Quixote."

QUIXOTE: "Money talks. Wake up. Besides, it will take major destruction in the U.S., for our citizens to face global warming."

SANCHO: "Thanks to media spin."

QUIXOTE: "You flatter me, Sancho."

SANCHO: "By the time you can no longer spin away the effects--it will be too late, Quixote."

QUIXOTE: "For many of them, that's true. Think of it as my friends' contribution to the population problem, Sancho."

SANCHO: "It's worse than just a bit of culling my Zarathustrian liege."

QUIXOTE: "We know that, Sancho."

SANCHO: "And still, your friends will do almost nothing about it."

QUIXOTE: "We raised gasoline prices didn't we, Sancho?"

SANCHO: "And cancelled home-owner's insurance across the East Coast."

QUIXOTE: "Who says altruism is dead, Sancho? Consider the current gas price squeeze--sure we make money hand over fist screwing the population--but look at it from our standpoint."

SANCHO: "I could use a laugh, Quixote."

QUIXOTE: "Instead of accepting the need to cut emissions, Junior is trying to get more gasoline out there."

SANCHO: "Quixote, he is a political ninny and an environmental pariah--you count on that."

QUIXOTE: "Sancho, it's a fact, but how could any rational effort ever be convened, when Junior's advisors have the insight of stale toast, the spine of jellyfish, and the morals of a crack dealer?"

SANCHO: "And so we all skip merrily off the cliff of global warming, our pockets empty, our TVs on, and a smile painted across our face."

QUIXOTE: "He who dies with the most toys wins--help me with this bird will you, Sancho? I need to get data on the greenhouse to the gang at CRRI."

SANCHO: "Quixote, which set of nihilists, suggested this research abomination?"

QUIXOTE: "The Chicken Ranch Research Institute thought it might help our efforts to prove global warming doesn't exist."

SANCHO: "What for? I thought that effort was winding down."

QUIXOTE: "Some scientists are still trying to convince us that global warming is real. Sancho, they think we don't get it."

SANCHO: "I bet you all laughed yourselves silly on that one, Quixote."

QUIXOTE: "Lackeys are sometimes made and not born. But they deserve it--some scientists think we are idiots about science. One of the new guys thinks we can use their ego to our use."

SANCHO: "I guess that sums it up, Quixote."

QUIXOTE: "Meaning what, Sancho?"

SANCHO: "The four horsemen of our apocalypse are: a lack of insight, a lack of grit, a lack of morality, and a lack of sense."

QUIXOTE: "Some would say cutting CO_2 by 75% shows a lack of sense as well, Sancho."

SANCHO: "I'd like to be wrong about that one, Quixote. I really would."

May 3, 2006
Sancho, Quixote, and the AGGI

QUIXOTE: "Sancho, did you see the AGGI came out yesterday?"

SANCHO: "What's an AGGI, Quixote?"

QUIXOTE: "The Atmospheric Grifters Grave Index."

SANCHO: "From the same folks who brought us carbon intensity?"

QUIXOTE: "Partly--it's in collaboration with the Department of Commerce. How did you know, Sancho?"

SANCHO: "Just a guess--and the AGGI assesses what, Quixote?"

QUIXOTE: "It quantifies the number of dead who have read ridiculous climate change reports and then forgot to protect themselves from the realities of their life."

SANCHO: "Truth is such an ugly word for you, Quixote, I know, but how are the numbers compiled?"

QUIXOTE: "Well they take the number of dead from global warming events in the last twelve months, then count the number of corporate-sponsored global warming reports, op-eds, and interviews, put out in the same period. They divide mortality by the number of bogus reports and then massage the trend using an exclusive network of monitoring stations--and adjust that with the uncounted dead--and a factor based on chocolate consumption in Duluth."

SANCHO: "With an attention to detail that baffles a sane mind. Quixote, how can one track the uncounted dead?"

QUIXOTE: "Sancho, once we get someone off the unemployment rolls and out of the workforce they are as good as forgotten. But we really don't lose track."

SANCHO: "So, Quixote, tell me, who gets onto this 'feel good' list? People like the dead of New Orleans?"

QUIXOTE: "And other disasters."

SANCHO: "Like FEMA?"

QUIXOTE: "Negligence, nonsense, nepotism, and numbers--they have their place--Sancho."

SANCHO: "Quixote, what's the use of your AGGI index, besides a heartwarming moment at the club?"

QUIXOTE: "It tells us quite a bit. First, its acceptance tells us how well we are doing at keeping the public deadened to climate change."

SANCHO: "This, despite the slowing climate change spin due to climate change slowing the Earth's spin?"

QUIXOTE: "I have gotten quite a bit of funding for that problem."

SANCHO: "All of which shows you that stupidity is not a class-based event, Quixote. Are your friends worried about the climate?"

QUIXOTE: "It's the upcoming hurricane season, Sancho."

SANCHO: "Just another excellent adventure--so what does AGGI say about storms, Quixote?"

QUIXOTE: "Nothing. The AGGI clarifies trends. When the numbers go up, we know we are doing a great job of keeping the public away from the key issues. And when the numbers go down, it says we are successful at keeping the public dulled."

SANCHO: "So in one case the trend is positive and in the opposite case, the trend is positive as well--a standard of deviation no doubt applauded by non-standard deviants. Has Junior added the Mad Hatter to his staff, Quixote?"

QUIXOTE: "He'd never take the job. We have a mountain of staffing problems. Ethics, corruption, graft--they are digging into our ranks."

SANCHO: "Indictments have a way of cutting down on employment applications."

QUIXOTE: "No one wants to leave a contrail in their wake of service."

SANCHO: "Or even admit such a thing exists, Quixote."

QUIXOTE: "Agreed, but overall we do work to keep a sunny, though somewhat diffused, outlook."

SANCHO: "The day is young, Quixote. Maybe by the PM, a fresh breeze of particles will blow through."

QUIXOTE: "I'm not holding my breath. Junior's second-in-command has a lean and hungry look."

SANCHO: "So that means we may have a new team trying the same old tactics, Quixote?"

QUIXOTE: "'Stay the course', that's their mantra."

SANCHO: "This all rates rather high on the TTTG--you know."

QUIXOTE: "What's that, Sancho?"

SANCHO: "The Titanic Theory of Government."

QUIXOTE: "Can we keep using it? Icebergs will be gone soon."

SANCHO: "Cogent to the end, Quixote. Tell me about the report."

QUIXOTE: "Well the numbers went up too much this year, but not as much as they might have gone up. In fact, the numbers might have gone up a lot more. So we are gratified at the inert response. It wasn't a remarkable year for super storms--even with the huge increase in death and destruction in 2005."

SANCHO: "Just another average ho-hum, solar-cyclical year, for the unconnected masses as they died in droves. So are things getting worse--fast--is that your cloudy sky, Quixote?"

QUIXOTE: "The death rate is escalating and the destruction is compounding. Global warming is accelerating far faster than imagined and we condemn a ton of people to die every year from climate change, Sancho."

SANCHO: "So you are saying?"

QUIXOTE: "In response to the crisis, we have upped our output of insipid reports and hired more bloggers. With God's help, we will be able to keep the ratio of disaster to bogus report right in line--and awareness low."

SANCHO: "That should make you proud, Quixote. On the other hand, there is water, food, disease, sea level rise, and storm issues on the horizon."

QUIXOTE: "With a few more reports like the AGGI, we'll have the planet--and its climate--drowning beneath the thundering hooves of the Wall Street bulls."

SANCHO: "Or turn Wall Street into a Pamplona meat stall."

QUIXOTE: "We are not dumb, Sancho. Don't you understand the depth of our commitment?"

SANCHO: "Is there a mystery?"

QUIXOTE: "Those who die from global warming can no longer buy goods and services."

SANCHO: "Oh, the humanity of it all--what will you do, Quixote?"

QUIXOTE: "Count them as voters--as soon as possible. After all, when you are given lemons, you make lemonade."

SANCHO: "Or as the AGGI shows us: When you are given doctored, irrelevant reports--you make jokes."

May 9, 2006
Sancho, Quixote, and a Positive Outlook
(Previously Unpublished)

QUIXOTE: "Sancho, did you hear, the Dow is going to hit a new high?"

SANCHO: "Quixote, the U.S., ranks second lowest in infant mortality among industrialized nations."

QUIXOTE: "So what? The stock market is booming."

SANCHO: "Quixote, children, infants, are dieing here in the U.S., at rates not seen for generations."

QUIXOTE: "Sancho, it is obviously the fault of the parents--either they didn't get pre-natal care, or the mother didn't watch her diet, or there were drugs. You know how they are."

SANCHO: "Who are they?"

QUIXOTE: "Sancho, can we dwell on the positive for once? I am so sick of your negative attitude."

SANCHO: "Sorry Quixote, let's talk about something positive--like oil."

QUIXOTE: "My friend and yours, Sancho."

SANCHO: "Oh, now I see what you mean by positive. Positive means anything that fits inside the fiscal quarter and allows your friends to manipulate the market."

QUIXOTE: "Sancho--you get smarter every day."

SANCHO: "You had better hope I am the only one."

May 10, 2006
Sancho, Quixote, and Joke Time

QUIXOTE: "Hi, Sancho, you are home late."

SANCHO: "That yellow rental truck broke down, twice. What a piece of junk."

QUIXOTE: "They're just trying to make a buck off unsuspecting consumers. It's America's way now."

SANCHO: "You wax poetic, Quixote. What are you doing out here in the chromatic dusk?"

QUIXOTE: "I love the corona in the clouds at dusk. It's so…natural."

SANCHO: "Quixote, spraying the air with pollutants to mask the effects of global warming--is hardly natural."

QUIXOTE: "Think of pollution as your friend."

SANCHO: "Introducing PM into the atmosphere to mitigate global warming is like introducing rabbits to Australia for food."

QUIXOTE: "Meaning?"

SANCHO: "It is going to backfire."

QUIXOTE: "Don't be silly. Did you hear, the Dow will hit a new high?"

SANCHO: "So we can all be emphysema-émigrés. But what's a little asthma among friends? I don't think I like your brand of hope, Quixote."

QUIXOTE: "Sancho, consider the alternatives to a weak economy."

SANCHO: "Well our strong economy has the U.S., ranked pretty low in infant mortality among industrialized nations."

QUIXOTE: "See what I mean? Sancho, relax, I was only kidding."

SANCHO: "I see, Quixote. It's joke time. How about--ah--how many wild-fires does it take to spin the idea that Florida has always had rampant fires?"

QUIXOTE: "I don't know Sancho, how many fires?"

SANCHO: "None, you need to fire the bush first."

QUIXOTE: "I don't get it."

SANCHO: "Of course not. Okay so why do bears in Yellowstone need cell phones?"

QUIXOTE: "I didn't think they did?"

SANCHO: "Exactly--how about this one--what do you say to an extinct butterfly?"

QUIXOTE: "I can't think of anything to say, Sancho."

SANCHO: "Perfect. So why do we need them? Tell me how a stock market brings hope when New York City has to brace for hurricanes and tornadoes?"

QUIXOTE: "That is no joke--that's going to cut the trading day--we'll have to work on that one. See, Sancho, we are working on real solutions to global warming as well as the nonsensical."

SANCHO: "A cavalier attitude towards the climate based in madness. No wonder you and I have the big time. In a decade, West Coast storms will regularly hit hurricane wind speeds. In twenty years, China and India will have to share a diminishing supply of water off a drying Tibetan plateau."

QUIXOTE: "Why are you so worried India and China?"

SANCHO: "The lesson of global warming Is we need to plan and adjust -not ravage and spin. The depleted glaciers in Tibet will cripple some of the largest river basins on the planet. That will impact many people."

QUIXOTE: "See that's what I mean. We need hope."

SANCHO: "We need sound policy. China and India battling each other for water is neither sound policy--nor a smiley-face event-- regardless of how you and your friends spray-paint the sky."

QUIXOTE: "Sancho, you talk so seriously."

SANCHO: "And you talk like America is a street corner crack-dealer."

QUIXOTE: "You can't argue with success, Sancho."

SANCHO: "Quixote, a lack of water will destabilize the whole of Asia."

QUIXOTE: "There you go again, worrying about unimportant events. Did you know crisis and opportunity are the same symbol in Chinese?"

SANCHO: "Quoting fortune cookie logic from godless commies?"

QUIXOTE: "You got me there. We are a consumption based society rather than a sustainable society--we hunt and harvest."

SANCHO: "Your friends plunder and loot like locusts, Quixote."

QUIXOTE: "Sancho, you are simply reacting to some miscues in spin by the media. Your concerns are merely the ebb and flow of doubt caused by uncontrolled thought patterns. Why don't you watch some TV, then go out and buy something?"

SANCHO: "Good joke. Now it's my turn."

QUIXOTE: "Lay it on me, Sancho."

SANCHO: "Economics are more important than climate."

QUIXOTE: "Very funny--but you needn't worry--people will always take care of their loyal servants, Sancho."

SANCHO: "And you might have made the funniest joke of all--if the realities of climate change were not so morose. Quixote, a destabilized climate leads to a destabilized population."

QUIXOTE: "So what are you complaining about? With a loss of economic activity, there will be a severe reduction in greenhouse gases. A few percentage points of drop in GDP, a little recession, some deflation and voi la--instant 40% reduction in GHGs."

SANCHO: "But 40% is not enough--and what about the destruction of infrastructure, society, and support systems?"

QUIXOTE: "The cycles starts anew. W build again and it's boom times for all--a GMO chicken in every pot."

SANCHO: "Quixote, CO_2 persists in the atmosphere for more than three generations. Do you really think you and your friends can cope with more than decades of increasing climate anarchy?"

QUIXOTE: "Are you saying the climate problems will continue even if we cut down on greenhouse gases going into the atmosphere?"

SANCHO: "You already knew that. Everyone does. But, just for clarification: No matter what we do at this point--the tragedy continues to get worse--especially since your aerosol system for mitigation pumps CO_2 directly into the upper atmosphere while here on the ground the output of CO_2 rises every year."

QUIXOTE: "Sancho, think dim."

SANCHO: "I don't need to, Quixote. You and your friends already have that covered."

May 11, 2006
Sancho, Quixote, and Oscillation

Quixote:	"Hi, Sancho, you're home late. That's a bad bruise on your forehead--what happened?"
Sancho:	"I was on the freeway in a new rental truck. Suddenly it started oscillating on me--rocking back and forth. Then without warning the swaying reinforced itself and the rocking got worse--even after I took my foot off the gas."
Quixote:	"It must have been chaos driving down the freeway, Sancho."
Sancho:	"Chaos is exactly right--even after my foot was off the gas--the truck tipped over on its side. The clowns at the rental company had the temerity to say it was my fault."
Quixote:	"Were you speeding, Sancho? Whose fault was it?"
Sancho:	"I was carrying the same load of sandbags as always. The same size truck, and I was driving well below the speed limit."
Quixote:	"Cheap springs, I bet. Once the truck's swaying reinforced itself, it went out of control."
Sancho:	"Those dunderheads almost killed me with their equipment."
Quixote:	"No one puts profits ahead of my servant. Do you want me to call one of the lawyers? Scooter isn't busy anymore and neither is Jack. Maybe Al is your man?"
Sancho:	"Quixote, think about what you are saying. Do you really want to make a commotion about putting corporate profits ahead of the tipping point?"
Quixote:	"I see. Maybe I'll let you handle it, Sancho."
Sancho:	"So what are you doing out here in the gray day looking up at the sun with polarized sunglasses?"
Quixote:	"I love the prismatic corona in the clouds near the sun, Sancho. It's so...Cheery. You know it has always been there."
Sancho:	"Quixote, desperately spraying the air with pollutants to mask the effects of global warming--is hardly cheery."

QUIXOTE:	"Sancho, think of pollution as hope. We're returning the atmosphere to a kinder, gentler, dirtier time."
SANCHO:	"The introduction of foreign agents into the climate randomizes an already energized situation--global warming--to say nothing of emphysema and asthma."
QUIXOTE:	"Don't be silly. It's just the gang from A.S.P., hard at work, spending tax dollars for a dimmer future."
SANCHO:	"Quixote, the climate buffers are worn by humanity forcing the radiative balance. The atmosphere might respond like that truck and start oscillating out of control."
QUIXOTE:	"So adding aerosols to the atmosphere is similar to speeding up a truck with bad shocks? Is that your point, Sancho?"
SANCHO:	"No. Aerosols are more like stomping on the brake peddle, then slamming on the gas pedal without knowing the effect--while rounding a turn in a truck with bad shock absorbers."
QUIXOTE:	"You know I love the sight of graying skies at end of the day."
SANCHO:	"Sorry to bother you with forethought, Quixote."
QUIXOTE:	"Sancho, you saw change coming as the truck began to rock back and forth. You took your foot off the gas and it still tipped over on you."
SANCHO:	"Quixote, after a certain point the oscillations were self-reinforcing. That's what the tipping point is all about. At some point there is nothing further we can do--"
QUIXOTE:	"--But crash."
SANCHO:	"And that's why we need to recognize the climate issues."
QUIXOTE:	"Maybe, the vehicle was simply reacting to corporate miscues. The crash might merely be a transportation ebb."
SANCHO:	"You are missing the point. The clowns at the rental company didn't understand a swaying truck falls over because of design."
QUIXOTE:	"They probably did. They were protecting their assets."
SANCHO:	"Fine. How do I get you to understand, or care about a chaotic response in the atmosphere due to the introduction of new atmospheric compounds?"

QUIXOTE: "Well if it is self-reinforcing--like the truck swaying--we'll know within a few years, Sancho."

SANCHO: "It may be too late by then. Consider this: The climate system is part of a larger planetary system. We are a small part of the planet. Is it so hard to see that the chaotic atmosphere compels us to further randomize it at this joint--and that's why your friends are pumping pollution into the atmosphere?"

QUIXOTE: "You are saying we humans are tools of the planet--pawns of its chaotic systems--and not the other way around?"

SANCHO: "Could it be more obvious, Quixote?"

QUIXOTE: "My friends will never accept a hypothesis which says they do not control their environment."

SANCHO: "Do you really think we can cope with more than sixty years of increasing climate anarchy? Can you imagine driving an out-of-control vehicle for thousands of miles, year after year?"

QUIXOTE: "That is an accident waiting to happen--like that truck."

SANCHO: "Quixote, the unstable vehicle is our atmosphere and it is randomized a bit more every day by our emissions."

QUIXOTE: "I see. Are you saying our climate problems may get worse, even though we feign cutting down on greenhouse gases while adding new pollution directly into the atmosphere?"

SANCHO: "Do you know how ridiculous that question sounds?"

QUIXOTE: "A bit--but we get away with it. Let me try again. So no matter what we do at this point--the climate tragedy will continue to get worse?"

SANCHO: "Especially since your mitigation system not only adds new components to the atmospheric engine--in the process--you infuse more CO_2 directly into the upper atmosphere. Of course here on the ground the output of CO_2 rises every year as you enhance albedo. So you support weather shifts with no clarity on the long term effects of the tactic."

QUIXOTE: "So what do we do, Sancho?"

SANCHO: "The only solution is to take your foot off the climate gas pedal--before the climate systems begin to randomize out of control like bad springs on a cheap truck."

QUIXOTE: "Sancho, my friends will not take their foot off the economic gas pedal."

SANCHO: "Quixote, that's because the notion of dim makes sense to them. Like vampires, they cannot tolerate the light. Of course that can change--if your friends fully engage their brains by altering the proximity of their frontal lobes to their posterior."

May 26, 2006
Sancho, Quixote, and the Black Box

SANCHO:	"Okay, Quixote, I've put the paint away. What next? Good heavens what did you do to the vacuum cleaner?"
QUIXOTE:	"I wanted to make room for it in that black box, Sancho."
SANCHO:	"It's too big--but I see you already know that. Which view of our economic albatross have you decided to blur this week?"
QUIXOTE:	"More is good and less is bad."
SANCHO:	"Something seems to be missing in your explanation."
QUIXOTE:	"I am making a climate model. The black box, the globe, the greenhouse, the refrigerator, the vacuum cleaner--they are all objects for the model."
SANCHO:	"Why the vacuum cleaner, Quixote?"
QUIXOTE:	"Sancho, I need to associate the vacuum of space with global warming--then I place the whole shebang inside the greenhouse along with the refrigerator."
SANCHO:	"It seems a poor model, Quixote."
QUIXOTE:	"The vacuum cleaner bags have become a definite issue, Sancho. The search for truth is a harsh mistress, isn't she?"
SANCHO:	"Plus she seems to have a sense of humor. What prompted you to simulate global warming using these objects?"
QUIXOTE:	"The guys at the Confusion Extension Institute, CEI, have recently stated that CO_2 influences our atmosphere."
SANCHO:	"Confirming for us all, their preeminence in the world of chicken-ranch-researchers."
QUIXOTE:	"Are you disagreeing with their theory? Are you disagreeing that the sun warms the planet and the atmosphere keeps the planet warm and that the resulting benign weather has made our good life possible?"
SANCHO:	"Oh, I agree with that."

QUIXOTE: "So, then maybe you'll agree with CEI's new public service advertisement which they titled, 'Science: Just Call It Lies'."

SANCHO: "Well their campaign targets them for litigation--even though they do appear to be a bit slow on the cognition side."

QUIXOTE: "CEI is a conservative organization, Sancho."

SANCHO: "I think I'll just leave that opening for a joke alone, Quixote. So your plan is to eviscerate truth with--oh of course--your black box model of the planet?"

QUIXOTE: "You understand our thrust."

SANCHO: "As so often happens--your friends' thrusts are out of sight. What facts are you seeking to impale to prove more is better?"

QUIXOTE: "That there has always been an atmosphere, and global warming has always existed."

SANCHO: "Quixote, you may be headed towards an epiphany."

QUIXOTE: "Don't count on it, Sancho."

SANCHO: "Silly me."

QUIXOTE: "I need to show more CO_2 as a positive event. Otherwise, people will see consumption as a curse--not a blessing."

SANCHO: "Imagine that--insight into our economic albatross."

QUIXOTE: "Our economy is a finally tuned machine of planetary subjugation and human degradation. Do you realize Gaia impacts policy without permission?"

SANCHO: "Think of Gaia as providing clarification on balance."

QUIXOTE: "Sancho, I have had enough of Gaia's clarification for a lifetime. How could more not be better? What about our economy--what about the stock market?"

SANCHO: "Is copulation between equities all your friends know?"

QUIXOTE: "Without portfolios, some of my friends might never copulate."

SANCHO: "Just another reason to support sustainability."

QUIXOTE: "Without an atmosphere, the Earth would have had too many extremes. Therefore carbon dioxide is our friend."

SANCHO: "Balance, Quixote--as in the opposite of avarice."

QUIXOTE: "And there is our disagreement. You are one of those foolish eco-nuts who will not accept our spin."

SANCHO: "Quixote, the excess heat in our atmosphere energizes the random nature of storms, sea level rise, heat, rain fall, disease, and so forth. That's why global warming is dangerous."

QUIXOTE: "Those are just facts; like temperature is just another way of saying we are keeping too much energy here on the planet. Energy we are better off sending out to space--isn't that right?"

SANCHO: "The lesson of climate change is all about balance, Quixote. You have an opportunity to enlighten your friends on the worth of balance over unmitigated consumption."

QUIXOTE: "Are you nuts? Help me empty the refrigerator. My friends are beginning to look like morons."

SANCHO: "They are passed that point, Quixote."

QUIXOTE: "Move the refrigerator into the greenhouse. Then I'll put the globe and the black box inside it--and make sure to open the door. When the refrigerator doesn't make ice, because the greenhouse is so hot, I'll make notes. Then I'll get in a band of friendly IT people to recreate the model and massage the data. Next stop: a few commercials, a feature story on the networks, an op-ed in the Journal, and there we are."

SANCHO: "Where are we?"

QUIXOTE: "The wonders of investing in a no-ice-globe. More is better!"

SANCHO: "What about the vacuum cleaner?"

QUIXOTE: "I'll label it a constant."

SANCHO: "Quixote, it's too late for propaganda."

QUIXOTE: "Without a doubt, Sancho, but if you think I plan to rock the self-satisfied leaders of this society out of their cradle of foolishness with the knowledge they are commandeering the blame for global warming by attacking facts--you're nuts."

SANCHO: "Quixote, the problem is bigger than their vanity."

QUIXOTE: "No, Sancho. It really isn't."

SANCHO: "I stand corrected. Quixote, there are horrors we can no longer avoid."

QUIXOTE: "Sancho, only a fool tells a band of ignorant sociopaths of their failures."

SANCHO: "Quixote, only a coward labels the righteous as fools."

May 30, 2006
Sancho, Quixote, and KISS

SANCHO: "That's a lot of paper, and pastel colors too--what for?"

QUIXOTE: "My friends have decided to address global warming and solve problems, Sancho."

SANCHO: "Forgive my lack of enthusiasm, Quixote, how do those little rectangular papers achieve this lofty goal?"

QUIXOTE: "Tickets."

SANCHO: "For what, Quixote?"

QUIXOTE: "First, we're tackling the transportation problem--so we need tickets. I'm coordinating the focus groups on ticket color appeal for the high end consumer."

SANCHO: "Minutia over momentum, Let them punch their own ticket."

QUIXOTE: "Without class distinction, we lose market leverage. A ticket says a lot about whom, and what, you are: first class, business class, coach class, frequent traveler, or budget traveler."

SANCHO: "Are we talking about air transportation?"

QUIXOTE: "No. That will not change, Sancho."

SANCHO: "Air travel is a significant contributor to global warming. It seems a good place to make changes."

QUIXOTE: "Sorry, no can do. We cannot curtail the air transportation industry. Then we have the hospitality industry on our backs, car rental, luggage, jet manufacturers, the list goes on."

SANCHO: "Quixote, moving bits and bytes around the globe is efficient, and far less energy intensive than moving people."

QUIXOTE: "Sorry. The teleconferencing lobby is just too small, Sancho."

SANCHO: "What about decreasing the output of CO_2 per mile traveled? An energy efficient light rail system between regional hubs or a mass transit system from hubs to cities might be fruitful. What about an electric car powered by residential solar cells?"

QUIXOTE: "Nope. We can't do that either. Do you know how hard it was to crush the electric car industry? Thank goodness, their lobby was small. Sancho, the American car companies are struggling. The oil companies have wilderness to ravage, and the construction companies are enjoying a boom in highway construction--to say nothing about concrete, aluminum, and steel. Nope, the car industry stays the same."

SANCHO: "What are the tickets for, Quixote?"

QUIXOTE: "It's something you will like. We have plans for individual trams that move people to small city shopping locations."

SANCHO: "Like enclosed bicycles?"

QUIXOTE: "Oh no, better than that. These are powered rail vehicles."

SANCHO: "And the tickets?"

QUIXOTE: "We match the ticket colors to the tram. That way class distinction flows over the waiting platforms. Don't you love simple solutions, Sancho? The different color pods will have various levels of amenities. Some will be small and austere; others will be large and luxurious. Our profit projections make Viagra look like the Edsel."

SANCHO: "What system are you replacing, Quixote?"

QUIXOTE: "Some cars, but mostly walking and bicycles."

SANCHO: "Are you insane, Quixote?"

QUIXOTE: "Our plan is to shut down bicycle manufacturers and thereby limit their CO_2 impact on the environment. Plus a reduction in the need for shoe leather will cut down on cow flatulence."

SANCHO: "Bicycles and cows must have a small lobby."

QUIXOTE: "Almost non-existent--in any case--our studies show people will not wait for mass transit if they need to shop on their lunch hour. Also, no one wants to bicycle to work because of the inconvenience and the need to freshen up afterwards."

SANCHO: "It would make far more sense to provide showers at corporate locations and longer lunch times to facilitate walking or bicycling? The health benefits are enormous and the resulting community links will go a long way to strengthening families and our ties to each other."

QUIXOTE: "Sancho, there is a huge untapped market of ignorant green investors and pie-in-the-sky technologists who understand nothing about climate change. They just want to invest in green projects. Do you understand?"

SANCHO: "Quixote, can you see beyond the deal--and start considering the energy expenditure and the resulting social impacts? Your myopic friends recognize decay in our society only to embrace social failures and therefore justify their gluttony. Has anyone focused on the energy exchange impact as people move from bicycling to little SUVs?"

QUIXOTE: "Sancho, that hardly matters. We get in, we build a project; we make our money and we are out. I think the pastel green ticket will be our business class ticket."

SANCHO: "So your strategy is to deal with global warming by economic slash and burn?"

QUIXOTE: "It works in the rain forests, Sancho. Our objective is to leverage our power through investor ignorance on global warming. Haven't you seen how nicely that strategy has worked with biodiesel, ethanol, nuclear, and a whole host of other alternative energy projects the public embraced without understanding the facts? Why not expand the concept as we sink deeper into the mire?"

SANCHO: "How can your friends be so loathsome, Quixote?"

QUIXOTE: "Sancho, my friends have come to terms with themselves. Maybe we'll use the dirty brown ticket for economy class. As long as the public is ignorant, we are not seen as loathsome. It's all about perception."

SANCHO: "Your friends have commandeered self-actualization as a way of giving themselves permission to be brats."

QUIXOTE: "Global warming is just another market, Sancho."

SANCHO: "So rather than fostering urban use of bicycles and improved walking spaces for people, or teleconferencing for meetings, or distributed energy production, regionalized manufacturing, and localized food production systems, your friends propose slash and burn projects, like ethanol, nuclear energy, and wasteful public transportation projects?"

QUIXOTE: "Exactly."

SANCHO: "Quixote, have you ever heard of the KISS principle?"

QUIXOTE: "The pink ticket is out--too much controversy. What's KISS?"

SANCHO: "Keep It Simple Stupid--it's an engineering term."

QUIXOTE: "Simplicity provides solutions, not the huge profits my friends seek. We govern with a sophisticated eye towards the inherent evil that is humanity."

SANCHO: "Part and parcel of that evil is unrestrained profits and corporate governance of the population--nothing self-serving about that viewpoint, Quixote."

QUIXOTE: "I'm sure my friends will not see the humor in that sarcasm."

SANCHO: "I never thought it was funny. Large complex projects will not work."

QUIXOTE: "That's obvious. Have you encountered any hyper-heat trapping events when they use aerosols at the wrong time?"

SANCHO: "I doubt they will admit their gnat-like complicity in the Chaotic equation of our horrors. Can you say tipping point?"

QUIXOTE: "They never use it with context. Why do you think I am researching the color of tickets? Minutia is the wave of the future. Do you think the deep red color has cache, Sancho?"

SANCHO: "Sooner or later the climate will reveal the truth about faux efforts to combat global warming, Quixote."

QUIXOTE: "So what? One day the population will understand the complexity of global warming and the interrelationship between climate and society--but that will take time--so long as we control the media."

SANCHO: "So you have plausible deniability and huge profits to boot."

QUIXOTE: "What do you think the term, 'No-Regrets Policy' means?"

SANCHO: "The pity is your friends don't recognize the scale of the event."

QUIXOTE: "The worst-case scenario says we get someone to make a movie to marginalize the problem. Or, we will claim our enlightenment mirrors the society's awareness. I don't think a red ticket is good--it looks too much like blood. Do you know why my friends care about colored tickets?"

SANCHO: "So they can cut down more trees?"

QUIXOTE: "Don't be cynical."

SANCHO: "Silly me, I thought your idiotic projects were base stupidity."

QUIXOTE: "Hah, see we even fooled you. My friends really aren't complete idiots. A ticket means control. And control means increasing profits. And transnational corporations exist for one purpose. Do you know what purpose that is?"

SANCHO: "A halfway house for sociopaths?"

QUIXOTE: "To make profit for its shareholders, Sancho."

SANCHO: "So supporting a godless, soulless, entity--the very essence of a demon--is okay? Quixote, corporate entities sacrifice anything for their own pursuits. Yet they have no life; they have no conscience. A transnational corporation has no concern for people except as profit tools. They are entities that exist purely for their own expansion, glorification, and dominion. Your friends support that and that's why I think your friends are stupid."

QUIXOTE: "Well almost, Sancho. There is a human element: A corporate entity can't exert dominion without lobbyists and corrupt politicians to foster corporate goals."

SANCHO: "Or minions dumb enough to issue tickets on their behalf to soul-centered entities."

June 6, 2006
Sancho Quixote, and More Rain

SANCHO: "It's like jungle out there. There is so much rain and humidity."

QUIXOTE: "What rain, Sancho?"

SANCHO: "You know, that wet stuff falling from the sky that's pounding on your thick skull."

QUIXOTE: "I don't see any rain, Sancho. Oh, remind me to get more sand bags."

SANCHO: "Quixote, look out! You're about to step into a big puddle of...Mud."

QUIXOTE: "Where did all these puddles come from--and so quickly?"

SANCHO: "Ah, well, Quixote, those--over there--came from the rain storm that doesn't exist. Those puddles by the door--in front of the sand bags--they're from the river that overflowed for a third time this year."

QUIXOTE: "No doubt caused by a hundred year flood."

SANCHO: "--And those really big puddles over there, they are what's left of the roadway after the ice damn from the glacier up the valley broke--which you claimed wasn't really melting."

QUIXOTE: "So water's draining from the glacier--it will go away soon. After a few more seasons it will never flood again, right?"

SANCHO: "Quixote, farmers count on glacial runoff for a balanced water supply all year long."

QUIXOTE: "Bah, let them eat cactus."

SANCHO: "Sure, Quixote, go tell that to those who rely on Himalayan glacial runoff."

QUIXOTE: "What do they normally eat?"

SANCHO: "Rice, lots of it. But speak loudly, there are over a billion waiting to hear your anti-global nonsense. Face it, Quixote, you're up to your knees in the mud--bud."

Quixote:	"What mud?"
Sancho:	"You're sinking, Quixote, denial time is coming to an end."
Quixote:	"Prove it, Sancho."
Sancho:	"Your Gucci's are drowning in mother Earth."
Quixote:	"Okay, fine so there's some mud and there's some rain. Help me get out of this mess."
Sancho:	"No problem. Cut your GHG emissions by 75%."
Quixote:	"Can't do that. Give me a hand will you?"
Sancho:	"Why not cut your emissions by 75%? It's already obvious new economies are developing--ones not based on fossil fuels."
Quixote:	"Sancho, don't blaspheme. Let's just go water skiing down Main Street instead? Ouch, what was that?"
Sancho:	"That was a hailstone. Here come the hail storms again--like the ones that broke the windshield on your SUV."
Quixote:	"Big hailstones--freak storms--come once every fifty years. Ouch, that one hurt also."
Sancho:	"That was a tree branch."
Quixote:	"I thought this Elm tree would protect me. You know it's getting damp around my posterior. Damn, was that thunder? Sancho, a lightning bolt just killed a cow."
Sancho:	"Pretty windy too. You suppose the Elm might blow over?"
Quixote:	"Never, this Elm tree's strong and well-tended. It's been here a long time."
Sancho:	"Like the economy, Quixote?"
Quixote:	"In many ways, yes, Sancho. Just like the economy. The Elm by the house is stable with deep healthy roots."
Sancho:	"But if it blows over the roots aren't worth a damn, Quixote. The tree dies."

QUIXOTE:	"That will never happen. Trust me. There, the sun has come out. Everything's fine--and look--a rainbow over the corn."
SANCHO:	"What's left of it. Quixote, knee-high-by-the-Fourth-of-July will soon mean the size of the stalk piles when we need to clean up."
QUIXOTE:	"Don't worry, Sancho, we'll turn the piles into ethanol. Ethanol good. Me like ethanol"
SANCHO:	"No, Quixote. Ethanol bad, Ethanol take too much energy to produce and too much land to grow. Ethanol bad. It only stretches our dwindling supply of gasoline."
QUIXOTE:	"That explains the deal with the big auto makers, Sancho."
SANCHO:	"You mean Toyota and Honda?"
QUIXOTE:	"No I mean Ford, and GM."
SANCHO:	"GM--as in--'What's good for General Motors is good for the USA?'"
QUIXOTE:	"It does sound kind of foolish these days, Sancho. You know those damn stockholders insisted GM create profits, not innovation. Anyway, we've just cut a deal with them to forget electric cars and hybrids for more PERS money. Off we go, on to ethanol, coal, and a hydrogen future!"
SANCHO:	"A hydrogen future is a good one but we've about run out of time."
QUIXOTE:	"Prove it."
SANCHO:	"Quixote, your friends plan to get the public drunk on ethanol hoping the public will see the pink elephant of a hydrogen future coping with global warming."
QUIXOTE:	"Or coal. We've got the lobbyists working overtime on it."
SANCHO:	"Quixote, the unending ignorance, vanity, and greed of our elected officials can only be explained by the stupidity and avarice of America's boardrooms."
QUIXOTE:	"It's what has made America what it is today, Sancho. Say, what's that in the storm cloud off to the side?"
SANCHO:	"That's called a rain-foot, Quixote. "

QUIXOTE: "I keep seeing whirly, spindly clouds dropping out of the bottom."

SANCHO: "Knowing the location of a rain-foot in a thunderstorm can help save your life--or the lives of your children. The rain-foot is where tornadoes form. Tornadoes aren't just for Kansas anymore, Toto."

QUIXOTE: "Is it important to really understand a rain-foot, Sancho? I have a stock portfolio to keep track of and I can't spend time keeping one eye on the clouds."

SANCHO: "Get used to it. The effects of global warming show themselves with increasing frequency now. We must recognize weather's warning signs."

QUIXOTE: "The increased storms can't be from global warming. The bad storms are a simple cyclical event--like the hurricanes."

SANCHO: "You were wrong about pollution, the ozone hole, and global warming, Quixote."

QUIXOTE: "I might be wrong about the cyclical nature of the climate. But the damage will not be as bad in an evolving economy."

SANCHO: "Quixote, you are an ignorant self-satisfied, patrician who pontificates outmodes ideas."

QUIXOTE: "There is no such thing as global warming caused by man."

SANCHO: "Exactly. Keep an eye on the rain-foot--you'll soon see those whirly formations develop further into funnel clouds then tornadoes. You might also keep an eye out for dust devils. You're going to be seeing them in places you never expected."

QUIXOTE: "Are the storms strong enough to uproot trees?"

SANCHO: "Like the Elm near the white house--yes--and more."

QUIXOTE: "More what?"

SANCHO: "Remember those huge hailstones?"

QUIXOTE: "No such thing as huge hailstones, Sancho."

SANCHO: "You know, Quixote, Maybe you can turn corpses into ethanol. Soon you'll have lots of them on your hands."

QUIXOTE: "Don't be so sure, Sancho."

SANCHO: "About the increased mortality due to global warming, Quixote?"

QUIXOTE: "No--about us waiting to turn the dead into fuel--I'm pretty sure Junior's friends are already using the dead in support of fuel."

SANCHO: "And that's the truth. Oops, there goes your Elm tree. Ethanol anyone?"

June 7, 2006
Sancho, Quixote, and the Chocolate Hammer

SANCHO: "Wow, Quixote, did you buy all that farm equipment?"

QUIXOTE: "No, Sancho. My friends are shipping this machinery south. I'm changing the labels from foreign manufacturers over to American corporations."

SANCHO: "I have heard Japanese is a difficult language to read. So, Quixote, what are those three big vehicles with the agent orange nozzles on the back for?"

QUIXOTE: "One is for spraying fertilizer, the one next to it sprays weed killer, and the other one sprays bug poisons."

SANCHO: "They are all petrochemicals, Quixote?"

QUIXOTE: "Sancho, can't you stop bothering me about the oil companies? We have a crisis."

SANCHO: "The hurricanes, Quixote?"

QUIXOTE: "No."

SANCHO: "Sea level rise?"

QUIXOTE: "No."

SANCHO: "Is the shill index falling, Quixote? Can't get enough shills to push your agenda? You know once the shills stop crawling out from under the rocks--and you have to start blackmailing them--and the end is near."

QUIXOTE: "Sancho, we're having a problem with chocolate production."

SANCHO: "I heard the cocoa plants are vulnerable to diseases fostered by global warming, Quixote."

QUIXOTE: "We can lie about science. We can spin a myth that hurricanes aren't getting stronger. We can even convince people not to worry about the melting ice caps and the oceans, but a loss of chocolate. That is a major crisis."

SANCHO: "I bet even Junior will understand this one, Quixote."

QUIXOTE: "You give him too much credit, Sancho."

SANCHO: "What will your friends do about decreased chocolate output?"

QUIXOTE: "Poison more land, what else?"

SANCHO: "Silly of me not to see the obvious option, Quixote. Why poison the land? You produce more crops--but the long term effects are toxic to the population."

QUIXOTE: "You worry about long term toxic effects on food and water, in the face of a global crisis? Now who is being silly?"

SANCHO: "I remain in awe of your erudite grasp of the facts, Quixote. So how did you all determine chocolate is a crisis?"

QUIXOTE: "A lack of chocolate will have a direct impact on consumers."

SANCHO: "You are worried people will react to the understanding that global warming can cause a decrease in chocolate production. Which breeds the word your friends fear most: Awareness."

QUIXOTE: "Sancho, we need to make the plantations toxic to everything except for the cocoa plants."

SANCHO: "Would that include humans, Quixote?"

QUIXOTE: "You bet your ganache it does--but don't worry there are always guest workers, Sancho."

SANCHO: "Quixote, why would farmers poison their own fields? Disease is a way of making a species stronger."

QUIXOTE: "My friends don't like giving farmers a choice, Sancho."

SANCHO: "I don't understand."

QUIXOTE: "Farmers are too damn close to the land. It makes them independent. We can't have that. Corporations have been blackmailing them for years to use more and more chemicals."

SANCHO: "If they don't poison the air, water, and ground your friends will run them out of business?"

QUIXOTE: "A financial hammer directed against the American family will work every time. The soul is a fertile target."

SANCHO: "So your friends pit farmers against what they know is right-
            -just so their families can survive?"

QUIXOTE: "The financial hammer is our main domestic weapon, Sancho.
            For it to work, we make sure there are no options. For farmers
            the key issue is eviscerating the term, Organic. It was a tough
            battle but we got it done. Add to that the distributors we
            own,the grocery stores, the FDA, and you have a nice profit
            package. Chemical dependency is our cornerstone."

SANCHO: "So in the name of corporate profits you have taken the
            beauty of farming and turned it into a toxic waste dump-
            -a repository for the poisonous chemicals created by the
            distillation of fossil fuels."

QUIXOTE: "That's about the size of it, Sancho. Isn't it amazing what spin
            can do for the bottom line?"

SANCHO: "And you want to keep this consumption-based economy
            strong for what reason? Its beauty? Its truth? Its respect for
            the planet and humanity?"

QUIXOTE: "We have a lot of people to feed, Sancho. My friends take
            that responsibly seriously."

SANCHO: "Don't hand me that nonsense, Quixote. Your keep artificially
            increasing yields so you can increase corporate profits--
            anyone can see poisoning the land, the water, and the air is
            proof the chemistry on the farm has gone too far."

QUIXOTE: "It may well be, Sancho, but we have the farmers over a
            barrel--and you too. Without our chemicals, food prices will
            skyrocket as yield decreases. And by the way--the bugs have
            become hardened to everything but the newest products. My
            friends work to leave the population with no choices."

SANCHO: "Just an illusion of freedom."

QUIXOTE: "Sancho, why don't you get me some 'I like GM' stickers?"

SANCHO: "Aren't you following this same strategy with global warming?"

QUIXOTE: "Don't you have something better to do, Sancho?"

SANCHO: "You back the population into a corner by denying global
            warming and its solutions until it is too late. Then when it
            gets too awful to ignore--by the population--you force them
            to accept any solution that benefits your friends."

QUIXOTE: "Show me the proof. Who told you that? It better not be a government scientist."

SANCHO: "And that's why the chocolate thing is a crisis for your friends. If the consumers can't get their chocolate then they will demand something be done about global warming too early, thereby exercising their right to self-determination."

QUIXOTE: "I think the sandbags need stacking, Sancho."

SANCHO: "But you could get the population on board to fight for global warming by letting the chocolate problem happen-- but your friends will do just the opposite."

QUIXOTE: "You said it yourself: Corporate profits have no conscience."

SANCHO: "All they need to do is show the link between human forcing of the climate and chocolate production--in a way the population will understand. What a great way to benignly align our resources to address climate change."

QUIXOTE: "Allowing chocolate production to drop or creating an artificial shortage is indecent. My friends will have none of that kind of deceit."

SANCHO: "Not without plausible deniability."

QUIXOTE: "Sancho, I'll talk with my friends about cutting off the supply of chocolate in a few years so people will pay attention to global warming--if you'll just keep quiet."

SANCHO: "My lips are sealed, though I can't speak for the EP. Ah, say, Quixote, there must be other items that global warming will remove from the consumer shelves."

QUIXOTE: "There are, but none of them are as persuasive as the chocolate hammer."

June 23, 2006
Sancho, Quixote, and Surf's Up

QUIXOTE:	"Sancho, would you get me some wax. It's in the barnyard."
SANCHO:	"I smell spin in the wind. Is that a surfboard, Quixote? "
QUIXOTE:	"It's a Rhino. And so rad, aye, dude?"
SANCHO:	"Totally ripped, and here is your wax, Sir Bajawaller."
QUIXOTE:	"I can't wait to hit the curl."
SANCHO:	"Quixote, we live a hundred miles from the coast. What's up?"
QUIXOTE:	"Sancho, my friends want me to take on a new project: Surfing. The campaign will be called: 'Surf the Big Ones!'"
SANCHO:	"The big ones what?"
QUIXOTE:	"Waves, Sancho."
SANCHO:	"Because...Waves getting bigger and more dangerous."
QUIXOTE:	"Totally gnarly, Sancho, what's the beef?"
SANCHO:	"Quixote, are your friends worried the public will tie destructive waves to global warming?"
QUIXOTE:	"Ah, maybe just a bit."
SANCHO:	"So they are not concerned about the damage that will be done by the enhanced waves?"
QUIXOTE:	"Ah, not so much."
SANCHO:	"Quixote, are the waves just higher, or longer as well?"
QUIXOTE:	"Ah, maybe just a bit."
SANCHO:	"So are you going to spin away the cause of increased wave height and length?"
QUIXOTE:	"Bogus is my business, Sancho."

SANCHO: "Are your friends worried about the weakening Gulf Stream?"

QUIXOTE: "Maybe just a bit."

SANCHO: "And they are worried about the increase in sea level rise, Quixote?"

QUIXOTE: "So narb! Can you believe it has gone from 1.5 mm per year to over 3 mm per year in 35 years?"

SANCHO: "And accelerating, Quixote. So they are worried about that as well."

QUIXOTE: "Ah, maybe just a bit, Sancho."

SANCHO: "Are they worried about the melting ice caps and the loss of albedo?"

QUIXOTE: "Maybe just a bit."

SANCHO: "Or perhaps it's the acidifying ocean, or the depleting fish stocks, maybe tsunamis, or the bleached coral?"

QUIXOTE: "Sancho, these days, those are minor issues."

SANCHO: "Sadly so, then it's the storms and hurricanes. The energized storms at sea are creating larger and larger waves and your friends are worried about a Katrina tie-in?"

QUIXOTE: "Isn't everyone?"

SANCHO: "So, Quixote, then energized storms are definitely causing increased wave height and length."

QUIXOTE: "Nonsense--the storms have nothing to do with the waves and the waves have nothing to do with the recent coastal damage in Guatemala and Nicaragua."

SANCHO: "Perish the thought, Quixote. By the way, do you think there is any tie-in between storms, rogue waves, and climate change?"

QUIXOTE: "Not a chance, Sancho."

SANCHO: "Silly to even bring it up, Quixote. So how are you going to spin it?"

QUIXOTE: "I am going to own The Conductor. We are going to create fear, doubt, and confusion--just as we are doing with global warming. With my surf tie-in, soon every major media outlet will be singing my song of how big waves are good for the economy. I am so ding dong!"

SANCHO: "I think the word is biscuit. So your spin is to make people see larger waves as a positive event?"

QUIXOTE: "Precisely, Sancho, and if they get rag-dolled, so what?"

SANCHO: "Then your friends already know that the waves will turn deadly. Quixote, you can help by supporting a cut in greenhouse gases. We must solve these problems."

QUIXOTE: "Sancho, you're just clucked. Our spin is this: Helping the environment will hurt our vibrant economy...You know I hate it when you laugh like that."

SANCHO: "Then stop making stupid jokes, Quixote."

QUIXOTE: "About the economy?"

SANCHO: "About vibrant."

QUIXOTE: "Sancho, aren't you impressed? Look at how we have turned the macking waves of global warming into a market."

SANCHO: "Too bad lay people will die because the waves will change faster than their experience. All because you and your band of skeeps refuses to admit your economy's hemo-ed and your market creation's crooked. Quixote, you're no surfer--you're just the man in a gray suit."

QUIXOTE: "It's what we do, Sancho. In surf, we trust. No fear, dude, surf's up!"

July 13, 2006
Sancho, Quixote, and the Corn

QUIXOTE:	"Sancho, get more fertilizer, will you? I want to sow another row of corn."
SANCHO:	"It's a little late in the season, Quixote. Perhaps you'd like to strip mine for coal instead?"
QUIXOTE:	"No, the money is in the corn, ethanol, you know."
SANCHO:	"Ethanol is a waste of time."
QUIXOTE:	"Sancho, it's never too late to make money. Speaking of that, did those microwave ovens get to the airport?"
SANCHO:	"I delivered them this morning. What are you going to do with them?"
QUIXOTE:	"Drop them out of an airplane. Was the logo changed when they were painted?"
SANCHO:	"Everything was just as you ordered. The labels were all changed to say 'The Morethanhail Company'."
QUIXOTE:	"Perfect."
SANCHO:	"So what are you going to so with them, corner the market on microwave pop corn--as a hedge--in case the marks discover the ethanol scam?"
QUIXOTE:	"By the time the dummies figure this ethanol market is a scam we'll be out of it waiting for the crash. Gosh, I love new markets--especially when we control them. You were right, Sancho, global warming can be fun, and economically vigorous. Care to buy a carbon credit, or ethanol futures?"
SANCHO:	"I wasn't talking about the carnival concession economy your friends are hawking, Quixote. Do you remember something about a sustainable economic system?"
QUIXOTE:	"Bread and circuses, Sancho, it's all bread and circuses."
SANCHO:	"Are you really going to drop microwave ovens from an airplane?"

QUIXOTE:	"If we have to, Sancho. Oh, what about that new hair shampoo, 'Rogue Wave', did you get the copyright on that and the logo completed?"
SANCHO:	"The attorneys have the copyright papers, and the logo is almost done. Pretty snappy jingle you have there, too."
QUIXOTE:	"You mean: 'Don't you wish all waves were Rogue Waves!' I like it as well. I know we can make money with it--and drown any ocean disaster reports we don't like."
SANCHO:	"And the long propagandistic chortle rolls on."
QUIXOTE:	"Exactly. More land, more oil, more nonsense, more of everything--bigger cars, bigger houses, private jets."
SANCHO:	"Quixote, you're starting to froth."
QUIXOTE:	"There's a great big wonderful world out there waiting to be subjugated, Sancho."
SANCHO:	"Says you, Quixote."
QUIXOTE:	"We stalled you ninnies on global warming and now we reap the rewards. Belly up to the bar, suckers--place your bets-- JI, CDM, offset your carbon footprint. Step right up E. U. Carbon Credits, Ethanol, Biodiesel, RECs, Nukes, we got 'em all. Hurry, hurry, hurry!"
SANCHO:	"Your friends think they are the major leagues don't they?"
QUIXOTE:	"Exactly."
SANCHO:	"Quixote, they are the bush league. It couldn't be more obvious. The planet wins. The ocean is a heavy hitter, period. And your friends--they're just the pre-game little league."
QUIXOTE:	"Whatever are you talking about, Sancho?"
SANCHO:	"Your friends have seen an increase in large waves, haven't they?"
QUIXOTE:	"Only because we are looking for them."
SANCHO:	"Amazing how things change once you open your eyes. Tell me about the microwave ovens?"

QUIXOTE:	"We've got reports of ice balls the size of microwave ovens falling from the sky."
SANCHO:	"So if the ice balls get noticed, you're planning to drop microwave ovens from an airplane--to blur the problem of tipped weather?"
QUIXOTE:	"My plan exactly, pretty good, huh?"
SANCHO:	"You need serious help, Quixote. Do you remember you used to say there were no giant ice balls, and then you said the ice came from jets?"
QUIXOTE:	"And now we call them megacryometeors. No spin lasts forever, Sancho."
SANCHO:	"Heaven forbid you do something about it, Quixote."
QUIXOTE:	"Like what?"
SANCHO:	"Help cut GHG output by 75% as soon as possible."
QUIXOTE:	"Wait. I need to say this with a straight face: It will ruin the economy. How'd I do?"
SANCHO:	"So, the spin continues, Quixote."
QUIXOTE:	"Oh, lighten up, Sancho. Did you hear the joke about the Arctic and Antarctic?"
SANCHO:	"Is it really a joke?"
QUIXOTE:	"Only the way we tell it. Okay here it comes, Sancho. How long before the Arctic and Antarctic melts enough to substantially increase sea level?"
SANCHO:	"About twenty years, Quixote."
QUIXOTE:	"Not funny, Sancho."
SANCHO:	"But true, Quixote."
QUIXOTE:	"The approved answer is a hundred years. Isn't that a hoot!"
SANCHO:	"What's funny about it, Quixote?"

QUIXOTE: "We get away with baloney like that all the time, Sancho. We've got the media so scared no one publishes the truth anymore. The only reason they admit to global warming is to blur the negative effects. We've even got the scientists scared. Do you know Exxon holds the big purse strings on climate research at MIT and Stanford?"

SANCHO: "Now that is funny--in a macabre sort of way--Quixote. By the way, aren't your fossilistic friends going to be a bit upset with all this support for ethanol?"

QUIXOTE: "No, we made a deal. It opened up off-shore drilling in the South East."

SANCHO: "Oh, good move, Quixote. So now you have a global warming problem--and what do you do? Encourage more sea-based oil and gas wells in the middle of hurricane alley. Very smart. You know between war, divisive policies, economic plunder, and global warming, it's hard to figure out which gaffe is the most idiotic."

QUIXOTE: "Oh, that's easy, Sancho. The idiotic blunder belongs to the citizens."

SANCHO: "How do you figure that?"

QUIXOTE: "They're sitting by, letting global warming--and all the rest-- happen to them."

SANCHO: "Quixote, you have that wrong. The citizens believe in the institutions of our country and our government."

QUIXOTE: "Talk about corn."

SANCHO: "Trusting in our institutions isn't a mistake, Quixote."

QUIXOTE: "With Junior and his friends it is, Sancho. Or isn't that obvious?"

July 24, 2006
Sancho, Quixote, and Infrastructure

QUIXOTE: "Sancho! That storm knocked over another tree. As it fell, it took down the power lines; when the limbs hit the ground, they pierced the water line. We've no power, we've no water, and the water heater is toast. What do we do?"

SANCHO: "You're rich, Quixote. What's the problem?"

QUIXOTE: "I called a dozen repair people, but they have others ahead of us--a few even have the temerity to fix their own homes first. It will be weeks before anyone can get out here. You know one repair-guy died."

SANCHO: "Storms are killers now, Quixote. Are we going to repair the damage ourselves?"

QUIXOTE: "I was thinking of that, but I can't get repair parts. I'd pay anything to get the power and water fixed, but without talent and spare parts I can't get anything done."

SANCHO: "So you see money doesn't help. Welcome to global warming, Quixote."

QUIXOTE: "Bah, global warming doesn't affect me."

SANCHO: "It already has, remember the airport delays? And you can't conduct business if you can't take a shower or use a computer. Remember when Kennedy said he was a Berliner--during the early sixties?"

QUIXOTE: "Did the Berlin repair people ignore the rich too?"

SANCHO: "Let me try another way: Quixote, we are all citizens of New York City, St. Louis, and New Orleans."

QUIXOTE: "You mean the outages. Were they caused by falling trees?"

SANCHO: "Almost, Quixote, those cities have infrastructure damage. The storms not only made the systems inoperable, the storms swamped the support and repair systems."

QUIXOTE: "Just like here at the house. Now I get it. You don't get invited to parties much do you?"

SANCHO: "The point is economics plays second fiddle to infrastructure repair--and the economy isn't even a player when it comes to the climate."

QUIXOTE: "I see where you are going with this, Sancho, but soon we'll have marvelous technological wonders to fix everything. They will make the bad thing go away. I wish I were in Kansas. I wish I were..."

SANCHO: "How will your technological wonders get developed if your capital and other resources are sapped by infrastructure destruction?"

QUIXOTE: "You worry too much--some day we will have a hydrogen economy, nuclear power, new photovoltaic systems, wind power, clean coal, off-shore generators and American dominion over the planet."

SANCHO: "And how will the engineering and development of those systems cope with energized weather patterns--plus how do we deploy and repair these systems in the face of violent storms?"

QUIXOTE: "This is all about global warming, isn't it?"

SANCHO: "That is correct, Quixote."

QUIXOTE: "My friends are implementing a CO_2 trading system."

SANCHO: "They are setting up a convenient carbon dioxide standard for systems that don't put out carbon dioxide. They will use these new systems as an excuse to continue emitting carbon dioxide."

QUIXOTE: "It's not an excuse, it's a trading system."

SANCHO: "Same thing--in this case. They will continue emitting carbon dioxide by selling carbon credits. Fact is, there will be no real GHG reduction because the system delivering the credit never emitted carbon dioxide in the first place."

QUIXOTE: "Future carbon dioxide emissions will be reduced as a result of carbon trading. You don't understand markets."

SANCHO: "And you don't understand ponzi schemes are irrelevant to the climate problem."

QUIXOTE: "Sancho, we can't cut carbon dioxide by 75%."

SANCHO: "You're going to do it sooner or later. Why would we wait until our national infrastructure and our global economies are weakened by global warming before you implement the inevitable cuts?"

QUIXOTE: "You want to talk about infrastructure, for the sake of argument, let's solve one issue: Let's cut CO_2 in a city."

SANCHO: "On issue at a time. That's the way to do it, Quixote."

QUIXOTE: "How does a city implement a 75% cut? By cutting energy--lighting for a start--do you know what happens if we cut lighting? Pure chaos, and we'd have to reduce a lot of lighting for a city to realize a 75% cut in GHGs."

SANCHO: "Do you know how much power a human can generate through exercise? Do you know how little power it takes to light an LED?"

QUIXOTE: "I don't get it."

SANCHO: "Localize the power generation for lighting. Open generating facilities that run on human power, just for lighting. Instead of sitting home and watching television--go out and exercise--generate a few watts for your neighborhood."

QUIXOTE: "That reduces it to a spin-problem. I like that, Sancho."

SANCHO: "I knew you would, Quixote."

QUIXOTE: "Sancho, your plan creates a whole new infrastructure system for city lighting."

SANCHO: "I am talking about creating a sustainable economy. Break the problems down and start thinking about decentralized solutions--that's the key."

QUIXOTE: "The cost will be enormous, Sancho."

SANCHO: "You mean the new economy will be enormous, Quixote."

QUIXOTE: "We can't bear the costs."

SANCHO: "Quixote, your friends label a project as costly, when they don't control it--on the other hand--when they control the project; they label it as an economic engine. Why?"

QUIXOTE: "Because it's a scam and my friends control the news, Sancho."

SANCHO: "Quixote, the climate isn't waiting for us to develop ethics. It's time to identify solutions to critical problems: security, food, and water."

QUIXOTE: "You seem to be forgetting about transportation, housing, and entertainment, Sancho."

SANCHO: "You just don't get it yet, Quixote. We're running out of time. You know the chaos you fear in cities?"

QUIXOTE: "Yes."

SANCHO: "It's all around you in the weather. Take that city chaos you fear and multiply it by the planet. And climate is the infrastructure of weather patterns--and that infrastructure has no more tolerance for humanity's unbridled consumption. We need to tow the line and cope with our place in things."

QUIXOTE: "Sancho, we humans can own the climate."

SANCHO: "Sure, Quixote whatever you say. Right now, you've got no water--and you've got no power. In a few years, the weather will get much, much worse. After that, the climate tips--and the benign climate disappears forever. Then we are stuck with generations of pain. Wake up, Quixote; it's the endgame, the oil portrait of reality is gone."

July 30, 2006
Sancho. Quixote, and Secrecy

SANCHO: "Quixote, why are your friends so secretive?"

QUIXOTE: "Without security we wouldn't have a functioning government, Sancho."

SANCHO: "Because we need to keep national secrets hidden from the terrorists?"

QUIXOTE: "No, Sancho, from the citizens, silly."

SANCHO: "Huh? Why?"

QUIXOTE: "Our Republican form of government is predicated on the notion that the masses cannot make informed decisions."

SANCHO: "Because they are stupid?"

"QUIXOTE: "Oh, we wish they were stupid. The TV goes just so far, in dumbing people down. Do you have any good ideas to make the population less aware? You'll be a rich man."

SANCHO: "Sorry, no can do. Quixote, if the population isn't stupid, then why not assume they will make prudent decisions?"

QUIXOTE: "Because they don't have access to information."

SANCHO: "But, Quixote, your friends are keeping the information from them."

QUIXOTE: "Exactly, Sancho, now you know why we are so secretive. You look upset."

SANCHO: "So then the reason your friends hide the facts about the climate is because, if they didn't, the population could make informed decisions about the dangers in their future and chart their own course."

QUIXOTE: "And those decisions might run contrary to certain transnational interests."

SANCHO: "This country isn't about corporations, Quixote. It's about its citizens."

QUIXOTE: "In the past perhaps, but now it's all about transnational corporate interests."

SANCHO: "And that's a problem, Quixote."

QUIXOTE: "Much more than that, Sancho. It's really about information. If information isn't spun just right it might lead to, anything."

SANCHO: "Like progress, a better economic model, a less divided country, self determination, self respect--"

QUIXOTE: "A loss of control for my friends."

SANCHO: "--Less centralized control, a sustainable system, freedom."

QUIXOTE: "Sadly the list goes on and on, Sancho."

SANCHO: "Quixote, when a corporate entity interferes with the rights of our citizens to know the truth about global warming, that corporate entity is committing treason."

QUIXOTE: "How, Sancho?"

SANCHO: "The corporate structure is betraying the interests of our country and its people for its own profit. That is treason."

QUIXOTE: "Of course to prove that, Sancho, you'll need information. Get it?"

SANCHO: "Regardless, it's still treason for a corporate entity to conscientiously undercut the right of self-determination by undermining the science of global warming and funding propaganda that damages the national interests--to say nothing of engaging in graft."

QUIXOTE: "Corporations have created a state of fear--but none of that matters, Sancho."

SANCHO: "Quixote, the corporate assault on our institutions heightens the dangers to our population, our country, and our world-- global warming is a crisis."

QUIXOTE: "I can get ten pin-head-commentators who will fight you on that--in between commercials of course--and don't forget the puppet researchers we own and operate."

SANCHO: "Quixote, we are a nation of strong citizens, not frightened consumers."

QUIXOTE: "Sancho, you need to keep clarity to yourself."

SANCHO: "Why."

QUIXOTE: "Certain corporate interests have no respect for our laws; they will fight you like a tiger."

SANCHO: "Which corporate interests? Do you mean Exxon/Mobil?"

QUIXOTE: "Shhhh."

August 7, 2006
Sancho, Quixote, and Epiphany

QUIXOTE:　　"Sancho, we need to talk."

SANCHO:　　"Certainly, Quixote, what can I do for you?"

QUIXOTE:　　"Global warming."

SANCHO:　　"What about it, Quixote?"

QUIXOTE:　　"We're in trouble, Sancho."

SANCHO:　　"No kidding."

QUIXOTE:　　"We want your help, Sancho."

SANCHO:　　"Cut corporate carbon dioxide output by 75%, Quixote."

QUIXOTE:　　"That's not the kind of help we want."

SANCHO:　　"I see. So what do you want, Quixote?"

QUIXOTE:　　"You need to tell people it will be okay."

SANCHO:　　"Me, Quixote?"

QUIXOTE:　　"Well, the EP, then."

SANCHO:　　"What do you mean by 'okay', Quixote?"

QUIXOTE:　　"You need to say life won't change because of global warming."

SANCHO:　　"Of course life will change--and radically."

QUIXOTE:　　"That's too dramatic, Sancho."

SANCHO:　　"Then try this, Quixote. Ten years ago, we had more choices. Our selections have become less and less because your friends tried to spin away truth. Today we are facing the options of cutting our carbon dioxide by 75% or getting burped off the planet. Don't you think I know how awful a 75% cut in GHGs is? It's a terrible option; however, it's a distinctly positive alternative to the paths awaiting us--if we ignore the science of global warming."

QUIXOTE: "Sancho, we're having trouble controlling the scientists."

SANCHO: "They are a brave group. How about this, Quixote: The only issue left to us now is the fact that we will kill millions-- without regard to race, creed, or color."

QUIXOTE: "That means the climate kills regardless of wealth or social status as well!"

SANCHO: "Now there's an epiphany for you, Quixote."

QUIXOTE: "My friends won't like that clarity, Sancho."

SANCHO: "And my friends don't like dying for dollars, Quixote."

QUIXOTE: "I don't see how this shows anything will be okay."

SANCHO: "Quixote, global warming is a leap forward for humanity. Anthropogenic forcing of the planet's radiative balance proves we must work together as a sustainable community. Imbalance is our enemy, not your friends' stupidity. Once we recognize that, we have begun to adjust to the larger truths that govern our world."

QUIXOTE: "Meaning?"

SANCHO: "Truth seeks us, Quixote. Only the questions matter."

QUIXOTE: "So the longer we wait to cope with the facts, the worse it will be for us."

SANCHO: "You understand part of it, Quixote. Most importantly, if we wait too long, we will abdicate our position in the ecosystem."

QUIXOTE: "That's too negative, Sancho."

SANCHO: "You misunderstand me, Quixote. You say you finally accept the signs--that's good news."

QUIXOTE: "Sancho, only a fool ignores the indicators."

SANCHO: "Or believes a madman who continually says they agree and does nothing. Regardless, the next step is: What are we going to do about it?"

August 12, 2006
Sancho, Quixote, and the Flywheel

QUIXOTE: "We can't beat global warming and maintain our free market."

SANCHO: "Free market? Is that a joke?"

QUIXOTE: "Climate change is depressing and too big to handle."

SANCHO: "Well it depends on how you are trying to spin it: To serve a failed economy or to grow with the challenge? What are you trying to do, Quixote?"

QUIXOTE: "Sancho, Coal plants put out 300 megawatts of reliable power day and night. How are we ever going to quickly replace them with enough clean energy quickly to reduce carbon dioxide by 75%?"

SANCHO: "Quixote, you're looking at the problem the wrong way."

QUIXOTE: "How so?"

SANCHO: "We don't need 300 megawatt generators."

QUIXOTE: "Lot you know, Sancho."

SANCHO: "Quixote, let's break the energy problem down to its three key areas. Let's start with households. Then we'll go to transportation, and after that, production systems. Today we'll talk about the average household in America."

QUIXOTE: "I'm listening, Sancho."

SANCHO: "Try considering three kilowatts instead of 300 megawatts."

QUIXOTE: "What for?"

SANCHO: "The average household can function well on three KWH."

QUIXOTE: "Do the math--there are a lot of households out there."

SANCHO: "You have that wrong. There is only one household. A model for every household that can be reduced to a single problem: three KWH. Solve that problem and the solution can be replicated over and over with total reliability."

QUIXOTE: "That's a distributed solution. My friends won't like that."

SANCHO: "You need to work with the utility engineers for solutions."

QUIXOTE: "Don't tell them that, okay?"

SANCHO: "My lips are sealed, Quixote."

QUIXOTE: "For just a minute, let's use this three kilowatt number--how can a home produce that? Plus there is the energy storage when the renewables are offline, there are the control systems. Woe is us--let's make ethanol instead and inject aerosols into the atmosphere--then we can forget the whole thing!"

SANCHO: "Idiotic solutions require idiotic leadership, Quixote."

QUIXOTE: "My friends are all there for that."

SANCHO: "And that's the truth, Quixote."

QUIXOTE: "The problem really isn't 3 kilowatts. The problem is the R&D, and the production of high tech generators, high tech control systems, and high tech batteries to power each home--to say nothing of installation and maintenance."

SANCHO: "A good sized solar cell manufacturing plant will put out 300 meg a year in solar cells. They can do that year after year. Let me make it easier for you. You need to use the physical properties of our world to our advantage. High tech equals energy use. It has its place but bypass it when you can."

QUIXOTE: "My friends love high tech. Besides, we need high tech to make a better battery--and keep my equities healthy."

SANCHO: "There are other ways to store energy, besides a battery."

QUIXOTE: "Like what, Sancho?"

SANCHO: "A flywheel. It's permanent, and more importantly it's repairable by local trades' people. It's cheaply reproduced and it's reliable. You need to get outside the notion of high technology for solutions. Right now we need answers that are easily reproduced and maintained on a regional level."

QUIXOTE: "For example?"

SANCHO: "In addition to flywheels, lighter than air hauling systems, sustainable mechanisms, a lever, gears, inclines, gravity--"

QUIXOTE: "How do we make money off the gravity market?"

SANCHO: "You're ranting, Quixote."

QUIXOTE: "Sorry, a loss of control. Wait, how will gravity help us?"

SANCHO: "Quixote, here are some facts for you. One KWH equals about 2, 655, 223 foot pounds. That means if you take the average SUV of 6,000 pounds and drop it off a 440 foot cliff a few times an hour, you can power a household--just put the energy into a flywheel."

QUIXOTE: "How do you lift it? Oh, I see, by using lighter-than-air systems. Seems dangerous to take ton-sized objects and drop them out of balloons to power your home."

SANCHO: "The point here is the SUVs are a lot of mass--and they roll."

QUIXOTE: "Sancho, I deal in facts. What are you laughing about?"

SANCHO: "You, facts?"

QUIXOTE: "No one is going to drop an SUV just to power their house."

SANCHO: "Do you understand what you have said? You are so smart."

QUIXOTE: "Thank you, I am perceptive about most kinds of problems... Wait a minute. What am I smart about?"

SANCHO: "Your home-sized energy generation system will define your future markets for everything that goes into the household. Plus, if the power is less convenient, people will use less energy. Plus if it's efficient enough, you can power a vehicle."

QUIXOTE: "Convenience is our secret weapon to control the consumer. Your proposal gives the population more choices. My friends can't allow that. It's a huge change."

SANCHO: "It's a huge economy waiting to be tapped."

QUIXOTE: "It doesn't matter. Sancho, you are proposing dozens of new markets. My friends can't control that many--let alone unbridled growth by regional entrepreneurs."

SANCHO: "That because we are discussing the formation of free markets. Don't ya' love how climate change fosters insight for all?"

September 7, 2006
Sancho, Quixote, and the Point

QUIXOTE: "Sancho, what are you doing with that microscope? Trying to find a hurricane?"

SANCHO: "Hi, Quixote, a hurricane, in a microscope? I don't get it."

QUIXOTE: "Last year your eco-terrorist friends told everyone the hurricanes were a sign of global warming. This year there hasn't been a hurricane to speak of here in the U.S., so I figured you were trying to find one. I wonder what happened to them?"

SANCHO: "I see the joke. You know, Quixote, if I was looking for hurricanes I wouldn't look under a microscope. I'd just look in the Pacific basin. There are lots of them there."

QUIXOTE: "Who cares, Sancho? They haven't been hitting the U.S., mainland. More importantly, we can claim the hurricane season is unusually slow. A little quick averaging and--hot damn, Martha--we have no connection between hurricanes and global warming."

SANCHO: "Nice spin, Quixote, has it worked?"

QUIXOTE: "In the U.S., it's taking hold--though that viewpoint seems to be less welcome in China and India."

SANCHO: "America will wake up, Quixote, don't worry."

QUIXOTE: "So what's with the microscope, Sancho?"

SANCHO: "You mean what's the point of it?"

QUIXOTE: "Well, yes."

SANCHO: "The point is the point, Quixote."

QUIXOTE: "You lost me, Sancho."

SANCHO: "Here, do you see this piece of paper? I'll take a pen and place a point on it."

QUIXOTE: "Okay. I see that."

SANCHO: "Now I take the pen-point and put it under a microscope. In doing this I will prove to you that a microscope can act as a time machine, Quixote."

QUIXOTE: "Nonsense, Sancho."

SANCHO: "Scale matters. Here, look down into the microscope. What do you see?"

QUIXOTE: "I see an arc of dark ink. It seems to be made of points. Funny the line isn't uniform. It's made of points too. Is that what I am supposed to see--a bunch of points inside points?"

SANCHO: "You bet your Mandelbrot, Quixote. Now watch, I'll increase the magnification so you are looking at a smaller area--right?"

QUIXOTE: "Wait I am off the line--all I see is the white paper. Oh, there, as you move the paper, the line is filling in. Now half of my view is dark and half is light."

SANCHO: "Good, Quixote. I'll move the paper. You see how the point takes a few seconds to pass by your point of reference?"

QUIXOTE: "I do...Okay, it's all white again."

SANCHO: "Look up. Now, when I take the paper from under the microscope and show it to you--you see the whole point at once. It doesn't take any time at all to fathom the point."

QUIXOTE: "So my relative viewpoint matters--oh that kind of a time machine--but you're talking about a relative system of reference. That's a parlor trick."

SANCHO: "Quixote, the scale of your interrogation to a particular point impacts your time reference to that point. Get it?"

QUIXOTE: "Huh?"

SANCHO: "What if the climate tipping point is that dot and humans always look at the tipping point through a microscope--or to put it another way--from a very narrow viewpoint?"

QUIXOTE: "Huh?"

SANCHO: "What if an arc to us is part of a point to the planet, and we can alter that arc by our actions because we are inside the temporal scale of the event?"

QUIXOTE: "So the human time-frame indicates a small scale view. That means the point, the climate tipping point, takes more time to pass by us."

SANCHO: "Exactly, Quixote. But if you step back--like before--you see the whole point. That's the planet's time scale on the tipping point."

QUIXOTE: "That's when I looked at the whole paper, Sancho, rather than looking through the microscope. What should I do?"

SANCHO: "Quixote, let me put it another way: Points are relative to the scale of the viewer. As a result, there is a temporal component based on scale. In truth, scale is time's master."

QUIXOTE: "You said that. Oh, I see. You mean we may have entered the climate tipping point, but because of our limited human scale of reference we see the point as events over time?"

SANCHO: "Good."

QUIXOTE: "You are saying the tipping point has started, Sancho?"

SANCHO: "I am saying points on the geologic time scale, when viewed from the human perspective, have a time-forward temporal component. That's our leverage. We need to be cognizant of that when considering options in global warming."

QUIXOTE: "Sancho, this is horrible news. That means the tipping point is occurring. Wait, I can make a fortune on this. Where can I buy Puts on humanity?"

SANCHO: "Quixote, I'd like you to know that greed is a joke. A planetary condition for the propagation of chaos, but somehow I don't think that is going to get through. Regardless, my point is this: If the tipping point has a temporal component from the human perspective, that also means we can alter that point because it has a beginning, middle, and an end for us. It is not binary--as it is on the planet's scale."

QUIXOTE: "That's great news, Sancho. How do we shut the tipping point off and keep things the same?"

SANCHO: "We can't, Quixote. We need to face the fact that we can alter the ensuing events, but it will take effort."

QUIXOTE: "Not from my friends."

SANCHO: "I don't expect effort from your friends. I've given up on your friends ever considering the public welfare above their comfort."

QUIXOTE: "We are a breed apart, that's true. Wait, Sancho. Does this mean low voltage light bulbs and more insulation will not allow us to adjust for global warming?"

SANCHO: "Humanity is a component in the Chaotic equation we call global warming. But, we have volition also. We have a chance to fix things--though I doubt half-assed measures based on defeatist attitudes will do any good."

QUIXOTE: "Defeatist? Us, just because we are us-centric. Just kidding. Okay, so how?"

SANCHO: "Need I say it again, Quixote? We need to cut our GHG output."

QUIXOTE: "Not that again. Sancho, don't you know it's impossible?"

SANCHO: "Quixote, are blind to options because you wish to be blind?"

QUIXOTE: "Sancho--going back to microscope--when I close my eyes, I never see the tipping point. How do you like that?"

SANCHO: "You will see it either way, Quixote--but only when it is too late--to continue with your metaphor. And that's always been the trump card the population has over your friends. You may cause them profound misery, but in the end your friends lose."

October 20, 2006
Sancho, Quixote, and Dinosaur Logic

QUIXOTE: "Sancho, do you really think the ozone hole matters?"

SANCHO: "Matters in what way, Quixote?"

QUIXOTE: "Well more than it has?"

SANCHO: "Well Quixote, the record loss of the ozone layer in the Antarctic means more ultraviolet light will strike the Earth and the recovery will take far longer than expected, say an additional 50 years."

QUIXOTE: "So our estimates of fixing it in a decade were off by a bit, Sancho."

SANCHO: "Yes, Quixote."

QUIXOTE: "Why was that, Sancho? We used only the best approved scientists with biggest budgets who knew that they had to say what we wanted to hear. I don't see how we got it wrong."

SANCHO: "So, ah, what's the question?"

QUIXOTE: "Is it true the ozone destroying compounds have a long life in the atmosphere--on the order of 40 years or so?"

SANCHO: "Right, Quixote. Coupled with that, the warming planet modifies the recovery rate, slowing down ozone recovery."

QUIXOTE: "So even though the output of ozone destroying chemicals peaked five years ago, the problem continues to get worse."

SANCHO: "We have the same kind of problem with carbon dioxide."

QUIXOTE: "You mean that carbon dioxide lasts in the atmosphere like the ozone destroying chemicals?"

SANCHO: "Well yes, but the persistence of carbon dioxide in the atmosphere is more like 80 years instead of 40 years."

QUIXOTE: "My, that's a long time, Sancho."

Sancho:	"And every gallon of gas you burn puts out 19.5 pounds of carbon dioxide into the atmosphere--and we are increasing our usage of gasoline every day."
Quixote:	"So it's a cumulative effect?"
Sancho:	"We are still seeing the effects of fossil fuels burned years ago."
Quixote:	"That means the cars that ran in the 'Roaring 20's, their carbon dioxide is still in the atmosphere?"
Sancho:	"Some, but the cars' exhaust from the 1930's, 40's, 50's, 60's, 70's, 80's, and 90's are still up there, and carbon dioxide retention has compounding effects we haven't even begun to understand."
Quixote:	"Boy, I'm glad I'm rich."
Sancho:	"A diaphanous piece of insight at best."
Quixote:	"Apathy and resignation are my allies, Sancho. The more you guys show the desperation and the unyielding imperative of global warming the less I worry about it. Why don't you start giving more solutions rather than dire warnings?"
Sancho:	"Cut GHG output by 75%, Quixote."
Quixote:	"That's never going to happen, Sancho. I've got legions of unemployed global warming denialists retrained to trumpet the impossibility of rapid reductions in GHG output."
Sancho:	"We are back to the argument of a decade ago. Sound science says we need to make major changes--but Junior and his band of sociopaths claim that either isn't true, or it can't be done."
Quixote:	"We stay with our winning strategies, Sancho."
Sancho:	"Their response is defeatist. But you know deep cuts in GHG output are the real answer."
Quixote:	"Prove it! Ha, got you again with that one, and wait I have another. The economic impacts of reduced GHG output will cripple our economy. I love the oldies, don't you? And just for you, I'm going to give you the newest slant on it all. Ready?"
Sancho:	"I wait with baited breath, Quixote."

QUIXOTE: "Why cut our GHGs when the Chinese and Indians--as well as other developing countries--will not cut their GHG output? All in all, I think we have you in a box on that one. The population may be concerned with global warming, but if we hit them in their pocketbooks, add racism, and a fear of losing what they have, I think we have a winning combination. We may lose the global warming battle but we are going to win the fear war."

SANCHO: "Which fear, Quixote?"

QUIXOTE: "The one that controls popular opinion and decimates the political will of the people."

SANCHO: "What about the destruction, the death, the suffering, the degradation of our people and our American way of life?"

QUIXOTE: "That's easy. We will say the damage we are incurring is because 'THEY' will not cut THEIR GHGs."

SANCHO: "But that's a bold faced lie--and you know it."

QUIXOTE: "But do Mr. and Mrs. America know? Do you really think people working 9-5, struggling to feed their families are going to research the problem in the face of a media blitz?"

SANCHO: "I would hope they would."

QUIXOTE: "Sancho, my noble servant, the American executive branch has stripped away First and Second amendment rights as if they were lilies in a field. We've got the population panicked about terrorists even while they can't feed themselves or get a living wage. Does anyone ask where the terrorist funding comes from? Of course not. We own the media. The general populace says nothing and does nothing because we brainwash them. By the time the population figures out the mess they are in, their freedoms will be so minute their collective voice of outrage will be nothing more than the pleading bleat of sheep waiting to be sheared."

SANCHO: "Junior and his friends are evil, Quixote."

QUIXOTE: "Ever hear the saying 'He who dies with the most toys wins?'"

SANCHO: "I have heard of it."

QUIXOTE: "Junior and his friends have now added the global warming corollary: He who dies last, really wins."

SANCHO: "So the reality is Junior and his friends don't care about the horrific life awaiting them?"

QUIXOTE: "Sancho, they care. They care enough to make sure Mr. and Mrs. America die first--and--frankly when enough of them die, the GHG output will plummet. Problem solved."

SANCHO: "And here I thought Junior and his friends were fiddling while Rome burned."

QUIXOTE: "Don't be silly. Junior and his friends aren't fiddling--Junior and his friends are lighting the fires."

SANCHO: "In the end, what do they think they will have?"

QUIXOTE: "Eden--because there will be less of the great unwashed."

SANCHO: "So they still think their wealth and power will protect them?"

QUIXOTE: "They do."

SANCHO: "That's flawed logic, I'm big so I can whip anyone. So how come the dinosaurs couldn't whip Gaia?"

QUIXOTE: "Just between us, Sancho. It's pure madness, but until Junior and his friends are unseated, we remain a country committed to sacrificing its population to the whims of dinosaur logic."

November 8, 2006
Sancho, Quixote, and the CDGI

SANCHO: "So Quixote, you've been fairly quiet since the elections. What now?"

QUIXOTE: "Sancho, all I know is Junior has had another case of scotch delivered to the back door, Dick bought a new shotgun, and Connie and Don may host a new talk show proving Nairobi ought to be the new dumping ground for U.S., nuclear waste."

SANCHO: "So your friends are worried, Quixote."

QUIXOTE: "Sancho, the world changed, but not in the way you might think."

SANCHO: "Meaning what, Quixote?"

QUIXOTE: "The CDGI, The Carbon Dioxide Generation Industry, they thought the population was a lot dumber than they seem to be."

SANCHO: "The benefits of elitist insulation are a two-way street."

QUIXOTE: "Regardless of all that has happened yesterday, the go-ahead was given for the lobbyists' to unleash a new barrage of unbridled terror and deceit aimed at science, honest news-people, and ethicists. From what I've seen, the plans would have made Saddam blush."

SANCHO: "So the plan is to ignore the American voters and the needs of the rest of the world?"

QUIXOTE: "With the CDGI--you can count on it."

SANCHO: "That's good. So the real question now is whether the profits and power of the CDGI will outweigh the American voters."

QUIXOTE: "You can count on a hell of a battle, Sancho."

SANCHO: "But it's finally in the open, Quixote. The whole world gets to see the corporate agenda of centralized power battle the agenda of liberty and freedom supported by the American people."

QUIXOTE: "That's what global warming has always been about, Sancho, political will. Nothing has changed except the addition of a big dose of fear. It will be interesting to see how much economic fear the CDGI can instill in the American people before the changes happen."

SANCHO: "You make it sound like America is entering fossil-fuel-menopause, Quixote."

QUIXOTE: "Sancho, you don't get to be a Senator or a Congressman in the United States of America by ignoring the corporate agenda. Heck, they run most of the mass media in the U.S. On the other hand, global warming has undoubtedly weakened the power of the CDGI corporations. To be frank, their demise is a fait accompli."

SANCHO: "So it's not a question of if the agenda of the American people will prevail, it's a question of when."

QUIXOTE: "As you have said, Sancho."

SANCHO: "Why clash at all, Quixote?"

QUIXOTE: "I couldn't agree more. Why don't you tell your eco-nut friends to roll over and let their children die from climate change? I think we can work out a small tax cut in exchange--or maybe even some kind of affordable health care."

SANCHO: "That's not funny, Quixote."

QUIXOTE: "Oh, I see. So you think the world knows the only question left is how many Americans will need to suffer--from global warming--before the CDGI and its lobbyists are either laughed out of the halls of power, or put in prison."

SANCHO: "Exactly, Quixote."

QUIXOTE: "A sobering thought, but what the hell--you can be sure of one thing--the CDGI will fight the American people at every turn."

SANCHO: "So what's all the paperwork on your desk? I thought you might be updating your resume, Quixote?"

QUIXOTE: "I am, but first I've got a major contract to green-wash nuclear power. Then there's the carbon trading scam to complete. Once that's done, it's time to freshen up the pointless plan of burying CO_2 underground. After that, iron filings in the ocean. By the time I'm done, the difference between me and the Sierra Club will be indistinguishable. Then, like the rest of Junior's friends, it will be time to slither back under the rocks so we can work to defeat the wishes of the American people, while looking as green as possible."

SANCHO: "Global warming and its effects are inevitable, Quixote. Don't you feel like you are wasting precious time that we could use to smooth the transition to a sustainable economy?"

QUIXOTE: "No question of that, Sancho. On the other hand, the longer Junior and his friends can undermine America's political will, the longer the CDGI can stay in power."

SANCHO: "That's insane. Why ignore the reality of a proven future?"

QUIXOTE: "Sancho, think about it. Junior and his friends have been ignoring the realities of anthropogenic forcing of the climate. What makes you think they will start paying attention to truth now?"

SANCHO: "Rationality, a sense of responsibility, culpability, lawsuits, jail time?"

QUIXOTE: "Sancho, for Junior and his friends, rationality--like liberty and freedom--take a back-seat to the vanity-fair that worships them and their lust for power."

SANCHO: "Which proves Junior and his friends are just sociopaths in business suits, Quixote."

QUIXOTE: "Once again the future has come home to roost, Sancho. But enough of that, before you go out in the field and put up that wind generator, please order more green ink for the ethanol brochures. With yesterday's election results, it's never too soon to take on the absurdity of converting food to fuel--and make it look harmless."

SANCHO: "Because people will starve, Quixote?"

QUIXOTE: "A dead person uses no power, Sancho. See how green we are?"

CHAPTER 11
2007

April 15, 2007
Sancho, Quixote, and Adaptation

SANCHO: "Quixote, you're back. Where have you been?"

QUIXOTE: "Adapting, Sancho."

SANCHO: "Adapting--to what?"

QUIXOTE: "The new climate regime: global warming, the storms, public awareness. It's taken a long time for you-all to face global warming, Sancho."

SANCHO: "Us? Are you kidding me, Quixote?"

QUIXOTE: "Let's not quibble over the past, Sancho. There's work to be done."

SANCHO: "Well I'm glad to hear that. It's time to face the climate impacts, and adjust our society to a sustainable model."

QUIXOTE: "What are you talking about? We're not going to change anything. I said we are going to adapt to climate change."

SANCHO: "How the heck are you going to adapt to climate change without changing anything?"

QUIXOTE: "Sancho, we're going to cap and trade, open the carbon markets, bring out ridiculous aerosol programs, fund research into nuclear, build coal plants, rape the arctic, blame China, and change light bulbs. We're adapting."

SANCHO: "None of that addresses the issues, Quixote."

QUIXOTE: "Sancho, my friends are adapting to climate change by opening markets. We'll make a fortune. I admire Al sometimes. I really do."

SANCHO: "What about research into climate change impacts and the time scale of events?"

QUIXOTE: "Sorry, we can't talk about science, research, or anything that might change the economy."

SANCHO: "I see: So you are responsible for all this nonsense about adapting to climate change, Quixote."

QUIXOTE: "Now you know where I have been, Sancho. My friends worry that the population will want something done about climate change. I know how to spin it."

SANCHO: "Which was?"

QUIXOTE: "I filled the nets with misinformation on scientists. Do you know how many shills it takes to push carbon trading, carbon offsets, the evil yellow empire, and changing light bulbs? Hey that sounds like the beginning of a joke."

SANCHO: "It is, Quixote. Regardless, you had me fooled. I thought the media barrage was the first steps to tackling the difficult task of climate change."

QUIXOTE: "They are the first steps...And we are putting together some substantial programs, Sancho."

SANCHO: "For example?"

QUIXOTE: "We are making ethanol a priority."

SANCHO: "And destroying the Amazon while raising food prices."

QUIXOTE: "If you and your eco-nut friends hadn't pushed this global warming agenda we wouldn't have had to destroy the Amazon. We were perfectly happy to rape the oil sands, build coal plants, and waste the Arctic National Refuge."

SANCHO: "So, Quixote, nothing has changed."

QUIXOTE: "We have research teams working in the Arctic and Antarctic, Sancho."

SANCHO: "That is substantial. So your friends are concerned about the first major pulses of melt water from the Antarctic and Greenland?"

QUIXOTE: "Pulse? What pulses? What are you talking about? The planet has no pulse."

SANCHO: "Quixote, why are you and your sociopathic friends pushing research in the cryosphere?"

QUIXOTE: "We have an opportunity to extract resources and we need good cost numbers. The public thinks it's about global warming. They get what they want and we get what we want."

SANCHO: "Quixote, it's all an excuse to pillage more from the planet?"

QUIXOTE: "You don't really think it's about research, do you?"

SANCHO: "Quixote, do you remember sea level rise and how global warming causes it?"

QUIXOTE: "Of course, Sancho. Insurance doubled last year for my beach homes. What does that have to do with anything? I can afford it."

SANCHO: "Quixote, do you really think the sea level will change just a few millimeters a year--in a nice linear fashion?"

QUIXOTE: "I never thought about it."

SANCHO: "Do you remember when we visited the Willamette Valley in Oregon? Do you know how the Willamette Valley was formed?"

QUIXOTE: "Farming loans to Monsanto and ConAgra?"

SANCHO: "Before that, Quixote."

Quixote: "Who cares?"

Sancho: "The Willamette Valley was formed by pulses of melt water from collapsed ice damns two states away. They were called the Missoula floods."

Quixote: "So?"

Sancho: "That flow will be insignificant when compared to the pulse from Greenland and the Antarctic, Quixote."

Quixote: "Are you saying the ice sheets in Greenland and Antarctica will do the same thing, pulse melt water in a big flood?"

Sancho: "Copiously--into the ocean."

Quixote: "Are you sure, Sancho?"

Sancho: "No question about it, Quixote. The ice sheets are already doing it; the ocean is just buffering the effect."

Quixote: "So what's the problem?"

Sancho: "The pulses will get larger due to climate change."

Quixote: "How big, Sancho?"

Sancho: "Quixote, imagine a single pulse that raises the oceans by a half inch or more."

Quixote: "Wow, dude, that's some wave!"

Sancho: "Very funny, Quixote--the effect will be catastrophic. We're not going to adapt to that by changing light bulbs or planting trees."

Quixote: "How soon, Sancho?"

Sancho: "That first major pulse could happen at any time, Quixote."

Quixote: "Hmm, did you get this information from any government scientists?"

Sancho: "No Quixote."

Quixote: "I had to know. The gang at the Department of Commerce have asked me to keep an eye on that for them and you seem to know so much. Okay, but first things first."

SANCHO: "Where are you going, Quixote, to tell your friends about the problem, to sound a warning?"

QUIXOTE: "Don't be a fool. I need to call my real estate agent and sell my homes on the coast. Then I need to buy some Puts on the insurance companies. Can you give me a better idea of when the first major pulse might happen?"

SANCHO: "Any time, Quixote."

QUIXOTE: "Damn, I hate the uncertainty of global warming. How am I supposed to time the securities market, Sancho?"

SANCHO: "That's the Quixote I know--always concerned about the other guy."

June 19, 2007
Sancho, Quixote, and Drought

Sancho: "Dusty isn't it, Quixote?"

Quixote: "Sancho, if you're going to tell me this drought is from global warming, don't bother."

Sancho: "I wasn't going to say that, Quixote. I am your loyal servant-- but it sure is dry in the south--and those ice sheets are melting pretty fast."

Quixote: "Well, what is your point, Sancho?"

Sancho: "My, we are prickly these days. Is something wrong?"

Quixote: "The disasters, the political groundswell, the science, the drought, the weather, the die-offs--they're laughing at us, Sancho. But we will have the last laugh."

Sancho: "How's that, Quixote?"

Quixote: "The people who are laughing at us will soon be huddled in shelters, covered in dust or swimming in mud. And we will still control them. They will be economically ruined, emotionally devastated by the death of a loved one, and just plain spun by the horrors of their life."

Sancho: "So basically the horrors of global warming are the friends of your friends?"

Quixote: "You make us sound demonic, Sancho, but the boys in Atlanta are worried. This global warming thing looks like it may even hurt us."

Sancho: "Oh, heavens no, Quixote."

Quixote: "You're making fun of me, Sancho."

Sancho: "I'm not making fun, Quixote. You just see my horror at a leadership that has led its citizens down the garden path of carbon trading, nuclear power, clean coal, ethanol, and changing out light bulbs to solve a civilization-shattering event."

QUIXOTE:	"Sancho, my friends and I took certain measures to ensure a healthy economy. Trouble is, Sancho, huge environmental disasters destroy large areas of the economy as well as dirt."
SANCHO:	"Ya' think?"
QUIXOTE:	"Sancho, the economic repercussions go on for years."
SANCHO:	"Imagine that, Quixote?"
QUIXOTE:	"Australia is a mess. Water wars are just around the corner. We are approaching the tipping point, even the stock market is taking a hit!"
SANCHO:	"Quixote, ignorance and myopia have a cost."
QUIXOTE:	"What are you talking about? We know what we are doing."
SANCHO:	"Doesn't sound like it."
QUIXOTE:	"You just don't like hearing me discuss the real state of the planet. Do you see why we do not discuss it?"
SANCHO:	"Quite. Your friends tell the population that useless systems like carbon trading, biodiesel, and ethanol are going to make a difference in global warming. Then, you follow that up with false information on the state of the problem saying it's manageable. People get a false sense of security and nothing gets done. Then suddenly it's hand wringing and concern."
QUIXOTE:	"We manage information for the good of the country."
SANCHO:	"How could current concentrations of CO_2 remained steady these last five years?"
QUIXOTE:	"They haven't."
SANCHO:	"The media reports the same number year after year. Most people think the concentration level is still at 382 PPMV. And these days your talking heads top it with cavalier comments that say 550 PPMV or 600 PPMV isn't out of the question."
QUIXOTE:	"So we take advantage of the media's ignorance--it's just a pay check for them anyway--so give them a break. They have families to feed and they know without our support they are in a pickle. Spin is spin, Sancho."

SANCHO: "Quixote, most people have no idea how important carbon dioxide concentrations are--just like they don't realize a 3 degree C change in planetary temperature is a 10% increase in the planetary greenhouse effect of our atmosphere. Then there's that nonsense about sea level rise maybe being an issue in 80 or 90 years. The last reliable measurements by the NASA GRACE system showed the sea rising at 3 mm per year. In the 19th century, that number was closer to ½ mm per year. In 1990 it was under 2 mm per year."

QUIXOTE: "Who cares about facts? We just don't like to be laughed at."

SANCHO: "So it's not just death-by-newbies that fosters the delivery of misinformation."

QUIXOTE: "We learned long ago you can't sell products with facts. You can sell products through fear, vanity, and greed. Though our favorite is addiction."

SANCHO: "Quixote, your friends are breaking the social contract between those who govern and the governed."

QUIXOTE: "Philosophy? Ethics? Do you really think that stuff matters?"

SANCHO: "Far more than you will ever understand, Quixote."

QUIXOTE: "So my friends and I will fake that too, Sancho. Look at the job we did with Junior. We had tens of millions Americans buffaloed with his supposed devotion to family--for years."

SANCHO: "But it didn't last, Quixote."

QUIXOTE: "So?"

SANCHO: "It wasn't sustainable. That's why you and your friends are dinosaurs. Your time has come and gone. What's sad is the pain you will cause the rest of us with your passing."

QUIXOTE: "Prove it, Sancho."

SANCHO: "I thought you might say that. Climate change is a shift in awareness about the 'forever' that ties us to the environment. With that tie comes a recognition of the deep connection to the planet and each other. It's a fact and people can no longer ignore it; soon every time you say different, people will laugh at you."

QUIXOTE: "So that's why they are laughing at us. We won't give up without a fight, Sancho."

SANCHO: "You have already lost--to the planet. You and your friends are a miniscule group of a minor species that resides on a small section this planet. You exist here at the pleasure of this planet. And it is no longer acceptable to this planet that you plunder it. That's the message of global warming. Unfortunately, your megalomaniac, sociopath-friends will kill millions of humans as you tilt at the windmill of your importance. In the end, justice will set the human record straight. It's as sure as the sunrise, clear as the sun, and firm as the Earth. You're friends are over, Quixote. They just don't know it yet."

QUIXOTE: "So what do you expect us to do?"

SANCHO: "You and your friends are limited-capability-beings. You will do as you have always done, and in doing that you will destroy yourselves leaving little more than a minor footnote in history."

QUIXOTE: "You're so smart--what will the footnote say, Sancho?"

SANCHO: "It will say: The oil-portrait-of-reality was flawed. It fed the ego rather than balance. God forgive the men and women who, through greed and self-importance killed so many for so little. We cannot."

QUIXOTE: "That sounds like a eulogy and it's not funny, Sancho."

SANCHO: "Nobody's laughing, Quixote."

August 11, 2007
Sancho, Quixote, and Gore

SANCHO: "Pew, what's stinks? Oh, my, what a mess, Quixote, is that blood?"

QUIXOTE: "I was working on a carbon offset project, Sancho, and it went haywire."

SANCHO: "So what's with all the blood?"

QUIXOTE: "Oh, the blood rivulets on the side of the path--that's for the sheep."

SANCHO: "For the sheep, or from the sheep, Quixote?"

QUIXOTE: "A little of both. Junior's dad was trying to come up with a way to keep the sheep in line as he marched them to the slaughterhouse. So he and his friends decided that showing them a little gore would keep then in line a little longer."

SANCHO: "And how does gore cut down on carbon output, Quixote?"

QUIXOTE: "All you need these days to call something a carbon reduction project to get the right backing--and boom--instant guilt offset."

SANCHO: "You mean carbon offset, don't you, Quixote?"

QUIXOTE: "No, I don't, Sancho. Only an idiot cannot see the legacy we are pushing. In this case, the gore offsets the guilt as the sheep and their progeny march toward destruction."

SANCHO: "How does it do that?"

QUIXOTE: "The gore distracts the sheep from the slaughterhouse ahead of them. At the same time, we use less energy to keep the sheep in line--voila, carbon reduction--the free market economy at work!"

SANCHO: "Incredible. So what happened with the sheep, Quixote?"

QUIXOTE: "The sheep panicked in that thunder storm, Sancho."

SANCHO: "Imagine that, Quixote."

QUIXOTE:	"You're not going to tell me the tornado was caused by global warming are you, Sancho?"
SANCHO:	"The thought had crossed my mind, Quixote."
QUIXOTE:	"What about hurricanes in the southeast, Sancho? We've haven't had any for two years."
SANCHO:	"And that's supposed to be good, Quixote?"
QUIXOTE:	"Global warming causes increased hurricane activity--blah, blah--what baloney!"
SANCHO:	"I guess we won't discuss moisture reduction in the Sahel."
QUIXOTE:	"Who told you about that, Sancho?"
SANCHO:	"Same guy who told you--your friend, Bill."
QUIXOTE:	"I don't want to discuss it, Sancho."
SANCHO:	"Quixote, what about your friends making plans to move off the Cape?"
QUIXOTE:	"Sancho, you know that's a lot of WHOI!"
SANCHO:	"See, Quixote, you can be elegant. So why don't you get it?"
QUIXOTE:	"We don't need to get it, Sancho."
SANCHO:	"Quixote, we're pumping energy into a chaotic system--the climate. Worse then that, you're friends are facilitating random events by altering the climate rhythm with their actions."
QUIXOTE:	"We are free thinking beings, Sancho."
SANCHO:	"Quixote--Junior, and his buddies are idiots. First, they add too much energy to the climate then they randomize the natural results of the climate system. You and your friends are pawns of the planet--but because of their control issues they can't see it."
QUIXOTE:	"I don't understand, Sancho."
SANCHO:	"Wonder of wonders, Quixote. Listen, we've entered the phase-shift portion of global warming. The system is getting more chaotic, surely you can see that much?"

QUIXOTE:	"Perhaps, but you're saying Junior is helping bring on the tipping point? Prove it."
SANCHO:	"A tornado in Brooklyn?"
QUIXOTE:	"A purely random event."
SANCHO:	"My, you are truly stupid aren't you?"
QUIXOTE:	"We like to call it committed."
SANCHO:	"You should be. Your friends think they own the weather?"
QUIXOTE:	"Well, yes, Sancho. We've cut down on moisture in the Sahel and as a result reduced hurricane activity. We've mitigated the warming with aerosols. We're dumping iron into the oceans to increase CO_2 uptake. We're going to win this climate battle. It's a triumph of the will."
SANCHO:	"Leni would be proud of you, Quixote, but there is no battle. If your friends could just step outside their vanity, they might see the climate as just another chaotic equation. We've randomized the climate equation by adding more energy--then you pinheads follow-through like good little mathematical functions to produce more random events-- and you call it weather control."
QUIXOTE:	"So you are saying we are insignificant, Sancho?"
SANCHO:	"Quixote, I am saying Junior and his friends are insignificant. The rest of us can make a difference by recognizing what's going on and cope with the reality of our time."
QUIXOTE:	"And do what, Sancho?"
SANCHO:	"Reduce the energy we add to the climate by severely cutting our GHG output while working to stabilize climate events."
QUIXOTE:	"Your 75% reduction in GHGs is suicide for the economy-- consumption first--sustainability later!"
SANCHO:	"You're consuming your children, Quixote. Look, your friends hate abortion. How can you condemn the next ten generations to horrific death and misery?"
QUIXOTE:	"Our studies show only five or six generations will be doomed to disease, suffering, poverty, starvation, and painful death from human induced global warming."

SANCHO: "Junior must be very proud that you've trumped the death-from-war numbers by killing members of six generations rather than just one."

QUIXOTE: "Those clouds look nasty. Where did those sheep go anyway?"

SANCHO: "I see. You and your friends will never accept the truth."

QUIXOTE: "It would have to hit us like a hammer in the skull. Where are those sheep?"

SANCHO: "They panicked and ran away in the storm, remember?"

QUIXOTE: "Sancho, the storm was a purely random event."

SANCHO: "Exactly, Quixote, intensely random."

September 9, 2007
Sancho, Quixote, and the Lake

Quixote: "So how was your trip to Lake Shasta, Sancho?"

Sancho: "There's no lake, Quixote. It's more like a wide river now. The flow is effectively gone."

Quixote: "The melt rates around the world are accelerating. Even I am surprised. But it is more amazing how docile people become once you convince them they are powerless."

Sancho: "I don't know about that, Quixote. People are awakening to the dangers of global warming."

Quixote: "You think so? You should have gone on to the conference in Palo Alto with me. People see climate change as just another market. Now that's progress."

Sancho: "Impossible."

Quixote: "We have a new strategy for climate change: We bore people into submission."

Sancho: "Did it work?"

Quixote: "Dead grass was more interesting than the conference."

Sancho: "That's surprising. Was that what the organizers wanted?"

Quixote: "No, but we have a new effort underway to confuse the public at large--and members of the news media. We're working hard to get them to move beyond climate change by making the climate issue appear boring."

Sancho: "Do you succeed, Quixote?"

Quixote: "We provided so much useless information on outdated topics of climate change that even I was bored."

Sancho: "I am sorry to hear that."

Quixote: "We kept debate to a minimum. New insights were squashed. We treated the participants as if they were idiots and told the same stupid stories. The most interesting people were the industry people."

SANCHO:	"So it was a spin-meister's wet-dream."
QUIXOTE:	"Beyond my wildest dreams, Sancho. We took the most interesting event of this generation and made it sound like math lecture on sand."
SANCHO:	"So no discussion on tectonic rebound?"
QUIXOTE:	"We avoided the link between plate tectonics and climate change."
SANCHO:	"What about the increase in sea level rise?"
QUIXOTE:	"Just the same stuff, none of the new research--none of the new debate."
SANCHO:	"Not a peep on the problems of adaptation?"
QUIXOTE:	"We just said it was underway and served sandwiches."
SANCHO:	"What about the problems of delivering Research and Development into the marketplace?"
QUIXOTE:	"They took the nonsense about solutions being a decade or so off and swallowed it hook, line, and sinker."
SANCHO:	"Don't they know that a decade off in R&D can mean a few months after never?"
QUIXOTE:	"Of course not--and we didn't tell them that. There was one mistake. Some idiot over at EPRI brought up the notion that the iron fertilization programs in the ocean is unproven. Thank goodness we squashed the debate before anyone could ask how an unproven technology like iron fertilization could gather so much funding and then make its way into the carbon markets."
SANCHO:	"Maybe the participants are so sophisticated they know it is a corrupt system and have given up fighting it?"
QUIXOTE:	"I can only hope that's the case, Sancho. We in the spin business live for that moment of controlled fear in our target audience."
SANCHO:	"Aldo Leopold would be proud of your commitment to tranquility."

November 5, 2007
Sancho, Quixote, and the Sick

QUIXOTE: "Sancho, I am having trouble breathing and my temperature is one-hundred-and-four."

SANCHO: "Your skin is damp and your eyes are puffy, Quixote. On the other hand, maybe you're like the planet, and just because there's an increase in temperature, that may not mean anything is wrong. Why don't we wait around and have a few conferences? Also, if we admit you're sick, do we need to consider its impact on our home economy? We need to make sure our money is safe before we do anything. Heck, maybe we'll discover it's really better for the human body to run at one-hundred-and-four instead of ninety-eight-point-six after that research. Science marches on!"

QUIXOTE: "Very funny."

SANCHO: "Or, I could write a Journal article on it? We could put it right next to the one on iron filings for carbon sequestration in the ocean making a difference. Or perhaps the research could go with that other propaganda jewel about how we might do geo-engineering that could include aerosol dispersion. Or, we could say the thermometer was flawed. It should be easy to find another thermometer that reads a bit differently. Then we could refute the whole notion of your being sick. It would dovetail nicely with the lies about the CO_2 concentrations in the atmosphere not increasing in the last few years. Oh, I know, let's see if we can get an op-ed on your being sick. We can say it is a scientific conspiracy and put it right under your friends' favorite bit of nonsense: The one about how the effects of global warming are way off in the future and that we have lots of time to do something about it."

QUIXOTE: "My stomach is queasy."

SANCHO: "I suppose it's too much to consider that the queasiness is caused by conscience? Hmm, your face is beginning to get red. Those blotches on your skin are turning orange too. I'll call a doctor, just in case rising temperature in the human body is serious."

QUIXOTE: "Sancho, is the room spinning? What's my temperature now?"

SANCHO: "Hmm, your temperature is one-hundred-and-five-point-one, and no, the room is not spinning--though that is an empirical observation on my part. Perhaps we should get some shill to come in and do a study on whether the room is really spinning or not? Then we can refute your temperature reading. Which response would you and your friends fund? To spin or not to spin--isn't that is the question? No, come to think of it, that's no question at all."

QUIXOTE: "That isn't funny. I feel terrible. Sancho, we control the research because we are entering a very difficult time. The effects of global warming will be horrific. We need to tighten our control over the population."

SANCHO: "You're delirious. You're repeating yourself."

QUIXOTE: "We keep the lobbyists happy. They give us money. Wow that was way too honest."

SANCHO: "Give it another shot, Quixote."

QUIXOTE: "Okay, Sancho. We are careful. We are prudent."

SANCHO: "There, now isn't that better, Quixote? A couple of good lies and you are right as rain."

QUIXOTE: "We govern. We have the right to lie, cheat and steal...What happened, Sancho?"

SANCHO: "You fell over. Your temperature is now one-hundred-and-five-point-nine. It seems like a couple of degrees of temperature rise might be bad for us humans. We need to call an ambulance--this looks serious."

QUIXOTE: "No I have to work on the media campaign for 'Green Fatigue'. We're trying to convince environmental reporters that global warming is a dead topic. I think a good lie will help me, Sancho."

SANCHO: "So what will it be? A fake FEMA news conference, bogus testimony on scientific research, more nonsense on why we should ignore droughts in a third of our country, the myth of melting glaciers, or the cyclical rising oceans? Or perhaps a position paper on why mega-fires are arson, or an unavoidable natural event. With those lies, you should feel fine, right?"

QUIXOTE: "Whew, it's hot in here. Would you open the window?"

SANCHO: "Glad to. There, that's a nice cool breeze for you. Hey, this opening a window to cool you down is kind of like geo-engineering you, isn't it? You got hot so we cooled you down. Gosh, it's all so simple, isn't it?"

QUIXOTE: "Sancho, I'm getting chills."

SANCHO: "Yup, look at those goose bumps. So maybe opening the window to lower the temperature was a bad idea, Quixote?"

QUIXOTE: "It seemed like a good idea at the time. Get me a blanket?"

SANCHO: "My pleasure. Now where are those old Indian blankets?"

QUIXOTE: "Not funny. We aren't evil, Sancho. Stop laughing--hear me out. We know what we are doing. We are showing the population that they cannot depend on the government or private industry to help them through the new climate regime. People have to learn to take care of themselves. Gosh, this blanket is musty. I can hardly breathe. Cough, cough."

SANCHO: "So, you were saying people have to take care of themselves?"

QUIXOTE: "Exactly. My mouth is dreadfully dry. My vision just went all sparkly for a moment. Do you think that's serious?"

SANCHO: "Could be, Quixote."

QUIXOTE: "Sancho, cooling me down by opening the window might not have been a good idea. I'm getting cold sweats and I feel like I am drowning in my own mucus."

SANCHO: "So an increase in our internal human humidity might be bad, too? Go figure. The window is now closed, Quixote."

QUIXOTE: "Sancho, I may not be able to take care of myself soon. I am awfully sick. Can I count on you?"

SANCHO: "Of course, Quixote."

QUIXOTE: "Don't pander to me--just how many times have I told you tree-hugging eco-freaks that it's every person for them self. These shivers are getting worse. Oh my, my temperature is almost one-hundred-and-six-point-five. Where is that damn doctor? I'll sue that SOB if he doesn't get here soon. Well anyway, it's a fait accompli, Sancho."

SANCHO: "What's that, Quixote? That sooner or later you consume everything, including yourself, and you still need help?"

QUIXOTE: "We're on this earth to stand on our own two feet... I'm getting nauseous, Sancho. I think I am going to faint again... Sancho, I can't see. The room is black and it's so hot! What am I doing on the floor? Help me, get me an ambulance. Sancho, where are you? Someone help me."

December 16, 2007
Sancho, Quixote, and Bali Hai

QUIXOTE: "Sancho, remove the scrim first and then get that passé picture of the American flag off the wall. It's covering the fossil fuel logos."

SANCHO: "You sound gruff, your directorship. I thought your production of South Pacific was pretty well attended."

QUIXOTE: "It went all right, Sancho, but a review or two did bother me. One said I was a dinosaur producing trite plots from a bygone era."

SANCHO: "Don't let that get you down, Quixote; they will never stop talking about your production of Grease."

QUIXOTE: "That one was easy, Sancho. It was near and dear to my heart. I guess the review put me in a bad mood. Do you know the review criticized the whole Bali Hai scene?"

SANCHO: "That scene where the actors stole things so they can party? That was a bit much. But like you have always told me, Quixote: Propaganda is a work in progress."

QUIXOTE: "Well at least the universities were quiet. I guess skewering them with corporate funding has focused them on where their bread is buttered."

SANCHO: "Which brings up your mastery of language: Think of what you had accomplished in the print media before your sojourn onto the world stage: You've gutted popular media so no one will dare speak against the oil portrait of reality. The AGU has agreed to publish a tabloid. Science Magazine spends so much ink on behavior modification that within a decade the 'Gulag Archipelago' will become a cult classic for hard science grad students."

QUIXOTE: "You're right, Sancho, I'm just not keeping to happy talk."

SANCHO: "Just like the song in your play, Quixote. In any case, tomorrow morning you can call up some friends and punish those media outlets that didn't suck up to your laughable laudations of a defunct economic model."

QUIXOTE: "Are you making fun of me, Sancho?"

SANCHO: "I'm just describing the way your friends get rid of nasty reviews."

QUIXOTE: "Okay. Keep that review from the WSJ--I want to talk to the new owners about it."

SANCHO: "See, I knew you can still gloat over the evisceration of a free press."

QUIXOTE: "Thank you for helping me recognize the worth of my profession."

SANCHO: "The faster we roll out your triumphs, Quixote. The quicker your greatness will come to light. By the way, that was a good idea to plant that baseball steroid story in the playbill. It took their minds off the background terror."

QUIXOTE: "You know, Sancho, sometimes I think the mind-numbing detritus bothers me; it's the meaningless of it all."

SANCHO: "Trust me, Quixote, that's the least of your worries. Any hint of ethics, relevance, or morality that creep into your consciousness quickly drowns in your deep-seated avarice."

QUIXOTE: "Sancho, you are making fun of me."

SANCHO: "You just completed a production where a stage full of actors, dancing to trite tunes, sang line after line about how death, destruction, and fear can be kinda' fun--as well as provide a healthy living."

QUIXOTE: "Sancho, it wasn't that insipid. Michener is an icon--he's a great author--like Crichton. What are you laughing about?"

SANCHO: "You choreographed a group of people stuck in the middle of a brutal conflict to act like morons. Quixote, every time I think of it, it brings a smile to my lips and chuckle to my belly."

QUIXOTE: "You are right. The way they danced, it was a thing of beauty."

SANCHO: "That would not be my choice of words, Quixote."

QUIXOTE: "Well no matter, Sancho, onto my next task."

SANCHO: "What's that, Herr Impresario?"

QUIXOTE: "A redo of 'Thriller'."

SANCHO: "Your friends are reproducing the music video by Michael Jackson?"

QUIXOTE: "It will be easy. When comes to ghoulish behavior, blood sucking monsters, nightmarish scenarios, evil intentions and just plain betrayal, there's not a soul on this planet that can stand up to my friends and their productions."

SANCHO: "Good point, Quixote."

CHAPTER 12
2008

February 15, 2008
Sancho, Quixote, and Cake

QUIXOTE: "Sancho, I don't see why you care and they don't."

SANCHO: "Who doesn't care, and about what, oh altruistic one?"

QUIXOTE: "Parts of the country are facing events that will kill cities, while places like Portland are facing floods that may wipe out large sections of the city overnight--and no one is paying attention. That's madness. You can't blame me for all of it."

SANCHO: "Perhaps the population doesn't have time to think about it."

QUIXOTE: "Sancho, do you have any idea how bad it is going to be?"

SANCHO: "I do."

QUIXOTE: "Exactly. Why do you bother caring? They get what they deserve."

SANCHO: "At some point the horrors that foster the population's apathy will turn into fear and anger--oh I see what is bothering you. Those that would-be-king fear a backlash from the tribe?"

QUIXOTE: "I didn't say that, Sancho."

SANCHO: "You didn't have to, Quixote."

QUIXOTE: "All right, let's say for a moment that you are correct. Do you think there will be a backlash?"

SANCHO: "Let's see, economic misery, the loss of loved ones, starvation, death, the realization that the oligarchy knew it was coming all along and hid it so they could keep control, hmm, ah, maybe."

QUIXOTE: "We've done a good job of hiding what we know, Sancho, I don't think our intelligence will be a problem."

SANCHO: "Never was in the past, Quixote, but just because your friends appear indolent, selfish, greedy, and stupid--it doesn't mean they have any plausible deniability on the dangers of climate change. There are enough people who understand the link between anthropogenic forcing and the coming horrors that anger will be everywhere. The backlash will make the Jacobins look like a cub-scout troop."

QUIXOTE: "So we need to increase the size of our military, train them better in urban warfare, legalize torture, and build up walled compounds to ride out the turmoil."

SANCHO: "You're not serious? Castles? Is the current ruling class really that ignorant?"

QUIXOTE: "Oh, I'm certain of that. We embrace ignorance--it's our friend."

SANCHO: "Quixote, if a strong military really kept the masses in line--if that strategy really worked--why then would rights have been granted to the masses in the 18th century?"

QUIXOTE: "A lack of computers?"

SANCHO: "You really believe that?"

QUIXOTE: "My friends do. But I see your point, Sancho."

SANCHO: "Quixote, the rulers and ruled, need to wake up to one reality: The climate wins."

QUIXOTE: "Sancho, we can own the weather."

SANCHO:	"Quixote--stop being a fool--the climate is out of control. There is nothing you can do about it. That's the reality of our lives."
QUIXOTE:	"You said cutting our output of carbon dioxide by 75% would save us."
SANCHO:	"At this point, Quixote, those reduction will cut down on the length of time that humanity suffers."
QUIXOTE:	"That's terrible. How can you say such a thing? It's defeatist."
SANCHO:	"I have just said we are facing mounting horrors. I also said we have passed the point where the transition to sustainable economic system will be benign. Reality is not defeatist."
QUIXOTE:	"Meaning we have passed the tipping point?"
SANCHO:	"The economic tipping point, yes. The climate tipping point is in motion, but it is not yet complete, though we will be there soon."
QUIXOTE:	"Sancho, the tipping point is the boogey man--like bird flu."
SANCHO:	"Quixote, you and your friends are laughable. The tipping point is the point of no return."
QUIXOTE:	"Meaning?"
SANCHO:	"Permanent hurricanes the size of states, droughts that never end, ocean waves the height of twenty story buildings washing ashore daily. Storms that pack the punch of tornadoes, increased tectonic activity, isotonic rebound in the Antarctic, three-meter sea level rise in less than a decade, uncontrollable disease, a lack of food and clean water, population migration, and oh yes: no economy to speak of."
QUIXOTE:	"But you say we can still make a difference."
SANCHO:	"If we cut carbon dioxide output immediately."
QUIXOTE:	"You are deranged. This is an election year. All we want to do is make money and control everything. The climate change problem is everybody's problem. Help me solve it."
SANCHO:	"So why have you and your friends installed a media machine that keeps the people in the dark about how bad it is going to get and how to fix it?"

QUIXOTE: "Some of my friends in the fossil fuels area are not willing to support dramatic changes--or any changes."

SANCHO: "So what passes for caring among your friends, Quixote?"

QUIXOTE: "Economic interests. Wait, are you are saying climate change is all about a lack of caring, a lack of political will, Sancho?"

SANCHO: "Ya' think, Quixote? The rulers are going to have to lead--not just take perqs--because they will get caught up in the madness and get swept away, just like everyone else."

QUIXOTE: "Well then, Sancho, the peasants are going to have to face the horrors of climate change and help us--immediately--or be annihilated by the thousands."

SANCHO: "Imagine it, Quixote. A breached social contract between the ruled and the rulers. America leaps boldly into the 18th century. Cake anyone?"

April 4, 2008
Sancho, Quixote, and the Recession

QUIXOTE: "So how do you like the recession so far, Sancho?"

SANCHO: "I see we've finally begun fighting global warming--Ukrainian style?"

QUIXOTE: "I don't know what you are referring to, Sancho."

SANCHO: "My auntie Albedo you don't. The only lasting CO_2 reduction ever achieved by a civilized nation was by the Ukraine, during its recession."

QUIXOTE: "I don't know what you are talking about, but did you hear the joke about the U.S., negotiator who told another climate negotiator addressing climate change would lead to a worldwide economic tailspin."

SANCHO: "Your friends are funny guys."

QUIXOTE: "But seriously, Sancho, you need to keep this quiet."

SANCHO: "Quixote, everyone knows that during the early nineties the Ukraine achieved a 30% reduction in its carbon dioxide output because it went into a deep recession. No one else has achieved so effective a cut in carbon dioxide so quickly."

QUIXOTE: "Sancho, people are listening."

SANCHO: "I hope to heck they are."

QUIXOTE: "The truth can be dangerous."

SANCHO: "I know your friends have control issues. Quixote, what happened? Why did they finally decide to bring on the recession? Was it the increasing rate of sea level rise, the lack of progress for A.S.P., the soil uptake issues, ethanol vs food, Dengue in Rio, frogs, bees, fish, bat, or moose extinction? Droughts, the tornadoes in the cities, tectonics--you can tell me. I am your humble servant."

QUIXOTE: "You are a tree-hugging, eco-terrorist, nut-case who has been pushing for deep CO_2 reduction for years now. And now we give it to you--so what are you complaining about?"

SANCHO:	"It took a long time for your friends to get their heads of their...Sands. Other than that, no complaints."
QUIXOTE:	"Do you think it will work?"
SANCHO:	"You're good for maybe a 15% reduction in carbon dioxide, Quixote, versus last year's output."
QUIXOTE:	"Well, that's not too bad. I can spin that, Sancho."
SANCHO:	"Oh, your friends are really scared."
QUIXOTE:	"Prove it, Sancho."
SANCHO:	"Quixote, for eight precious years, they played dumb when they could have used those eight years to prepare for the inevitable adjustment to the new climate regime. Now any adjustment to a low carbon economy will be brutal. That's why they are scared."
QUIXOTE:	"For the last eight years...They've been a little too flexible in their use of the truth."
SANCHO:	"The word cowardly springs to mind, Quixote. This climate mess has gotten much worse while your friends' have had the reins of power. Do they have a plan to deal with climate change--I mean besides the recession?"
QUIXOTE:	"What do you think they should do, Sancho?"
SANCHO:	"The same answer as always, CO_2 reduction, immediately."
QUIXOTE:	"Can't be done, Sancho, it'll be a mess."
SANCHO:	"We need to reduce the energy retained by the climate system. Therefore we need to reduce our output of CO_2 into the storage mechanism, the atmosphere."
QUIXOTE:	"They'll never do it."
SANCHO:	"You're wrong again, Quixote. As soon as there has been enough destruction, your friends will shut down the carbon economy. That's a fait accompli."
QUIXOTE:	"Sancho, the economic hardships will be unending."

SANCHO: "No fooling? Gosh, that shocks me. Quixote, just because an answer comes with huge a challenge that doesn't mean the answer is wrong--especially when our leadership has pissed away other options over the years."

QUIXOTE: "Don't you think your attitude is a bit harsh, Sancho?"

SANCHO: "Wait fifteen years, Quixote. Then you'll see harsh."

April 29, 2008
Sancho, Quixote, and Ethanol

QUIXOTE: "Sancho, I have to work on the rice scam. So please, I want you to finish the work on alcohol distiller and then call the attorney to make sure we have the foreclosure papers completed on those family farms. Then I can buy more grain futures. Oh, and the advertisement I am working on called 'Water For All' needs to be delivered to Junior as soon as possible. Put it on the 'War is Peace" disc. Sancho! Sancho? Hey, Sancho, what are you doing? Where are you going on that bicycle? Sancho!"

May 8, 2008
Sancho, Quixote, and Sea Ice

QUIXOTE: "Sancho, the summer Arctic sea ice will melt off completely in the next few years."

SANCHO: "I know, Quixote. It's awful. You need to get this information to the public."

QUIXOTE: "Sancho. For Junior and his friends, science is their bitch and the media is their puppy."

SANCHO: "That's not something to be proud of, Quixote."

QUIXOTE: "Depends on which side of the government committee you sit on, Sancho."

SANCHO: "The melting sea ice is a tragedy. If the Arctic is ice free in summer the devastation might be unlimited."

QUIXOTE: "What does that have to do with anything? Let me tell you the real issue: Junior and his friends think it will take at least a generation or so to negotiate and control the mineral and sea lane rights in the Arctic. If we are ice free in less than a decade, their negotiating position is useless. Global warming is becoming an economic problem. Why didn't you tell me?"

SANCHO: "Quixote, with Arctic albedo disappearing in the summer, that will make a huge difference in the amount of heat retained by the planet. Global warming will accelerate. We have to take substantive steps now."

QUIXOTE: "Stop being an eco-terrorist."

SANCHO: "Your friends are the real eco-terrorists. A consumptive economic system based on fossil fuels has been outmoded for over a decade. Your friends and their nonsensical, megalomaniacal, self-aggrandizing behavior will certainly kill millions--and destroy our economy."

QUIXOTE: "Prove it, Sancho."

SANCHO: "The planet proves my point. Fund the transition to a sustainable economic system as if it were a war."

QUIXOTE: "You mean cut CO_2 output by 75%. That will never happen."

SANCHO: "Quixote, you are an idiot. Don't you see we are entering the triage phase? How bad does it have to get before you and friends dislodge their heads from their anal cavity?"

QUIXOTE: "Power has its percs."

SANCHO: "Quixote, there is no question we will reduce the human CO_2 output by 75%. Does it happen by plan or by tragedy? A steep reduction in CO_2 is a fait accompli, your friends have guaranteed it with their childish response to change. We need to implement economic redirection right away. Focus on wind, solar, and other renewables. Our current economic system is not sustainable and a recession won't protect anyone in the long run Why don't you get it?"

QUIXOTE: "Sancho, that kind of change will never happen, at least as long as my friends run the roost. My friends have hog-tied the scientists with skewed funding requirements, and if that doesn't work; they use political pressure from lobbyists to bury any climate research they don't like with an absurd review process."

SANCHO: "Sadly, you speak the truth."

QUIXOTE: "And don't expect to get the word out either. We own the media and we own the pundits."

SANCHO: "Well...Most of the media, Quixote."

CHAPTER 13
2009

April 20, 2009
Sancho, Quixote, and Three Degrees
(Previously Unpublished)

QUIXOTE: "Sancho, we don't care about the numbers--unless they are on a balance sheet. Only the economy matters."

SANCHO: "I see so if we humans force a 3 degree Celsius rise in temperature, that's okay."

QUIXOTE: "Why not?"

SANCHO: "You and your friends are a bit too cavalier about that in conversation. Do you remember when you were sick?"

QUIXOTE: "I am not going to talk about the past here. We have issues to deal with."

SANCHO: "Like say the Earth's scale. When you measure a 3 degree rise in human terms, it seems like a slight cold or flu--but when you compare it to the atmosphere's influence on the Earth, a 3 degrees C change is huge."

QUIXOTE: "Impossible. Prove it."

SANCHO: "Funny, I knew that was coming. Quixote, without an atmosphere our planet would be 33 degrees C cooler."

QUIXOTE: "So the atmosphere and its ability to trap heat made a 33 degree Celsius difference in the temperature of the planet. That's like 91 degrees Fahrenheit. How?"

SANCHO: "By retaining heat. The atmosphere acts like a blanket."

QUIXOTE: "Why didn't it keep heating up with all this heat from the sun?"

SANCHO: "A balance was formed with the cold vacuum of space. The planet achieved a radiative balance due to the thickness of the blanket and that fostered human growth."

QUIXOTE: "Oh so that's what a radiative balance means."

SANCHO: "Right, and now humans are forcing the radiative balance up by retaining more blankets--in the form of greenhouse gases like carbon dioxide."

QUIXOTE: "This is a disaster. Is it really that simple?"

SANCHO: "To a point--33 degrees is a black box number, but in effect--yes it is that simple. We're modifying a very large energy system by 10% or more. And that's a lot."

QUIXOTE: "Can I make money off it?"

SANCHO: "Carbon trading, I suppose."

QUIXOTE: "Nah, one of the guys already has that covered for us."

SANCHO: "Why am I not surprised to hear that."

July 4, 2009
Sancho, Quixote, and What Ain't
(Previously Unpublished)

SANCHO: "Quixote, I need to ask you why you've given up on America."

QUIXOTE: "Sancho, I haven't. On the other hand I am limiting my investments to other ruthless enterprises for a while."

SANCHO: "Why?"

QUIXOTE: "It's not the market it once was."

SANCHO: "See that's what I mean, Quixote. You and your friends have plundered what they could from the country and now you are letting it go to ruin while you plunder another country."

QUIXOTE: "Prove it."

SANCHO: "Infrastructure, medical care, a free press, investments in scientific research, banking, real estate."

QUIXOTE: "Now hold on a minute. We invest in scientific research, as long as it benefits us. I suppose now you are going to say we are holding science hostage to greed."

SANCHO: "You are holding science hostage to sociopathic tendencies."

QUIXOTE: "Oh, that's harsh, Sancho. I am so upset."

SANCHO: "Quixote, you and your friends are subjugating everything that made this country great--to your control issues."

QUIXOTE: "It's always been that way, Sancho."

SANCHO: "No it hasn't, Quixote. A previous generation kept their control issues in check by the rule of law."

QUIXOTE: "Sancho, doesn't matter. No matter what happens with the climate, we win. We we ride through it at the top of the heap."

SANCHO: "And your friends can tolerate a heap of dead bodies to rest on? I think you're spinning a tale here, Quixote."

QUIXOTE:	"So perhaps I pick and choose my investments in the truth."
SANCHO:	"And you don't feel any responsibility for the coming problems. You and your friends have hidden the problem from objective eyes and spent millions doing it. There's a smoking gun and it is in your hands. The population will eventually get the information. Don't you get it?"
QUIXOTE:	"Ever listen to some of my friends discuss the climate problem?"
SANCHO:	"I just don't get to the club as much as I used to…"
QUIXOTE:	"Sancho, let me clue you in. We think we've solved the problem of an angry response to our deceit and avarice."
SANCHO:	"How?"
QUIXOTE:	"We'll pick a fall-person or group. Anyway, we'll find a mark and focus the media on them. They get obliterated and the rest of us walk away. That's part one."
SANCHO:	"And part two?"
QUIXOTE:	"As far as my friends are concerned, the real issue isn't the climate. It's the population."
SANCHO:	"So population control is now policy?"
QUIXOTE:	"Though the climate."
SANCHO:	"That's not funny, Quixote."
QUIXOTE:	"I wasn't trying to be funny. Less people means less usage of resources, and less need for energy. And by the time we are done, the desire to reduce our population will be the definition of an environmentalist."
SANCHO:	"Quixote, there is difference between being a mass murderer and being an environmentalist."
QUIXOTE:	"Not by the time we are done. You think we were rough on the climate scientists--just wait until you see how we deal with environmentalists for getting us into this mess."
SANCHO:	"An interesting plan so long as no one knows you are doing it."

QUIXOTE: "And you think we don't know what we are doing."

SANCHO: "The thought has crossed my mind. Do you remember all the clowns in the think tanks who said there was no climate change a decade ago?"

QUIXOTE: "Hey watch it; those were my clowns. But yes I remember. What about them?"

SANCHO: "Those people are your best and your brightest."

QUIXOTE: "We need to be careful who we let in on the team. If you get people on the team who are too smart then the guys at the top might get toppled--and they would never let that happen."

SANCHO: "Cheer up, Quixote, that will change in time."

QUIXOTE: "Impossible, it would have to be a life and death circumstance."

SANCHO: "Imagine that. What would happen to your friends if they culled or angered the best minds of a generation? No one would help them."

QUIXOTE: "Money. We'll pay them a fortune."

SANCHO: "In a crisis situation your friends plan to use murder of the population as a solution. Do you think you can pay off the best and the brightest to help you? You really think the best and brightest will sell their souls to take on your problem? You've been dealing with shills too long."

QUIXOTE: "They are all shills. It's just a question of price."

SANCHO: "You really are a funny lackey, Quixote."

CHAPTER 14
2010

February 26, 2010
Sancho, Quixote, and Sacrifice
(Previously unpublished)

QUIXOTE: "Hello Sancho, long time no see."

SANCHO: "Quixote, how are you?"

QUIXOTE: "Oh just fine. We've begun our jobs program and things are going very well."

SANCHO: "A jobs, program, Quixote? You and your friends? Let's see that means cutting down your labor costs, right?"

QUIXOTE: "Well it's our version of employment. I've put together a program to hire people who will poison the Web by filling the net, the blogs, posting locations, social networks, and other popular sites with obscenity, racism, climate change misinformation, health care falsehoods, and economic anger. We are adding hundreds of gutless, greedy shills to our employment rolls every day to spew our hatred. We pay them nothing and the beauty of it is there is no need for honesty. These independent contractors have the moral fiber of jelly fish. I kinda' feel like their father."

SANCHO: "They are you're kind of folk, Quixote. You must be proud."

QUIXOTE: "Sancho, it's the kind of strategy that has brought America to current place in the world."

SANCHO: "Sounds right. Quixote. What are going to do about the facts? The storms, the science, the melting poles, sea level rise, false market moves, and disease?"

QUIXOTE: "Sancho, don't you see? The facts don't matter when you confuse the population with so many lies they can't tell who, or what, to believe. People become idiots."

SANCHO: "Because they believe no one, aye, Quixote? Add to that gutless politicians and a corrupt media afraid of falling off the gravy-train and you have the recipe for seppalyte success."

QUIXOTE: "We thought we'd lost the opportunity when TV began to fade. Luckily, facts have become irrelevant because no one will stand up for them anymore. If they do, we hit them with the economic hammer."

SANCHO: "In your world, the truth has been sacrificed to greed. In the process, you and your friends are deconstructing freedom. Has this been your battle strategy all along, Quixote?"

QUIXOTE: "Only an idiot would doubt the science of climate change or the ethical and moral certainty to provide health care for the citizens of this nation. But so long as the citizens grovel under fear--we make money. When we stop making money--so what? We watch the landscape and make new investments while our psychologically raped population withers under a barrage of new lies while the politicians run for cover."

SANCHO: "But if you recognize the immorality of it why do you do it?"

QUIXOTE: "Sancho, I've learned something about my friends these last few years. You see, Sancho, they're evil. And as long as you and your friends are afraid of evil, afraid of how evil may hinder your lifestyle, or even hurt you, we win. We have the winning formula, and it's called evil. You have a losing formula and it's called cowardice."

SANCHO: "So you believe you have been successful in turning America into a land of cowards--a nation of shop keepers?"

QUIXOTE: "We own the media, the Supreme Court, and the politicians. They all exist for our benefit."

SANCHO: "What about the United States of America and its people, Quixote?"

QUIXOTE: "Screw that, Sancho. This is the Corporate States of America. The United States of America is dead."

SANCHO: "So your friends wage war against the citizens of this country and the country as a whole to gain control? Quixote, that's treason."

QUIXOTE: "Stop being paranoid. It's not just a battle for control against America."

SANCHO: "Oh, I see. That's much better. So your friends are targeting the concept of a united nation."

QUIXOTE: "Just call it our adaptation to the changing climate. And what are you doing these days, Sancho?"

SANCHO: "Listening to you. And I am wondering why the security agencies of the United States of America, and its military do not defend her against you and your treasonous band of bastards. You know, I bet it wouldn't take much for the CIA, FBI, NSA, Homeland Security, or the military to destabilize your revenue base. I bet that would be a wake-up call, don't you?"

QUIXOTE: "Sancho, we have the military off fighting our wars while we destroy the nation. In the process, we kill off the patriots left and right, and fatten our wallets. You know, I think some of them really believed the people of the U.S., were the owners of their liberties."

SANCHO: "I still do."

QUIXOTE: "Hell, we stole your nation while you and your neighbors were watching TV. Now we have the web to get you to fight with your neighbor--that's the core of our jobs' bill. You're a dreamer, Sancho. My friends and I own it all now."

SANCHO: "Really? Now who is being the idiot, Quixote?"

May 1, 2010
Sancho, Quixote and Solar Cycles
(Previously Unpublished)

QUIXOTE: "Sancho, what is a solar cycle?"

SANCHO: "Radiance from the sun, it goes up and down. We are at the bottom of a cycle now and it will peak around 2020, then start heading down again."

QUIXOTE: "So does the solar cycle have an effect on the temperature of the earth?"

SANCHO: "It has an effect on the amount of energy that is retained by the atmosphere, so in a way, yes. That's part of the reason the temperatures have been cooler. Remember the issue is the radiative balance between the energy we get from the sun and the amount we release into space. In 2010, we are at the lowest point--an ebb--but we are still seeing the problems mount."

QUIXOTE: "Prove it."

SANCHO: "Been to Nashville recently?"

QUIXOTE: "It must have been El Nino."

SANCHO: "If it makes you feel better Quixote."

QUIXOTE: "What happens when the sun's radiance starts going up?"

SANCHO: "Well, I guess there will be an increase in the energy from the sun."

QUIXOTE: "You know we have been telling the bloggers to hit the sun's effect on the climate pretty hard recently to confuse people. I've got to tell the bloggers to keep the solar influence on the changing climate to a minimum for the next few years."

SANCHO: "Because someone might make sense of it?"

QUIXOTE: "Exactly. We can't have that. This is going to be tough--we have a full scale assault going on against the climate scientist conspiracy and the solar cycle thing was a keystone. Now we can't use it."

SANCHO: "You wouldn't want to dull the blade of deceit. Your lordship."

QUIXOTE: "I am not worried about that. I am worried that Mr. and Mrs. America might put two and two together and make sense of climate change event and see their confusion was just spin."

SANCHO: "Clarity--perish the thought, Quixote."

QUIXOTE: "Wait a minute, if there is an increase in the radiance then there is an increase in the energy that the greenhouse gases retain. So do we get a double whammy in the next eight or nine years?"

SANCHO: "Looks that way."

QUIXOTE: "Looks like I have a lot of work ahead of me. But you, know it could get really bad in the next decade."

SANCHO: "Yup. It might get a bit unpleasant."

QUIXOTE: "Maybe I should dust off that plan for a set of greenhouse laws? At least then it will look like we are doing something."

May 29, 2010
Sancho, Quixote, and Oil Drilling
(Previously Unpublished)

QUIXOTE: "Sancho, isn't it terrible?"

SANCHO: "The worst, Quixote. I was always worried that oil drilling might lead to big problems like this."

QUIXOTE: "And here we are with this Gulf mess. I swear I just don't know what to do. My best slogan is down the tubes!"

SANCHO: "What do you mean, Quixote?"

QUIXOTE: "Drill Baby Drill! That was one of mine you know. And now here it is dead, dead, dead. All because of a few million gallons of oil, a destroyed ecosystem, and some angry Gulf residents making a stink."

SANCHO: "And so your concern here is…Your slogan?"

QUIXOTE: "We had three maybe four seats with that slogan. Now all we have bupkis. Zilch. Did you know that they are saying that maybe the oil guys weren't taking enough precautions with drilling? Don't they know there are costs involved here, stock prices, bonus money? Even the media is getting pressure."

SANCHO: "What kind of pressure?"

QUIXOTE: "To report real events."

SANCHO: "It's enough to make you sick."

QUIXOTE: "Those guys really screwed up. Some heads are going to roll."

SANCHO: "I thought you said the guys on the rigs did a great job."

QUIXOTE: "I'm not talking about those workers, I'm talking about the scores of oil lobbyists who put their careers on the line for deep water drilling. You know, without them there'd be no drilling. And now this, I swear it's a disaster for them."

SANCHO: "Uh, huh, and the sea life, and the people who live on the Gulf? The tar dispersal patterns and the toxicity events? A hurricane or two. What about that?"

QUIXOTE: "You're right. I should be looking on the sunny side of things. The lobbyists can always find some cash dealing on that side of it. Once the oil hits the shores of New Jersey, there will be plenty of spin. It'll go on for years."

SANCHO: "Heck, Quixote, they'll be cover-ups. Patsy's to set up, legal maneuvering and your favorite: A history rewrite of the event and the inevitable sacrifice of an engineer or two, perhaps even a scientists. It's enough to make your mouth water. Picked a set of patsy's yet?"

QUIXOTE: "We're already working on that--but we are having trouble finding a credible environmentalist within a hundred miles of the event."

SANCHO: "My sympathies. That could be a problem."

QUIXOTE: "I know. It's a disaster, Sancho. Think about it. First, we have the Arctic ice melting like a snowball in hell, the floods in Nashville, the nonstop earthquakes, Iceland, now this."

SANCHO: "Makes you wonder when it will all stop doesn't it? Quixote, do you remember our discussion about solar radiance cycles?"

QUIXOTE: "No, should I? Are you looking for an investment in green tech? Who are they, another bicycle company?"

SANCHO: "Funny, my liege. Not quite."

QUIXOTE: "What if there is a real investigation? Junior is attending the scribbling festival and then he is off to the Lego competition. He can't help us. It isn't like the old days when we could just get a prosecutor fired if Justice didn't go as we said."

SANCHO: "What is this world coming to? But why worry about little things like the law. You never have before."

QUIXOTE: "Corruption has its limits and this oil spill is a disaster. Global Warming will be this bad and worse, will it not?"

SANCHO: "Too true--but as things get brighter, amazing things happen."

QUIXOTE: "When I look on the brighter side I do feel more energy."

SANCHO: "See? When it's dim there is less energy. When it is bright, there's more energy. More energy means more can be affected. I bet soon you'll be radiating ideas that squash freedom just like the old days."

QUIXOTE: "You're strange, Sancho. But I guess I should be looking on the sunny side. Without avarice, stupidity, and second line talent in upper management I'd be out of a job. Who needs spin when you're doing the job correctly?"

SANCHO: "So all you really need now is to wait for your increase in radiance. It'll all be much clearer then."

QUIXOTE: "Anything is possible, Sancho. I do have a good record of subversion and rumor mongering. Do you know, we just got through a conversation and I didn't hear a word from you about humans forcing the radiative balance of the planet?"

SANCHO: "Quixote--maybe some things are just so obvious--I just don't bring them up. Or perhaps it's just a cycle of mine. You can call me Sunny-Sancho."

QUIXOTE: "That's good, Sancho. Keep looking on the brightening side of things."

SANCHO: "Yup, it's only the planet we're toying with here."

QUIXOTE: "And don't worry, be happy. We've got it all solved. Trust me and my transnational friends to take care of your country while you sit at home. What, you worry? Turn on the TV, it's safe. After all, you can't trust your neighbors."

SANCHO: "Spin at its finest, Quixote."

www.ingramcontent.com/pod-product-compliance
Lightning Source LLC
Chambersburg PA
CBHW031458270326
41930CB00006B/144